Revised 4th Edition

Elegant Glassware of the Depression Era

By Gene Florence

COLLECTOR BOOKS

A Division of Schroeder Publishing Co., Inc.

The current values in this book should be used only as a guide. They are not intended to set prices, which vary from one section of the country to another. Auction prices as well as dealer prices vary greatly and are affected by condition as well a demand. Neither the Author nor the Publisher assumes responsibility for any losses that might be incurred as a result of consulting this guide.

DEDICATION

This book is dedicated to three special people, Nora, Austin, and George, friends in and of Depression Glass, who spent years of their lives promoting every aspect of the glass collecting field and who willingly shared their vast knowledge with us. We miss you, but we are all richer for your having lived, albeit too briefly, among us.

FOREWORD

"Elegant" glassware, as defined in this book, refers to the handmade and etched glassware that was sold in the department stores and jewelry stores during the Depression era through the 1950's as opposed to the dime store and give-away glass that is known as Depression Glass.

The rapid growth of collecting "Elegant" glassware has been phenomenal and many dealers who wouldn't touch that crystal stuff a few years ago are stocking up on as much "Elegant" as basic Depression Glass.

The success of the first three books has spawned this fourth. The term "Elegant" is now standard terminology for glass collectors and dealers.

I hope you enjoy the book, and I hope you will feel the weeks of effort to give you the best book possible on "Elegant" glassware were well spent.

PRICING

ALL PRICES IN THIS BOOK ARE RETAIL PRICES FOR MINT CONDITION GLASSWARE. This book is intended to be only **A GUIDE TO PRICES.** There are regional price differences which cannot be reasonably dealt with herein.

You may expect dealers to pay from thirty to fifty percent less than the prices quoted. My personal knowledge of prices comes from my experience of selling glass in my Grannie Bear Antique Shop in Lexington, from my traveling to and selling at shows in various parts of the United States, and (immediately prior to the pricing of this book) from setting up as a dealer at the National Heisey and Cambridge Glass shows. I readily admit to soliciting price information from persons I know to be expert in these various fields so as to provide you with the latest, most accurate pricing information possible. However, final pricing judgment is mine; so, for any errors (or praises), the buck stops here.

MEASUREMENTS AND TERMS

All measurements and terms in this book are from factory catalogues or actual measurements from the piece. It has been my experience that actual measurements vary slightly from those listed in catalogues; so don't get unduly concerned over slight variations.

ACKNOWLEDGMENTS

There are so many people behind the scenes in the production of a book like this that you would not believe it unless you were there! These people have lent glass, their precious time, talents and information to make this book what it is. Many of these people became friends (and most still are) after enduring hours of packing, unpacking, arranging and sorting glass! They have spent hours discussing and writing down their prices, often after long show hours. Some have travelled hundreds of miles to show you their glass because it is for YOU, the public, that these fine people have been willing to share glass collections of years in the making. I get the credit, but without these special people, this book would not exist: Dick and Pat Spencer, Earl and Beverly Hines, George and Veronica Sionakides, Arline Moffett, Dan Tucker and Lorrie Kitchen, Ronnie Marshall Vickers, Charles and Cecelia Larson, Paul and Margaret Arras, Gary and Sue Clark, John and Judy Bine, Bill and Lottie Porter, Vivian McMahon, Dennis Bialek, Ralph Leslie, John and Kathy Oppelt, Yvonne Heil, Parke and Joyce Bloyer, Kathy Hoertel, Steve Quertermous, Jane White, Tom Clouser, Teri Hatch, Karen Geary, Bill and Barbara Adt, Michelle Fredrickson, Pat and Sue McGrain and numerous unnamed readers from throughout the U.S. and Canada who shared pictures of their heretofore unlisted pieces.

The photography sessions this time were spread over a three-year period with one one session lasting a whole week! A special thanks for the extra help involved in these processes.

Family is the most important aid in my work. Were it not for my mom, "Grannie Bear," listing and packing the glass after Dad cleans it for each of the photography sessions, some of it might never be seen in these books. Charles carted boxes from storage and Sybil spent two weeks with Cathy out in the cold sorting glass into various patterns and boxes. Chad and Marc have both helped loading and unloading full vanloads of glass.

Cathy, with her editing pencil, still labors to make sense out of the material that I write. I deal in concepts; she deals with subjects and verbs. She's had nineteen years of this glass and book business (research, editing, proofing, travel, packing and unpacking, both me and the glassware.)

Thanks also to Della Maze of Collector Books for translating all my Microsoft Words into Quark.

You, my readers, are the inspiration to continue. So keep sending me any pertinent information and listings that I may have omitted. You help immensely!

INDEX

INDEX BY COMPANY

AMERICAN, Line #2056, Fostoria Glass Company, 1915–1986

Colors: crystal; some amber, blue, green, yellow in late 1920's; white, red in 1980's

Most of my mail about American concerns questions as to authenticity of pieces. Since the closing of the Fostoria factory in 1986, Lancaster Colony has continued to market its "Whitehall" glassware line which is similar to American, and made by Indiana Glass at Dunkirk, Indiana. You will find an abundance of this in pink at the present, although an avocado green and a smoky blue have also been made. That does not take into account the many pieces being sold in the "outlet" stores in crystal and red.

Red was never made until the 1980's and then it was made by Viking Glass for Fostoria. Dalzell Viking is now making the red for Lancaster Colony who now owns Fostoria. You can see the true green color on the top of pages 7 and 11, the true blue color on the top of page 13, and the true purple/pink color made by Fostoria on page 13.

Colored pieces of older American are in demand, but know from whom you are buying if you are a novice. If the price seems too good, then there is probably a good reason!

Look at the "western" style (rolled edge) hat on the right front side of the picture on top of page 9. Many collectors are missing that hat from their collections. At the bottom of that page are shown a hexagonal sugar and creamer that I found in Texas. These sell in the $50.00 range for each piece.

Also, the ice cream saucers (two styles) in the foreground of the picture on page 11 are selling for $75.00 on the West Coast as I was amazed to see on the two trips I made out there this Spring. These are only shown in a 1941 catalogue, so they may be in shorter supply than we suspect.

	*Crystal		*Crystal
Appetizer, tray, 10½", w/6 inserts	210.00	Bowl, 5½", preserve, 2 hdld., w/cover	55.00
Appetizer, insert, 3¼"	25.00	Bowl, 6", bonbon, 3 ftd.	15.00
Ashtray, 2⅞", sq.	6.00	* Bowl, 6", nappy	12.00
Ashtray, 3⅞", oval	9.00	Bowl, 6", olive, oblong	9.00
Ashtray, 5", sq.	27.50	Bowl, 6½", wedding,	
Ashtray, 5½", oval	12.00	w/cover, sq., ped.ft., 8" h.	77.50
Basket, w/reed handle, 7" x 9"	70.00	Bowl, 6½", wedding, sq., ped. ft., 5¼" h.	35.00
Basket, 10", new in 1988	25.00	Bowl, 7", bonbon, 3 ftd.	10.00
Bell	65.00	Bowl, 7", cupped, 4½" h.	37.50
Bottle, bitters, w/tube, 5¾", 4½ oz.	55.00	* Bowl, 7", nappy	22.50
Bottle, condiment or catsup w/stopper	80.00	Bowl, 8", bonbon, 3 ftd.	17.50
Bottle, cologne, w/stopper, 6 oz., 5¾"	55.00	Bowl, 8", deep	42.50
Bottle, cologne, w/stopper, 7¼", 8 oz.	52.50	Bowl, 8", ftd.	47.50
Bottle, cordial, w/stopper, 7¼", 9 oz.	75.00	Bowl, 8", ftd., 2 hdld., "trophy" cup	75.00
Bottle, water, 44 oz., 9¼"	375.00	* Bowl, 8", nappy	12.50
Bowl, banana split, 9" x 3½"	175.00	* Bowl, 8", pickle, oblong	13.00
Bowl, finger, 4½" diam., smooth edge	22.00	Bowl, 8½", 2 hdld.	13.50
Bowl, 3½", rose	16.00	* Bowl, 8½", boat	10.00
Bowl, 3¾", almond, oval	12.50	Bowl, 9", boat, 2 pt.	10.50
Bowl, 4¼", jelly, 4¼" h.	15.00	* Bowl, 9", oval veg.	25.00
* Bowl, 4½", 1 hdld.	8.00	Bowl, 9½", centerpiece	27.50
Bowl, 4½", 1 hdld., sq.	8.00	Bowl, 9½", 3 pt., 6" w.	37.50
Bowl, 4½", jelly, w/cover, 6¾" h.	18.00	Bowl, 10", celery, oblong	14.00
* Bowl, 4½", nappy	10.00	Bowl, 10", deep	20.00
Bowl, 4½", oval	7.00	Bowl, 10", float	35.00
Bowl, 4¾", fruit, flared	15.00	Bowl, 10", oval, float	32.50
Bowl, 5", cream soup, 2 hdld.	45.00	Bowl, 10", oval, veg., 2 pt.	25.00
Bowl, 5", 1 hdld., tri-corner	11.00	Bowl, 10½", fruit, 3 ftd.	15.00
* Bowl, 5", nappy	7.00	Bowl, 11", centerpiece	40.00
Bowl, 5", nappy, w/cover	25.00	Bowl, 11", centerpiece, tri-corner	30.00
Bowl, 5", rose	22.00	Bowl, 11", relish/celery, 3 pt.	30.00
Bowl, 5½", lemon, w/cover	32.50	Bowl, 11½", float	47.50

* See note on new American on page 12.

*Crystal

Bowl, 11½", fruit, rolled edge, 2¾" h. ..	40.00
Bowl, 11½", oval, float	45.00
Bowl, 11½", rolled edge	37.50
Bowl, 11¾", oval, deep........................	37.50
Bowl, 12", boat..................................	16.00
Bowl, 12", fruit/sm. punch, ped. ft.,	
(Tom & Jerry)	125.00
Bowl, 12", lily pond	55.00
Bowl, 12", relish "boat," 2 pt.	19.00
Bowl, 13", fruit, shallow	45.00
Bowl, 14", punch, w/high ft. base (2 gal.)	175.00
Bowl, 14", punch, w/low ft. base........	155.00
Bowl, 15", centerpiece, "hat" shape	135.00
Bowl, 16", flat, fruit, ped. ft.	115.00
Bowl, 18", punch, w/low ft. base (3¾ gal.)	250.00
Box, pomade, 2" square......................	195.00
* Box, w/cover, puff, 3⅛" x 2¾"	115.00
Box, w/cover, 4½" x 4½"......................	100.00
Box, w/cover, handkerchief, 5⅝" x 4⅝" .	150.00
Box, w/cover, hairpin, 3½" x 1¾"........	95.00
Box, w/cover, jewel, 5¼" x 2¼"	125.00
Box, w/cover, jewel, 2 drawer, 4¼" x 3¼".1,000.00	
* Box, w/cover, glove, 9½" x 3½"	175.00
* Butter, w/cover, rnd. plate, 7¼"	95.00
* Butter, w/cover, ¼ lb.	15.00
Candelabrum, 6½", 2-lite, bell base	
w/bobeche & prisms	75.00
Candle lamp, 8½", w/chimney, candle	
part, 3½".......................................	95.00
Candlestick, twin, 4⅛" h., 8½" spread .	50.00
Candlestick, 2", chamber with fingerhold	30.00
Candlestick, 3", rnd. ft.......................	13.50
Candlestick, 4⅜", 2-lite, rnd. ft.	30.00
Candlestick, 6", octagon ft...................	20.00
Candlestick, 6½", 2-lite, bell base........	65.00
Candlestick, 6¼", round ft...................	150.00
* Candlestick, 7", sq. column.................	90.00
Candlestick, 7¼", "Eiffel" tower	100.00
Candy box, w/cover, 3 pt., triangular ..	60.00
Candy, w/cover, ped. ft.	27.50
Cheese (5¾" compote) & cracker	
(11½" plate)...................................	45.00
Cigarette box, w/cover, 4¾".................	30.00
Coaster, 3¾"	5.00
Comport, 4½", jelly............................	8.00
* Comport, 5", jelly, flared	12.00
* Comport, 6¾", jelly, w/cover...............	30.00
Comport, 8½", 4" high	35.00
Comport, 9½", 5¼" high......................	30.00
Comport, w/cover, 5".........................	22.50
* Cookie jar, w/cover, 8⅞" h..................	300.00

*Crystal

Creamer, tea, 3 oz., 2⅜" (#2056½)	7.50
Creamer, individual, 4¾ oz.	7.50
Creamer, 9½ oz.	10.50
Crushed fruit, w/cover & spoon, 10" ...	750.00
Cup, flat	5.00
Cup, ftd., 7 oz.	8.00
Cup, punch, flared rim........................	10.00
Cup, punch, straight edge	9.00
Decanter, w/stopper, 24 oz., 9¼" h.	85.00
Dresser set: powder boxes w/covers	
& tray	225.00
Flower pot, w/perforated cover, 9½"	
diam.; 5½" h.	650.00
Goblet, #2056, 2½ oz., wine, hex ft.,	
4⅜" h.	12.00
Goblet, #2056, 4½ oz., oyster cocktail,	
3½" h.	16.00
Goblet, #2056, 4½ oz., sherbet, flared,	
4⅜" h.	9.00
Goblet, #2056, 4½ oz., fruit, hex ft.,	
4¾" h.	9.00
Goblet, #2056, 5 oz., low ft., sherbet,	
flared, 3¼" h.	9.00
Goblet, #2056, 6 oz., low ft., sundae,	
3⅛" h.	9.00
Goblet, #2056, 7 oz., claret, 4⅞" h.	35.00
* Goblet, #2056, 9 oz., low ft., 4⅜" h.	11.00
Goblet, #2056, 10 oz., hex ft., water,	
6⅞" h.	11.00
Goblet, #2056, 12 oz., low ft., tea, 5¾" h..	13.00
Goblet, #2056½, 4½ oz., sherbert, 4½" h. .	10.00
Goblet, #2056½, 5 oz., low sherbert,	
3½" h.	10.00
Goblet, #5056, 1 oz., cordial, 3⅛",	
w/plain bowl	27.50
Goblet, #5056, 3½ oz., claret, 4⅝",	
w/plain bowl	12.00
Goblet, #5056, 3½ oz., cocktail, 4",	
w/plain bowl	12.00
Goblet, #5056, 4 oz., oyster cocktail, 3½",	
w/plain bowl	10.00
Goblet, #5056, 5½ oz., sherbert, 4⅛",	
w/plain bowl	10.00
Goblet, #5056, 10 oz., water, 6⅛",	
w/plain bowl	12.00
Hair receiver, 3" x 3"...........................	175.00
Hat, 2⅛", (sm. ash tray)	11.00
Hat, 3" tall.......................................	22.50
Hat, 4" tall.......................................	40.00
Hat, western style..............................	125.00
Hurricane lamp, 12" complete.............	125.00

* See note on new American on page 12.

	*Crystal
Hurricane lamp base	47.50
Ice bucket, w/tongs	50.00
Ice cream saucer (2 styles)	60.00
Ice dish for 4 oz. crab or 5 oz. tomato liner	30.00
Ice dish insert	9.00
Ice tub, w/liner, 5⅝"	47.50
Ice tub, w/liner, 6½"	55.00
Jam pot, w/cover	45.00
Jar, pickle, w/pointed cover, 6" h.	225.00
Marmalade, w/cover & chrome spoon	35.00
* Mayonnaise, div.	7.50
Mayonnaise, w/ladle, ped. ft.	32.50
Mayonnaise, w/liner & ladle	30.00
Molasses can, 11 oz., 6¾" h., 1 hdld.	225.00
* Mug, 5½ oz., "Tom & Jerry," 3¼" h.	30.00
* Mug, 12 oz., beer, 4½" h.	40.00
Mustard, w/cover	27.50
Napkin ring	7.00
Oil, 5 oz.	27.50
Oil, 7 oz.	27.50
Picture frame	5.50
Pitcher, ½ gal. w/ice lip, 8¼", flat bottom	65.00
Pitcher, ½ gal., 8", ftd.	55.00
Pitcher, 1 pt., 5⅜", flat	22.00
Pitcher, 2 pt., 7¼", ftd.	55.00
Pitcher, 3 pt., 8", ftd.	55.00
Pitcher, 3 pt., w/ice lip, 6½", ftd., "fat"	45.00
* Pitcher, 1 qt., flat	20.00
Plate, cream soup liner	12.00
Plate, 6", bread & butter	11.00
Plate, 7", salad	8.50
Plate, 7½" x 4⅜", crescent salad	39.50
Plate, 8", sauce liner, oval	20.00
Plate, 8½", salad	10.00
Plate, 9", sandwich (sm. center)	14.00
Plate, 9½", dinner	18.00
Plate, 10", cake, 2 hdld.	16.00
Plate, 10½" sandwich (sm. center)	16.00
Plate, 11½", sandwich (sm. center)	16.00
Plate, 12", cake, 3 ftd.	22.50
Plate, 13½", oval torte	40.00
Plate, 14", torte	16.75
Plate, 18", torte	90.00
Plate, 20", torte	110.00
* Platter, 10½", oval	37.50
Platter, 12", oval	55.00
Ring holder	110.00
Salad set: 10" bowl, 14" torte, wood fork & spoon	67.50
Salt, individual	6.00
Salver, 10", sq., ped. ft. (cake stand)	67.50

	*Crystal
Salver, 10", rnd., ped. ft. (cake stand)	50.00
* Salver, 11", rnd., ped. ft. (cake stand)	27.50
Sauce boat & liner	45.00
Saucer	3.00
Set: 2 jam pots w/tray	95.00
Set: decanter, 6 - 2 oz. whiskeys on 10½" tray	185.00
Set: toddler, w/baby tumbler & bowl	52.50
Set: youth, w/bowl, hdld. mug, 6" plate	70.00
Set: condiment, 2 oils, 2 shakers, mustard w/cover & spoon w/tray	235.00
Shaker, 3", ea.	9.50
Shaker, 3½", ea.	5.50
Shaker, 3¼", ea.	9.50
Shakers w/tray, individual, 2"	15.00
Sherbet, handled, 3½" high, 4½ oz.	60.00
Shrimp bowl, 12¼"	310.00
Spooner, 3¾"	32.50
** Strawholder, 10"	230.00
Sugar, tea, 2¼" (#2056½)	7.50
Sugar, hdld., 3¼" h.	7.50
Sugar shaker	40.00
Sugar, w/o cover	9.00
Sugar, w/cover, no hdl., 6¼" (cover fits strawholder)	55.00
Sugar, w/cover, 2 hdld.	17.50
Syrup, 6½ oz., #2056½, Sani-cut server	40.00
Syrup, 6 oz., non pour screw top, 5¼" h.	85.00
Syrup, 10 oz., w/glass cover & 6" liner plate	95.00
Syrup, w/drip proof top	25.00
Toothpick	20.00
Tray, cloverleaf for condiment set	100.00
Tray, tid bit, w/question mark metal handle	27.50
Tray, 5" x 2½", rect.	65.00
Tray, 6" oval, hdld.	35.00
Tray, pin, oval, 5½" x 4½"	45.00
Tray, 6½" x 9" relish, 4 part	35.00
Tray, 9½", service, 2 hdld.	27.50
Tray, 10", muffin (2 upturned sides)	25.00
Tray, 10", square, 4 part	70.00
Tray, 10", square	105.00
Tray, 10½", cake, w/question mark metal hdl.	25.00
Tray, 10½" x 7½", rect.	65.00
Tray, 10½" x 5", oval hdld.	42.50
Tray, 10¾", square, 4 part	90.00
Tray, 12", sand. w/ctr. handle	35.00
Tray, 12", round	100.00
Tray, 13½", oval, ice cream	52.50
Tray for sugar & creamer, tab. hdld., 6¾"	9.00

* See note on new American on page 12.
** Bottom only

	*Crystal			*Crystal
Tumbler, hdld. iced tea	165.00		Urn, 7½", sq. ped. ft	30.00
Tumbler, #2056, 2 oz., whiskey, 2½" h.	10.00		Vase, 4½", sweet pea	75.00
Tumbler, #2056, 3 oz.,			Vase, 6", bud, ftd.	10.00
ftd. cone, cocktail, 2⅞" h	13.50	*	Vase, 6", bud, flared	10.00
Tumbler, #2056, 5 oz., ftd., juice, 4¾".	10.00		Vase, 6", straight side	25.00
Tumbler, #2056, 6 oz., flat, old			Vase, 6½", flared rim	15.00
fashioned, 3⅜" h.	11.00		Vase, 7", flared	67.50
Tumbler, #2056, 8 oz. flat, water, flared,		*	Vase, 8", straight side	40.00
4⅛" h.	12.00	*	Vase, 8", flared	77.50
* Tumbler, #2056, 9 oz. ftd., water, 4⅞" h.	12.00		Vase, 8", porch, 5" diam.	265.00
Tumbler, #2056, 12 oz.,			Vase, 8½", bud, flared	20.00
flat, tea, flared, 5¼" h.	12.50		Vase, 8½", bud, cupped	20.00
Tumbler, #2056½, 5 oz.,			Vase, 9", w/sq. ped. ft.	37.50
straight side, juice	12.00		Vase, 9½", flared	85.00
Tumbler, #2056½, 8 oz.,			Vase, 10", cupped in top	150.00
straight side, water, 3⅞" h.	12.00		Vase, 10", porch, 8" diam.	195.00
Tumbler, #2056½, 12 oz.,		*	Vase, 10", straight side	90.00
straight side, tea, 5" h.	15.00		Vase, 10", swung	125.00
Tumbler, #5056, 5 oz., ftd.,			Vase, 10", flared	85.00
juice, 4⅛" w/plain bowl	10.00		Vase, 12", straight side	100.00
Tumbler, #5056, 12 oz.,			Vase, 12", swung	125.00
ftd., tea, 5½" w/plain bowl	12.00		Vase, 14", swung	225.00
Urn, 6", sq., ped. ft	25.00		Vase, 20", swung	275.00

* Note: July 1990. Fostoria Outlet stores are saying 90+ pieces of American are going to be re-issued. I have placed an asterisk by all pieces that I am sure will be made. Additionally, a creamer, sugar, salt (dip or shaker?) and several dishes (?) and bowls (?) are being made. I do not know all sizes, but I suspect all pieces with asterisks in my previous editions will be made since these moulds should be in working order. Lancaster Colony is having these remade at Dalzell Viking. They have even hired former Fostoria employees to get the color right!

The cookie jars mentioned above are good copies, but **most** of the ones I have seen have wavy lines in the pattern and crooked knobs on the top. Old cookie jars did not. This is a tremendous setback to longtime collectors of American, but it is not unusual for a company to put monetary concerns above concerns for collectors.

A special thanks to Miki's Crystal Registry, P.O. Box 22506GF, Robbinsdale, MN 55422 for some of the above information.

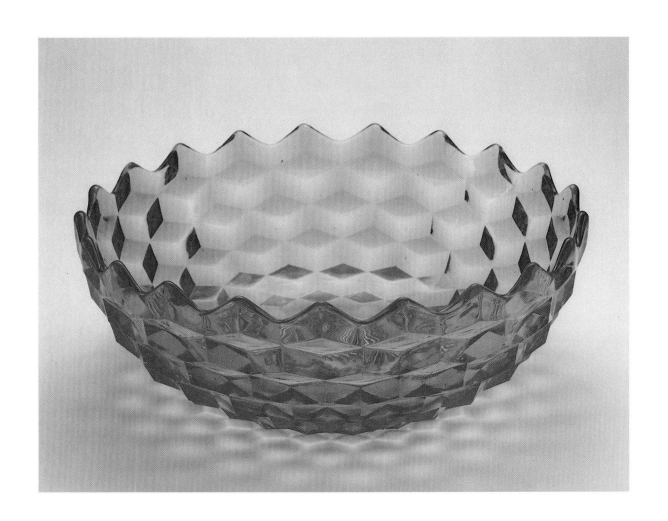

APPLE BLOSSOM, Line #3400, Cambridge Glass Company, 1930's

Colors: blue, pink, light and dark green, yellow, crystal, amber

I have endeavored to show you a multitude of new items, but the Cambridge line numbers for each of the pieces will have to wait until next time. I bought three different collections that had yellow Apple Blossom sets and one with green since the last book. Hence the great photographs!

Demand is for serving and unusual pieces. Enjoy the photographs and in your travels see if you can find something that is not shown.

	Crystal	Yellow Amber	Pink *Green
Ashtray, 6", heavy	50.00	135.00	
Bowl, #3025, ftd., finger, w/plate	15.00	30.00	35.00
Bowl, #3130, finger, w/plate	30.00	30.00	35.00
Bowl, 5¼", 2 hdld., bonbon	10.00	25.00	25.00
Bowl, 5½", 2 hdld., bonbon	10.00	25.00	25.00
Bowl, 5½", fruit "saucer"	8.00	12.00	14.00
Bowl, 6", 2 hdld., "basket" (sides up)	12.00	25.00	30.00
Bowl, 6", cereal	10.00	22.00	25.00
Bowl, 9", pickle	11.00	30.00	35.00
Bowl, 10", 2 hdld.	20.00	65.00	75.00
Bowl, 10", baker	20.00	60.00	70.00
Bowl, 11", fruit, tab hdld.	20.00	70.00	75.00
Bowl, 11", low ftd.	19.00	75.00	85.00
Bowl, 12", relish, 4 pt.	20.00	50.00	55.00
Bowl, 12", 4 ftd.	25.00	65.00	75.00
Bowl, 12", flat	28.00	50.00	55.00
Bowl, 12", oval, 4 ftd.	25.00	60.00	70.00
Bowl, 12½", console	20.00	50.00	55.00
Bowl, 13"	20.00	55.00	60.00
Bowl, cream soup, w/liner plate	13.00	27.50	35.00
Butter w/cover, 5½"	100.00	200.00	275.00
Candelabrum, 3-lite, keyhole	17.50	35.00	40.00
Candlestick, 1-lite, keyhole	12.00	22.50	25.00
Candlestick, 2-lite, keyhole	15.00	27.50	32.50
Candy box w/cover, 4 ftd. "bowl"	35.00	85.00	110.00
Cheese (compote) & cracker (11½" plate)	30.00	55.00	75.00
Comport, 4", fruit cocktail	11.00	18.00	22.00
Comport, 7", tall	20.00	40.00	50.00
Creamer, ftd.	11.00	17.50	20.00
Creamer, tall ftd.	11.00	20.00	22.50
Cup	12.00	22.00	26.00
Cup, A.D.	25.00	45.00	75.00
Fruit/oyster cocktail, #3025, 4½ oz.	11.00	17.50	20.00
Mayonnaise, w/liner & ladle, (4 ftd. bowl)	25.00	50.00	65.00
Pitcher, 50 oz., ftd., flattened sides	85.00	150.00	200.00
Pitcher, 64 oz., #3130	100.00	175.00	225.00
Pitcher, 64 oz., #3025	100.00	195.00	240.00
Pitcher, 67 oz., squeezed middle, loop hdld.	110.00	210.00	250.00
Pitcher, 76 oz.	100.00	195.00	240.00
Pitcher, 80 oz., ball	110.00	135.00	250.00
Pitcher w/cover, 76 oz., ftd., #3135	150.00	350.00	450.00
Plate, 6", bread/butter	4.00	7.00	8.00
Plate, 6", sq., 2 hdld.	7.00	9.00	10.00
Plate, 7½", tea	7.00	12.00	13.00
Plate, 8½"	10.00	20.00	22.00
Plate, 9½", dinner	35.00	65.00	75.00
Plate, 10", grill	18.00	35.00	40.00
Plate, sandwich, 11½", tab hdld.	20.00	30.00	32.50
Plate, sandwich, 12½", 2 hdld.	23.00	32.50	35.00

APPLE BLOSSOM, Line #3400, Cambridge Glass Company, 1930's (continued)

	Crystal	Yellow Amber	Pink *Green
Plate, sq., bread/butter	4.00	7.00	8.00
Plate, sq., dinner	35.00	65.00	75.00
Plate, sq., salad	9.00	12.00	13.00
Plate, sq., service	15.00	20.00	22.00
Platter, 11½	30.00	55.00	60.00
Platter, 13½" rect., w/tab handle	35.00	75.00	85.00
Salt & pepper, pr.	37.50	75.00	90.00
Saucer	2.50	5.00	5.00
Saucer, A.D.	7.50	12.50	15.00
Stem, #1066, parfait	65.00	95.00	135.00
Stem, #3025, 7 oz., low fancy ft., sherbet	11.00	15.00	16.00
Stem, #3025, 7 oz., high sherbet	12.00	18.00	20.00
Stem, #3025, 10 oz.	17.00	22.00	25.00
Stem, #3130, 1 oz., cordial	50.00	90.00	125.00
Stem, #3130, 3 oz., cocktail	15.00	24.00	27.50
Stem, #3130, 6 oz., low sherbet	10.00	15.00	16.00
Stem, #3130, 6 oz., tall sherbet	10.00	18.00	20.00
Stem, #3130, 8 oz., water	14.00	22.00	25.00
Stem, #3135, 3 oz., cocktail	13.00	24.00	27.50
Stem, #3135, 6 oz., low sherbet	10.00	15.00	16.00
Stem, #3135, 6 oz., tall sherbet	10.00	18.00	20.00
Stem, #3135, 8 oz., water	14.00	22.00	25.00
Stem, #3400, 6 oz., ftd., sherbet	9.00	15.00	16.00
Stem, #3400, 9 oz., water	10.00	22.00	25.00
Sugar, ftd.	9.00	16.00	18.00
Sugar, tall ftd.	9.00	18.00	20.00
Tray, 11" ctr. hdld. sand.	22.00	35.00	37.50
Tumbler, #3025, 4 oz.	12.00	17.00	19.00
Tumbler, #3025, 10 oz.	14.00	20.00	22.00
Tumbler, #3025, 12 oz.	18.00	30.00	32.50
Tumbler, #3130, 5 oz., ftd.	11.00	20.00	25.00
Tumbler, #3130, 8 oz., ftd.	12.00	25.00	27.50
Tumbler, #3130, 10 oz., ftd.	13.00	25.00	27.50
Tumbler, #3130, 12 oz., ftd.	16.00	32.50	35.00
Tumbler, #3135, 5 oz., ftd.	10.00	20.00	25.00
Tumbler, #3135, 8 oz., ftd.	12.00	25.00	27.50
Tumbler, #3135, 10 oz., ftd.	13.00	25.00	27.50
Tumbler, #3135, 12 oz., ftd.	15.00	32.50	35.00
Tumbler, #3400, 2½ oz., ftd.	12.00	40.00	50.00
Tumbler, #3400, 9 oz., ftd.	12.00	25.00	27.50
Tumbler, #3400, 12 oz., ftd.	14.00	32.50	35.00
Tumbler, 12 oz., flat (2 styles) - 1 mid indent to match 67 oz. pitcher	17.00	30.00	35.00
Tumbler, 6"	15.00	30.00	35.00
Vase, 5"	22.00	40.00	45.00
Vase, 6", rippled sides	23.00	50.00	55.00
Vase, 8", 2 styles	30.00	65.00	75.00
Vase, 12", keyhole base w/neck indent	35.00	135.00	195.00

* Blue prices 25% to 50% more.
Note: See Pages 182-183 for stem identification.

BAROQUE, Line #2496, Fostoria Glass Company, 1936-1966

Colors: crystal, "Azure" blue, "Topaz" yellow, green, pink, red, cobalt blue, black amethyst

The red and green candlesticks "jump out" at you on the opposite page. I have recently seen these in cobalt blue and black amethyst; so keep a lookout for other colors. The green was photographed for my first rare book as I had never seen them before. Right after the book came out, I ran into a red pair in Hillsville, Virginia, at the Labor Day extravaganza. It has always amazed me how that seems to happen. A single red candlestick just sold at a recent show for the price shown below.

The blue shakers shown on the right are the individual size. These are difficult to find in color.

Several items need to be discussed on the top of page 21. The 9" tall covered piece in the back is the sweetmeat. If anyone has a cup for the pink saucer, let me know. The cream soup is not found often, and I can only show you one in crystal. Note the tops on the shakers. They came both with metal and glass tops, although most collectors prefer the glass lids. Metal lids were replacements if the catalogues can be believed.

Remember that Baroque's blanks (#2496) were used on many of Fostoria's etched lines including Chintz and Navarre.

	Crystal	Blue	Yellow
Ashtray	7.50	15.00	13.00
Bowl, cream soup	25.00	60.00	50.00
Bowl, ftd., punch	295.00	1,500.00	
Bowl, 3¾", rose	18.00	47.50	37.50
Bowl, 4", hdld. (4 styles)	9.00	17.50	15.00
Bowl, 5", fruit	9.00	18.00	15.00
Bowl, 6", cereal	15.00	30.00	25.00
Bowl, 6", sq.	8.00	17.00	14.00
Bowl, 6½", 2 pt.	9.00	18.00	15.00
Bowl, 7", 3 ftd.	12.50	25.00	20.00
Bowl, 7½", jelly, w/cover	25.00	75.00	55.00
Bowl, 8", pickle	8.50	25.00	20.00
Bowl, 8½", hdld.	14.00	35.00	30.00
Bowl, 9½", veg., oval	25.00	55.00	37.50
Bowl, 10", hdld.	15.00	45.00	35.00
Bowl, 10½", hdld., 4 ftd.	17.50	45.00	35.00
Bowl, 10" x 7½"	22.00		
Bowl, 10", relish, 3 pt.	17.50	32.50	25.00
Bowl, 11", celery	12.00	30.00	22.50
Bowl, 11", rolled edge	20.00	45.00	37.50
Bowl, 12", flared	21.50	40.00	32.50
Candelabrum, 8¼", 2-lite, 16 lustre	37.50	75.00	60.00
Candelabrum, 9½", 3-lite, 24 lustre	47.50	95.00	75.00
Candle, 7¾", 8 lustre	12.50	35.00	27.50
Candlestick, 4"	8.00	15.00	12.50
Candlestick, 4½", 2-lite	15.00	25.00	20.00
Candlestick, 5½"	9.00	25.00	20.00
* Candlestick, 6", 3-lite	17.50	40.00	30.00
Candy, 3 part w/cover	30.00	95.00	65.00

* Red $125.00
  Green $95.00
  Black Amethyst $100.00
  Cobalt Blue $100.00

	Crystal	Blue	Yellow
Comport, 4¾"	9.00	22.50	16.50
Comport, 6½"	10.00	32.00	23.00
Creamer, 3¼", indiv.	6.00	25.00	22.00
Creamer, 3¾", ftd.	7.00	14.00	12.00
Cup	6.50	20.00	14.00
Cup, 6 oz., punch	8.00	17.50	
Ice bucket	27.50	65.00	50.00
Mayonnaise, 5½", w/liner	15.00	45.00	35.00
Mustard, w/cover	22.00	45.00	37.50
Oil, w/stopper, 5½"	45.00	450.00	210.00
Pitcher, 6½"	100.00	650.00	425.00
Pitcher, 7", ice lip	100.00	600.00	375.00
Plate, 6"	3.00	5.00	4.00
Plate, 7"	4.00	9.00	7.00
Plate, 8"	6.00	11.00	9.00
Plate, 9"	15.00	45.00	35.00
Plate, 10", cake	10.00	21.50	20.00
Plate, 11", ctr. hdld., sand	15.00		
Plate, 14", torte	13.00	30.00	25.00
Platter, 12", oval	22.00	40.00	35.00
Salt & pepper, pr.	30.00	130.00	95.00
Salt & pepper, indiv., pr.	50.00	250.00	140.00
Saucer	2.00	5.00	4.00
Sherbet, 3¾", 5 oz.	8.00	17.50	15.50
Stem, 6¾", 9 oz., water	12.50	23.00	18.00
Sugar, 3", indiv.	5.00	22.00	20.00
Sugar, 3½", ftd.	6.00	12.00	11.00
Sweetmeat, covered, 9"	75.00	135.00	125.00
Tray, 11", oval	10.00	25.00	20.00
Tray, 6¼" for indiv. cream/sugar	6.00	12.50	10.00
Tumbler, 3½", 6½ oz., old fashioned	15.00	55.00	35.00
Tumbler, 3", 3½ oz., ftd., cocktail	10.00	20.00	16.00
Tumbler, 6", 12 oz., ftd., tea	12.00	30.00	25.00
Tumbler, 3¾", 5 oz., juice	12.00	30.00	22.00
Tumbler, 5½", 9 oz., ftd., water	10.00	20.00	18.00
Tumbler, 4¼", 9 oz., water	14.00	26.00	21.00
Tumbler, 5¾", 14 oz., tea	18.00	50.00	35.00
Vase, 6½"	15.00	40.00	35.00
Vase, 7"	15.00	50.00	40.00

BLACK FOREST, Possibly Paden City for Van Deman & Son, Late 1920's – Early 1930's

Colors: amber, black, ice blue, crystal, green, pink, red, cobalt   **See "Deerwood" for more information.**

	Amber	Black	Crystal	Green	Pink	Red
Bowl, 4½", finger				12.00		
Bowl, 9¼", center hdld.				65.00	65.00	
Bowl, 11", console	50.00	50.00	35.00	30.00	30.00	
Bowl, 11", fruit		30.00		25.00	25.00	
Bowl, 13", console		65.00				
Bowl, 3 ftd.			60.00			
Cake plate, 2" pedestal	25.00	40.00		30.00	25.00	
Candlestick, mushroom style	25.00	25.00	15.00	25.00	25.00	
Candlestick double			25.00			
Candy dish, w/cover, several styles	75.00	75.00			65.00	
Creamer, 2 styles		30.00	20.00	30.00	30.00	50.00
Comport, 4", low ftd.				25.00	25.00	
Comport, 5½", high ftd.		30.00		28.00	25.00	
Cup and saucer, 3 styles		75.00		75.00	75.00	95.00
Decanter, w/stopper			75.00	95.00	95.00	
Ice bucket				75.00	75.00	
Ice tub, 2 styles (Ice blue $150.00)	75.00	60.00			50.00	
Mayonnaise, with liner		60.00		60.00	60.00	
Night Set: pitcher, 6½", 42 oz. & tumbler				350.00	350.00	
Pitcher, 8", 62 oz.			150.00	300.00	300.00	
Plate, 6½", bread/butter		22.00		22.00		
Plate, 8", luncheon		25.00			25.00	30.00
Plate, 11", 2 hdld.		45.00		25.00	25.00	
Salt and pepper, pr.			100.00		100.00	
Server, center hdld.	50.00	40.00	35.00	35.00	35.00	
Stem, 2 oz., wine, 4¼"			15.00	50.00		
Stem, 6 oz., champagne, 4¾"			15.00		30.00	
Stem, 9 oz., water, 6"			20.00			
Sugar, 2 styles		30.00	20.00	30.00	30.00	50.00
Tumbler, 3 oz., juice, flat or footed, 3½"			25.00	20.00		
Tumbler, 8 oz., old fashioned, 3⅞"					30.00	
Tumbler, 9 oz., ftd., 5½"	20.00					
Tumbler, 12 oz., tea, 5½"				40.00	40.00	
Vase, 6½" (Cobalt $100.00)		55.00		50.00	50.00	
Vase, 10"		75.00		65.00	65.00	
Whipped cream pail	75.00					

CADENA, Tiffin Glass Company, Early 1930's

Colors: crystal, yellow; some pink

One of my biggest problems in organizing these books is the failure of pictures taken to materialize when I need them. I am looking at a photo that I took of a new set-up for this book, but the photograph taken by the professional studio has never been seen! So you will not get to see a cup this time in yellow as I had hoped. Meanwhile, you can help me find a yellow saucer to go with it.

I still have not found a yellow or pink cordial for my collection. Very little of this pattern is found at shows and this probably means that there are few collectors. You will find a piece or two in your travels, but seeing a whole set for sale is a thing of the past. Evidently, Tiffin did not market this pattern as extensively as Cherokee Rose, Flanders or some of their other patterns.

Remember that the pitcher cover is plain (no pattern is etched on it).

	Crystal	Pink/Yellow
Bowl, cream soup	15.00	25.00
Bowl, finger, ftd.	12.00	20.00
Bowl, grapefruit, ftd.	17.50	35.00
Bowl, 6", hdld.	10.00	20.00
Bowl, 10", pickle	12.50	25.00
Bowl, 12", console	22.50	45.00
Candlestick	13.50	22.00
Creamer	15.00	25.00
Cup	20.00	45.00
Goblet, 4¾", sherbet	15.00	22.00
Goblet, 5¼", cocktail	17.50	25.00
Goblet, 5¼", ¾ oz., cordial	35.00	65.00
Goblet, 6", wine	22.00	35.00
Goblet, 6½", champagne	17.00	30.00
Goblet, 7½", water	20.00	35.00
Mayonnaise, ftd., w/liner	25.00	37.50
Oyster cocktail	15.00	25.00
Pitcher, ftd., w/cover	200.00	300.00
Plate, 6"	5.00	8.00
Plate, 7¾"	7.00	12.00
Plate, 9¼"	30.00	37.50
Saucer	5.00	10.00
Sugar	15.00	23.00
Tumbler, 4¼", ftd., juice	15.00	25.00
Tumbler, 5¼", ftd., water	17.00	27.50
Vase, 9"	35.00	55.00

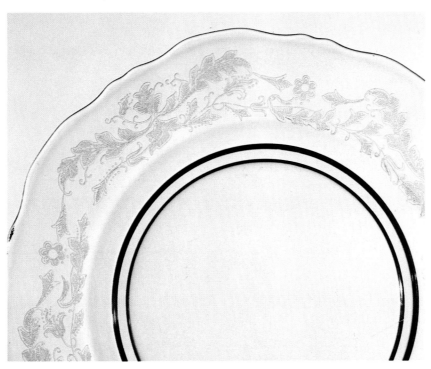

CANDLEWICK, Line #400, Imperial Glass Company, 1936 – 1984

Colors: crystal, blue, pink, yellow, black, red, cobalt blue; a few items in color recently

Collecting Candlewick is almost never ending. This pattern just keeps surprising us with newly found pieces. Someone once asked me what it takes to have a "complete" collection of this pattern. I believe that there is no such thing. There are too many experimental pieces and whimsies (worker's "play" projects) to ever get a "complete" set.

Prices on colored (red, black and light blue) Candlewick pieces escalated very fast. Lately, these prices have slowed considerably which is usually the fate of a too rapid rise. I have seen three different red center handled servers at shows priced from $300.00 to $595.00 in the last few months. Guess which one sold? Most of the red and black fancy bowls have steadied in price around $200.00 with the blue bringing about a third of that.

I should point out a few of the hard to find items shown on the following pages. I might also remind you that there are several unusual Candlewick items shown in my two volumes of *Very Rare Glassware of the Depression Years.*

On the bottom of page 27 is a setting of cut Candlewick purchased in late 1939 or 1940. Unfortunately, the owner sold all the dinner plates, cups and saucers before I had a chance to buy the set. The 7½" lily bowl shown on the right was only made in 1939 and is quite hard to find. That covered three part dish (400/216) shown in the foreground at the top of page 29 is found most often without the cover.

The bottom photo on page 29 shows just about any kind of candlestick you could want in Candlewick. Note the green and silver decorated one as well as several different hurricane lamps. Also shown are several lamp globes. The oval one in the center has an original Candlewick sticker. The one shown on the right with the yellowish cast is of questionable origin, but the others are most likely the "real" thing.

The top of page 31 (left rear) shows the 400/18 hard to find line of tumblers. The bottom photo shows the family punch bowl, some DeVilbis perfumes and a dresser set.

Page 33 (top left) shows the straight-topped vase normally found ruffled, and the bottom photo (back right) shows some of the goblets that should have been gold decorated, but were not. Enjoy these new pictures and let me know of any new discoveries!

Bulletin: July 1990. A trial run of red and black plates (dinner and other sizes) has just been made. More pieces are sure to follow.

	Crystal
Ashtray, eagle, 6½", 1776/1	40.00
Ashtray, heart, 4½", 400/172	9.00
Ashtray, heart, 5½", 400/173	13.00
Ashtray, heart, 6½", 400/174	15.00
Ashtray, indiv.	5.00
Ashtray, oblong, 4½", 400/134/1	6.00
Ashtray, round, 2¾", 400/19	4.50
Ashtray, round, 4", 400/33	9.00
Ashtray, round, 5", 400/133	8.00
Ashtray, square, 3¼", 400/651	9.00
Ashtray, square, 4½", 400/652	12.00
Ashtray, square, 5¾", 400/653	15.00
Ashtray, 6", matchbook holder center, 400/60	60.00
Ashtray set, 3 pc. rnd. nest. (crys. or colors), 400/550	20.00
Ashtray set, 3 pc. sq. nesting, 400/650	36.00
Ashtray set, 4 pc. bridge (cig. hold at side), 400/118	35.00
Basket, 5", beaded hdld., 400/273	165.00
Basket, 6½", hdld., 400/40/0	27.50
Basket, 11", hdld., 400/73/0	110.00
Bell, 4", 400/79	32.50
Bell, 5", 400/108	37.50
Bottle, bitters, w/tube, 4 oz., 400/117	40.00
Bowl, bouillon, 2 hdld., 400/126	27.50
Bowl, #3400, finger, ftd.	13.50
Bowl, #3800, finger	13.50

	Crystal
Bowl, 4½", nappy, 3 ftd., 400/206	50.00
Bowl, 4¾", round, 2 hdld., 400/42B	10.00
Bowl, 5", cream soup, 400/50	39.50
Bowl, 5", fruit, 400/1F	12.00
Bowl, 5", heart w/hand., 400/49H	17.50
Bowl, 5", square, 400/231	50.00
Bowl, 5½", heart, 400/53H	13.00
Bowl, 5½", jelly, w/cover, 400/59	45.00
Bowl, 5½", sauce, deep, 400/243	25.00
Bowl, 6", baked apple, rolled edge, 400/53X	25.00
Bowl, 6", cottage cheese, 400/85	17.50
Bowl, 6", fruit, 400/3F	11.00
Bowl, 6", heart w/hand., 400/51H	19.00
Bowl, 6", mint w/hand., 400/51F	14.00
Bowl, 6", round, div., 2 hdld., 400/52	22.00
Bowl, 6", 2 hdld., 400/52B	11.00
Bowl, 6", 3 ftd., 400/183	37.50
Bowl, 6", sq., 400/232	55.00
Bowl, 6½", relish, 2 pt., 400/184	18.00
Bowl, 6½", 2 hdld., 400/181	20.00
Bowl, 7", round, 400/SF	16.00
Bowl, 7", round, 2 hdld., 400/62B	17.00
Bowl, 7", relish, sq., div., 400/234	50.00
Bowl, 7", ivy, high, bead ft., 400/188	135.00
Bowl, 7", lily, 4 ft., 400/74J	50.00
Bowl, 7", relish, 400/60	20.00
Bowl, 7", sq., 400/233	70.00

	Crystal
Bowl, 7¼", rose, ftd. w/crimp edge, 400/132C	200.00
Bowl, 7½", pickle/celery	15.00
Bowl, 7½", lily, bead rim, ftd., 400/75N	100.00
Bowl, 7½", belled, (console base), 400/127B	45.00
Bowl, 7½", pickle/celery, 400/57	15.00
Bowl, 8", round, 400/7F	25.00
Bowl, 8", relish, 2 pt., 400/26/1	17.50
Bowl, 8", cov. veg., 400/65/1	150.00
Bowl, 8½", rnd., 400/69	27.50
Bowl, 8½", nappy, 4 ftd., 400/74B	32.50
Bowl, 8½", 3 ftd., 400/182	85.00
Bowl, 8½", 2 hdld., 400/72B	20.00
Bowl, 8½", pickle/celery, 400/58	15.00
Bowl, 8½", relish, 4 pt., 400/55	18.00
Bowl, 9", round, 400/10F	30.00
Bowl, 9", crimp, ftd., 400/67C	45.00
Bowl, 9", sq., fancy crimp edge, 4 ft., 400/74SC	45.00
Bowl, 9", heart, 400/49H	85.00
Bowl, 9", heart w/hand., 400/73H	100.00
Bowl, 10", 400/13F	32.00
Bowl, 10", banana, 400/103F	1,000.00
Bowl, 10", 3 toed, 400/205	90.00
Bowl, 10", belled, (punch base), 400/128B	50.00
Bowl, 10", cupped edge, 400/75F	40.00
Bowl, 10", deep, 2 hdld., 400/113A	45.00
Bowl, 10", divided, deep, 2 hdld., 400/114A	55.00
Bowl, 10", fruit, bead stem (like compote), 400/103F	75.00
Bowl, 10", relish, oval, 2 hdld., 400/217	22.50
Bowl, 10", relish, 3 pt., 3 ft., 400/208	57.50
Bowl, 10", 3 pt., w/cover, 400/216	195.00
Bowl, 10", 2 handled, 400/113A	75.00
Bowl, 10½", belled, 400/63B	60.00
Bowl, 10½", butter/jam, 3 pt., 400/262	65.00
Bowl, 10½", salad, 400/75B	35.00
Bowl, 10½", relish, 3 section, 400/256	22.00
Bowl, 11", celery boat, oval, 400/46	45.00
Bowl, 11", centerpiece, flared, 400/13B	40.00
Bowl, 11", float, inward rim, ftd., 400/75F	35.00
Bowl, 11", oval, 400/124A	125.00
Bowl, 11", oval w/partition, 400/125A	100.00
Bowl, 12", round, 400/92B	27.50
Bowl, 12", belled, 400/106B	70.00
Bowl, 12", float, 400/92F	37.50
Bowl, 12", hdld., 400/113B	35.00
Bowl, 12", shallow, 400/17F	40.00
Bowl, 12", relish, oblong, 4 sect., 400/215	50.00
Bowl, 13", centerpiece, mushroom, 400/92F	47.50
Bowl, 13", float, 1½" deep, 400/101	42.50
Bowl, 13½", relish, 5 pt., 400/209	65.00
Bowl, 14", belled, 400/104B	85.00
Bowl, 14", oval, flared, 400/131B	150.00
Butter and jam set, 5 piece, 400/204	200.00
Butter, w/ cover, rnd., 5½", 400/144	27.50
Butter, w/ cover, no beads, California, 400/276	110.00
Butter, w/ bead top, ¼ lb., 400/161	23.00
Cake stand, 10", low foot, 400/67D	45.00
Cake stand, 11", high foot, 400/103D	55.00
Calendar, 1947, desk	100.00
Candleholder, 3 way, beaded base, 400/115	65.00
Candleholder, 2-lite, 400/100	17.50
Candleholder, flat, 3½", 400/280	20.00
Candleholder, 3½", rolled edge, 400/79R	10.50

	Crystal
Candleholder, 3½", w/fingerhold, 400/81	35.00
Candleholder, flower, 4", 2 bead stem, 400/66F	37.50
Candleholder, flower, 4½", 2 bead stem, 400/66C	40.00
Candleholder, 4½", 3 toed, 400/207	37.50
Candleholder, 3-lite on cir. bead. ctr., 400/147	22.50
Candleholder, 5", hdld. /bowled up base, 400/90	35.00
Candleholder, 5" heart shape, 400/40HC	30.00
Candleholder, 5½", 3 bead stems, 400/224	60.00
Candleholder, flower, 5", (epergne inset), 400/40CV	75.00
Candleholder, 5", flower, 400/40C	20.00
Candleholder, 6½", tall, 3 bead stems, 400/175	60.00
Candleholder, flat, 3½", 400/280	25.00
Candleholder, flower, 6", round, 400/40F	17.50
Candleholder, urn, 6", holders on cir. ctr. bead, 400/129R	60.00
Candleholder, flower, 6½", square, 400/40S	25.00
Candleholder, mushroom, 400/86	22.00
Candleholder, flower 9" centerpiece, 400/196FC	125.00
Candy box, round, 5½", 400/59	32.50
Candy box, sq., 6½", rnd. lid, 400/245	95.00
Candy box, w/ cover, 7", 400/259	125.00
Candy box, w/ cover, 7" partitioned, 400/110	50.00
Candy box, w/ cover, round, 7", 3 sect., 400/158	125.00
Candy box, w/ cover, beaded, ft., 400/140	125.00
Cigarette box w/cover, 400/134	25.00
Cigarette holder, 3", bead ft., 400/44	25.00
Cigarette set: 6 pc., (cigarette box & 4 rect. ash trays), 400/134/6	55.00
Clock, 4", round	100.00
Coaster, 4", 400/78	6.00
Coaster, w/spoon rest, 400/226	12.50
Cocktail, seafood w/bead ft., 400/190	45.00
Cocktail set: 2 pc., plate w/indent; cocktail, 400/97	27.50
Compote, 4½", 400/63B	17.50
Compote, 5", 3 bead stems, 400/220	40.00
Compote, 5½", 4 bead stem, 400/45	18.00
Compote, 5½, low, plain stem, 400/66B	15.00
Compote, 5½", 2 bead stem, 400/66B	15.00
Compote, 8", bead stem, 400/48F	65.00
Compote, 10", ftd. fruit, crimped, 40/103C	100.00
Compote, ft. oval, 400/137	95.00
Condiment set:	
4 pc., (2 squat bead ft. shakers, marmalade), 400/1786	57.50
Console sets:	
3 pc. (14" oval bowl, two 3-lite candles), 400/1531B	225.00
3 pc. (mushroom bowl, w/mushroom candles), 400/8692L	90.00
Creamer, domed foot, 400/18	65.00
Creamer, 6 oz., bead handle, 400/30	7.50
Creamer, indiv. bridge, 400/122	5.00
Creamer, plain ft., 400/31	6.00
Creamer, flat, bead handle, 400/126	12.50
Cup, after dinner, 400/77	15.00
Cup, coffee, 400/37	7.50
Cup, punch, 400/211	6.00
Cup, tea, 400/35	7.00
Decanter, w/stopper, 15 oz. cordial, 400/82/2	250.00

CANDLEWICK, Line #400, Imperial Glass Company, 1936 – 1984 (continued)

	Crystal
Decanter, hdld., with stopper, 400/82/2	275.00
Decanter, w/stopper, 26 oz., 400/163	210.00
Deviled egg server, 12", ctr. hdld., 400/154	80.00
Egg cup, bead. ft., 400/19	30.00
Fork & spoon, set, 400/75	22.00
Hurricane lamp, 2 pc. candle base, 400/79	70.00
Hurricane lamp, 2 pc., hdld. candle base, 400/76	95.00
Hurricane lamp, 3 pc. flared & crimped edge globe, 400/152	75.00
Ice tub, 5½" deep, 8" diam., 400/63	75.00
Ice tub, 7", 2 hdld., 400/168	120.00
Icer, 2 pc., seafood/fruit cocktail, 400/53/3	95.00
Icer, 2 pc., seafood/fruit cocktail #3800 line, one bead stem	50.00
Jam set, 5 pc., oval tray w/2 marmalade jars w/ladles, 400/1589	65.00
Jar tower, 3 sect., 400/655	150.00
Knife, butter, 4000	150.00
Ladle, marmalade, 3 bead stem, 400/130	6.00
Ladle, mayonnaise, 6¼", 400/135	6.00
Marmalade set, 3 pc., beaded ft. w/cover & spoon, 400/1989	30.00
Marmalade set, 3 pc. tall jar, domed bead ft., lid, spoon, 400/8918	47.50
Marmalade set, 4 pc., liner saucer, jar, lid, spoon, 400/89	35.00
Mayonnaise set, 2 pc. scoop side bowl, spoon, 400/23	32.50
Mayonnaise set, 3 pc. hdld. tray/hdld. bowl/ladle, 400/52/3	37.50
Mayonnaise set, 3 pc. plate, heart bowl, spoon, 400/49	33.00
Mayonnaise set, 3 pc. scoop side bowl, spoon, tray, 400/496	40.00
Mayonnaise 4 pc., plate, divided bowl, 2 ladles, 400/84	40.00
Mirror, 4½", rnd., standing	75.00
Mustard jar, w/spoon, 400/156	30.00
Oil, 4 oz., bead base, 400/164	35.00
Oil, 6 oz., bead base, 400/166	37.50
Oil, 4 oz., bulbous bottom, 400/274	37.50
Oil, 4 oz., hdld., bulbous bottom, 400/278	42.00
Oil, 6 oz., hdld., bulbous bottom, 400/279	50.00
Oil, 6 oz., bulbous bottom, 400/275	40.00
Oil, w/stopper, etched "Oil," 400/121	45.00
Oil, w/stopper, etched "Vinegar," 400/121	45.00
Party set, 2 pc., oval plate w/indent for cup, 400/98	20.00
Pitcher, 14 oz., short rnd., 400/330	65.00
Pitcher, 16 oz., low ft., 400/19	200.00
Pitcher, 16 oz., no ft., 400/16	150.00
Pitcher, 20 oz., plain, 400/416	30.00
Pitcher, 40 oz., juice/cocktail, 400/19	125.00
Pitcher, 40 oz., manhattan, 400/18	195.00
Pitcher, 40 oz., plain, 400/419	30.00
Pitcher, 64 oz., plain, 400/424	35.00
Pitcher, 80 oz., plain, 400/424	35.00
Pitcher, 80 oz., 400/24	100.00

	Crystal
Pitcher, 80 oz., beaded ft., 400/18	165.00
Plate, 4½", 400/34	4.50
Plate, 5½", 2 hdld., 400/420	6.50
Plate, 6", bread/butter, 400/1D	6.00
Plate, 6", canape w/off ctr. indent, 400/36	10.00
Plate, 6¾", 2 hdld. crimped, 400/52C	20.00
Plate, 7", salad, 400/3D	8.00
Plate, 7½", 2 hdld., 400/52D	8.00
Plate, 7½", triangular, 400/266	50.00
Plate, 8", oval, 400/169	17.50
Plate, 8", salad, 400/5D	8.00
Plate, 8", w/indent, 400/50	11.00
Plate, 8¼", crescent salad, 400/120	40.00
Plate, 8½", 2 hdld., crimped, 400/62C	20.00
Plate, 8½", 2 hdld., 400/62D	12.00
Plate, 8½", salad, 400/5D	9.00
Plate, 8½", 2 hdld. (sides upturned), 400/62E	22.00
Plate, 9", luncheon, 400/7D	12.50
Plate, 9", oval, salad, 400/38	25.00
Plate, 9", w/indent, oval, 400/98	12.50
Plate, 10", 2 hdld., sides upturned, 400/72E	22.50
Plate, 10", 2 hdld. crimped, 400/72C	25.00
Plate, 10", dinner, 400/10D	32.50
Plate, 10", 2 hdld., 400/72D	15.00
Plate, 12", 2 hdld., 400/145D	25.00
Plate, 12", 2 hdld. crimp., 400/145C	32.50
Plate, 12", service, 400/13D	25.00
Plate, 12½", cupped edge, torte, 400/75V	27.50
Plate, 12½", oval, 400/124	35.00
Plate, 13½", cupped edge, serving, 400/92V	35.00
Plate, 14" birthday cake (holes for 72 candles), 400/160	285.00
Plate, 14", 2 hdld., sides upturned, 400/113E	32.00
Plate, 14", 2 hdld., torte, 400/113D	30.00
Plate, 14", service, 400/92D	30.00
Plate, 14", torte, 400/17D	35.00
Plate, 17", cupped edge, 400/20V	42.50
Plate, 17", torte, 400/20D	42.50
Platter, 13", 400/124D	65.00
Platter, 16", 400/131D	125.00
Punch ladle, 400/91	20.00
Punch set, family, 8 demi cups, ladle, lid, 400/139/77	400.00
Punch set, 15 pc. bowl on base, 12 cups, ladle, 400/20	200.00
Relish & dressing set, 4 pc. (10½" 4 pt. relish w/marmalade), 400/1112	67.50
Salad fork & spoon set, 400/75	22.00
Salad set, 4 pc., buffet; lg. rnd. tray, div. bowl, 2 spoons, 400/17	75.00
Salad set, 4 pc. (rnd. plate, flared bowl, fork, spoon), 400/75B	60.00
Salt & pepper, bead ft., straight side, chrome top, 400/247	16.00
Salt & pepper, bead ft., bulbous, chrome top, 400/96	12.50
Salt & pepper, bulbous w/bead stem, plastic top, 400/116	75.00

	Crystal
Salt & pepper, pr., indiv., 400/109	10.00
Salt & pepper, pr., ftd. bead base, 400/190	35.00
Salt dip, 2", 400/61	6.00
Salt dip, 2¼", 400/19	6.50
Salt spoon, 3, 400/616	5.00
Salt spoon, w/ribbed bowl, 4000	7.00
Sauce boat, 400/169	95.00
Sauce boat liner, 400/169	30.00
Saucer, after dinner, 400/77AD	5.00
Saucer, tea or coffee, 400/35 or 400/37	250.00
Set: 2 pc. hdld. cracker w/cheese compote, 400/88	35.00
Set: 2 pc. rnd. cracker plate w/indent; cheese compote, 400/145	45.00
Snack jar w/cover, bead ft., 400/139/1	300.00
Stem, 1 oz., cordial, 400/190	65.00
Stem, 4 oz., cocktail, 400/190	18.00
Stem, 5 oz., tall sherbet, 400/190	14.50
Stem, 5 oz., wine, 400/190	22.00
Stem, 6 oz., sherbet, 400/190	14.00
Stem, 10 oz., water 400/190	16.00
Stem, #3400, 1 oz., cordial	35.00
Stem, #3400, 4 oz., cocktail	14.00
Stem, #3400, 4 oz. oyster cocktail	14.00
Stem, #3400, 4 oz., wine	24.00
Stem, #3400, 5 oz., claret	35.00
Stem, #3400, 5 oz., low sherbet	10.00
Stem, #3400, 6 oz., parfait	45.00
Stem, #3400, 6 oz., sherbet/saucer champagne	13.00
Stem, #3400, 9 oz., goblet, water	15.00
Stem, #3800, low sherbet	14.00
Stem, #3800, brandy	20.00
Stem, #3800, 1 oz. cordial	35.00
Stem, #3800, 4 oz., cocktail	18.00
Stem, #3800, 4 oz. wine	24.00
Stem, #3800, 6 oz., champagne/sherbet	15.00
Stem, #3800, 9 oz. water goblet	18.00
Stem, #3800, claret	30.00
Stem, #4000, 1¼ oz., cordial	30.00
Stem, #4000, cocktail	22.00
Stem, #4000, 5 oz., wine	28.00
Stem, #4000, 6 oz., tall sherbet	14.00
Stem, #4000, 11 oz., goblet	18.00
Stem, #4000, 12 oz., tea	20.00
Strawberry set, 2 pc. (7" plate/sugar dip bowl), 400/83	40.00
Sugar, domed foot, 400/18	50.00
Sugar, 6 oz., bead hdld., 400/30	6.50
Sugar, flat, bead handle, 400/126	20.00
Sugar, indiv. bridge, 400/122	6.00
Sugar, plain ft., 400/31	6.50
Tete-a-tete 3 pc. brandy, a.d. cup, 6½" oval tray, 400/111	47.50
Tid bit server, 2 tier, cupped, 400/2701	40.00
Tid bit set, 3 pc., 400/18TB	90.00
Toast, w/cover, set, 7¾", 400/123	150.00

	Crystal
Tray, 5½", hdld., upturned handles, 400/42E	18.00
Tray, 5½", lemon, ctr. hdld., 400/221	13.50
Tray, 5¼" x 9¼", condiment, 400/148	40.00
Tray, 6½", 400/29	15.00
Tray, 6", wafer, handle bent to ctr. of dish, 400/51T	22.00
Tray, 10½", ctr. hdld. fruit, 400/68F	45.00
Tray, 11½", ctr. hdld. party, 400/68D	30.00
Tray, 13½", 2 hdld. celery, oval, 400/105	30.00
Tray, 13", relish, 5 sections, 400/102	45.00
Tray, 14", hdld., 400/113E	40.00
Tumbler, 3½ oz., cocktail, 400/18	38.00
Tumbler, 5 oz., juice, 400/18	35.00
Tumbler, 6 oz., sherbet, 400/18	35.00
Tumbler, 7 oz., parfait, 400/18	35.00
Tumbler, 9 oz., water, 400/18	35.00
Tumbler, 12 oz., tea, 400/18	40.00
Tumbler, 3 oz., ftd., cocktail, 400/19	12.00
Tumbler, 3 oz., ftd., wine, 400/19	14.00
Tumbler, 5 oz., low sherbet, 400/19	12.00
Tumbler, 5 oz., juice, 400/19	10.00
Tumbler, 7 oz., old fashioned, 400/19	13.50
Tumbler, 10 oz., 400/19	10.00
Tumbler, 12 oz., 400/19	14.00
Tumbler, 14 oz., 400/19, tea	17.00
Tumbler, #3400, 5 oz., ft., juice	15.00
Tumbler, #3400, 9 oz., ftd.	14.00
Tumbler, #3400, 10 oz., ftd.	12.50
Tumbler, #3400, 12 oz., ftd.	15.00
Tumbler, #3800, 5 oz., juice	16.00
Tumbler, #3800, 9 oz.	14.00
Tumbler, #3800, 12 oz.	18.00
Vase, 4", bead ft., sm. neck, ball, 400/25	40.00
Vase, 5¾", bead ft., bud, 400/107	45.00
Vase, 5¾", bead ft., mini bud, 400/107	40.00
Vase, 6", flat, crimped edge, 400/287C	40.00
Vase, 6", ftd., flared rim, 400/138B	60.00
Vase, 6" diam., 400/198	160.00
Vase, 6" fan, 400/287 F	27.50
Vase, 7", ftd., bud, 400/186	175.00
Vase, 7", ftd., bud, 400/187	145.00
Vase, 7", ivy bowl, 400/74J	45.00
Vase, 7", rolled rim w/bead hdld., 400/87 R	35.00
Vase, 7", rose bowl, 400/142 K	65.00
Vase, 7¼", ftd., rose bowl, crimped top, 400/132C	200.00
Vase, 7½", ftd., rose bowl, 400/132	125.00
Vase, 8", fan, w/bead hdld., 400/87F	30.00
Vase, 8", flat, crimped edge, 400/143C	55.00
Vase, 8", fluted rim w/bead hdlds., 400/87C	27.50
Vase, 8½", bead ft., bud, 400/28C	60.00
Vase, 8½", bead ft., flared rim, 400/21	75.00
Vase, 8½", bead ft., inward rim, 400/27	75.00
Vase, 8½", hdld. (pitcher shape), 400/227	250.00
Vase, 10", bead ft., straight side, 400/22	130.00
Vase, 10", ftd., 400/193	110.00

CAPE COD, Imperial Glass Company, 1932 – 1980's

Colors: crystal, cobalt blue, red

Cape Cod seems to the stepchild of Imperial. While there are many unusual pieces of Cape Cod that were made for a long time, just as was the case for Candlewick, there is not the devotion to collecting it as there is with Candlewick. Perhaps that will come.

One of the "fun" things for me is to pick up unusual pieces not shown in previous books for the new book. I found many unusual and hard to find pieces this time, but I also found out that these pieces are also hard to sell!

This was not the case for the Tom and Jerry punch bowl set at the bottom of page 35. This was purchased (at an estate sale) in Idaho with thirty-six mugs for $50.00 last year. It was wrapped in 1954 paper. Very few of these have been found. The mug is also considered a handled cigarette holder.

Colored Cape Cod has its devotees, but it is cobalt blue and red that are most in demand. Prices are not that much more than crystal with most of the latter colors selling at reasonable prices - if at all!

I still do not know what a "Pokal" jar is used for, but they are the wicker handled jars shown on the bottom of page 37. I'm wondering if anyone can enlighten me on that!

	Crystal		Crystal
Ashtray, 4", 160/134/1	6.00	Bowl, 11¼", oval, 1602	45.00
Ashtray, 5½", 160/150	7.00	Bowl, 12", 160/75B	37.50
Basket, 9", handled, crimped, 160/221/0	125.00	Bowl, 12", oval, 160/131B	45.00
Basket, 11" wide, 160/221/0	115.00	Bowl, 12", oval crimped, 160/131C	65.00
Basket, 11" tall, handled, 160/40	95.00	Bowl, 12", punch, 160/20B	50.00
Bottle, bitters, 4 oz., 160/235	32.50	Bowl, 12½", punch, ftd., 160/120	65.00
Bottle, cologne, w/stopper, 1601	35.00	Bowl, 13", console, 160/75L	40.00
Bottle, condiment, 6 oz., 160/224	45.00	Bowl, 15", console, 16010L	50.00
Bottle, cordial, 18 oz., 160/256	75.00	Butter, 5", w/cover, handled, 160/144	22.00
Bottle, decanter, 26 oz., 160/244	70.00	Butter, w/cover, ¼ lb., 160/161	42.50
Bottle, ketchup, 14 oz., 160/237	85.00	Cake plate, 10", 4 toed, 160/220	85.00
Bowl, 3", handled mint, 160/183	8.00	Cake stand, 10½", footed, 160/67D	32.50
Bowl, 3", jelly, 160/33	5.00	Cake stand, 11", 160/103D	55.00
Bowl, 4" finger, 1602	8.00	Candleholder, twin, 160/100	45.00
Bowl, 4½", finger, 1604½A	6.00	Candleholder, 3", single, 160/170	12.00
Bowl, 4½", handled spider, 160/180	10.00	Candleholder, 4", 160/81	12.00
Bowl, 4½", dessert, tab handled, 160/197	8.00	Candleholder, 4", Aladdin style, 160/90	45.00
Bowl, 5", dessert, heart shape, 160/49H	10.00	Candleholder, 4½", saucer, 160/175	15.00
Bowl, 5", flower, 1605N	12.00	Candleholder, 5", 160/80	17.50
Bowl, 5½", fruit, 160/23B	6.00	Candleholder, 5", flower, 160/45B	35.00
Bowl, 5½", handled spider, 160/181	11.00	Candleholder, 5½", flower, 160/45N	40.00
Bowl, 5½", tab handled, soup, 160/198	10.00	Candleholder, 6", centerpiece, 160/48BC	65.00
Bowl, 6", fruit, 160/3F	6.00	Candy, w/cover, 160/110	60.00
Bowl, 6", baked apple, 160/53X	8.00	Carafe, wine, 26 oz., 160/185	135.00
Bowl, 6", handled, round mint, 160/51F	13.50	Celery, 8", 160/105	15.00
Bowl, 6", handled heart, 160/40H	14.50	Celery, 10½", 160/189	22.50
Bowl, 6", handled mint, 160/51H	18.00	Cigarette box, 4½", 160/134	30.00
Bowl, 6", handled tray, 160/51T	12.50	Cigarette holder, ftd., 1602	12.50
Bowl, 6½", handled portioned spider, 160/187	22.50	Cigarette holder, Tom & Jerry mug, 160/200	30.00
Bowl, 6½", handled spider, 160/182	20.00	Cigarette lighter, 1602	15.00
Bowl, 6½", tab handled, 160/199	12.00	Coaster, w/spoon rest, 160/76	9.50
Bowl, 7", nappy, 160/5F	15.00	Coaster, 3", square, 160/85	7.00
Bowl, 7½", 160/7F	13.00	Coaster, 4", round, 160/78	5.00
Bowl, 7½", 2-handled, 160/62B	20.00	Coaster, 4½", flat, 160/1R	5.00
Bowl, 8¾", 160/10F	22.00	Comporte, 5¼", 160F	17.50
Bowl, 9", footed fruit, 160/67F	50.00	Comporte, 5¾", 160X	20.00
Bowl, 9½", 2-handled, 160/145B	35.00	Comporte, 6", 160/45	17.50
Bowl, 9½", crimped, 160/221C	45.00	Comporte, 6", w/cover, ftd., 160/140	50.00
Bowl, 9½", float, 160/221F	40.00	Comporte, 7", 160/48B	25.00
Bowl, 10", footed, 160/137B	55.00	Comporte, 11¼", oval, 1602, 6½" tall	75.00
Bowl, 10", oval, 160/221	40.00	Creamer, 160/190	8.00
Bowl, 10", round, 160/8A	32.50	Creamer, 160/30	8.00
Bowl, 11", flanged edge, 1608X	65.00	Creamer, ftd., 160/31	9.00
Bowl, 11", oval, 160/124	40.00	Cruet, w/stopper, 4 oz., 160/119	15.00
Bowl, 11", oval divided, 160/125	42.50	Cruet, w/stopper, 5 oz., 160/70	22.00
Bowl, 11", salad, 160/8B	35.00	Cruet, w/stopper, 6 oz., 160/241	35.00

	Crystal
Jar, cookie, w/lid, wicker hand., 6½" h., 160/195..	75.00
Jar, peanut butter w/lid, wicker hand., 4" h., 160/193	50.00
Ladle, marmalade, 160/130	6.00
Ladle, mayonnaise, 160/165	6.00
Ladle, punch	20.00
Lamp, hurricane, 2 pc., 5" base, 160/79	65.00
Lamp, hurricane, 2 pc., bowl-like base, 1604	75.00
Marmalade, 3 pc. set, 160/89/3	25.00
Marmalade, 4 pc. set, 160/89	30.00
Mayonnaise, 3 pc. set, 160/52H	25.00
Mayonnaise, 3 pc., 160/23	22.00
Mayonnaise, 12 oz., hdld., spouted, 160/205	45.00
Mug, 12 oz., handled, 160/188	40.00
Mustard, w/cover & spoon, 160/156	17.50
Nut dish, 3", hdld., 160/183	6.00
Nut dish, 4", hdld., 160/184	8.00
Pepper mill, 160/236	20.00
Pitcher, milk, 1 pt., 160/240	22.00
Pitcher, ice lipped, 40 oz., 160/19	60.00
Pitcher, martini, blown, 40 oz., 160/178	125.00
Pitcher, ice lipped, 2 qt., 160/239	85.00
Pitcher, 2 qt., 160/24	75.00
Pitcher, blown, 5 pt., 160/176	110.00
Plate, 4½" butter, 160/34	3.00
Plate, 6", cupped, (liner for 160/208 salad dressing), 160/209	18.00
Plate, 6½", bread & butter, 160/1D	2.50
Plate, 7", 160/3D	4.00
Plate, 7", cupped (liner for 160/205 Mayo), 160/206	15.00
Plate, 8", center handled tray, 160/149D	22.50
Plate, 8", crescent salad, 160/12	40.00
Plate, 8", cupped, (liner for gravy), 160/203	20.00
Plate, 8", salad, 1605D	6.00
Plate, 8½", 2-handled, 160/62D	20.00
Plate, 9", 160/7D	10.00
Plate, 9½", 2 hdld., 160/62D	27.50
Plate, 10", dinner, 160/10D	32.50
Plate, 11½", 2-handled, 160/145D	32.00
Plate, 12½" bread, 160/222	42.00
Plate, 13", birthday, 72 candle holes, 160/72	185.00
Plate, 13", cupped torte, 160/8V	30.00
Plate, 13", torte, 160/8F	35.00
Plate, 14", cupped, 160/75V	30.00
Plate, 14", flat, 160/75D	30.00
Plate, 16", cupped, 160/20V	40.00
Plate, 17", 2 styles, 160/10D or 20D	35.00
Platter, 13½", oval, 160/124D	45.00
Puff Box, w/cover, 1601	35.00
Relish, 8", hdld., 2 part. 160/223	30.00
Relish, 9½", 4 pt., 160/56	32.50
Relish, 9½", oval, 3 part, 160/55	32.50
Relish, 11", 5 part, 160/102	40.00
Relish, 11¼", 3 part, oval, 1602	40.00
Salad dressing, 6 oz., hdld., spouted, 160/208	40.00

	Crystal
Salad set, 14" plate, 12" bowl, fork & spoon, 160/75	90.00
Salt & pepper, individual, 160/251	12.00
Salt & pepper, pr., ftd., 160/116	15.00
Salt & pepper, pr., ftd., stemmed, 160/243	22.50
Salt & pepper, pr., 160/96	9.00
Salt & pepper, pr. square, 160/109	18.00
Salt dip, 160/61	10.00
Salt spoon, 1600	3.00
Saucer, tea, 160/35	1.50
Saucer, coffee, 160/37	1.50
Server, 12", ftd. or turned over, 160/93	65.00
Spoon, 160/701	7.50
Stem, 1½ oz., cordial, 1602	10.00
Stem, 3 oz., wine, 1602	7.00
Stem, 3½ oz., cocktail, 1602	7.00
Stem, 5 oz., claret, 1602	12.00
Stem, 6 oz., low sundae, 1602	7.00
Stem, 6 oz., parfait, 1602	12.00
Stem, 6 oz., sherbet, 1600	7.50
Stem, 6 oz., tall sherbet, 1602	8.50
Stem, 9 oz., water, 1602	9.50
Stem, 10 oz., water, 1600	10.00
Stem, 11 oz., dinner goblet, 1602	10.00
Stem, 14 oz., goblet, magnum, 160	22.50
Stem, oyster cocktail, 1602	8.00
Sugar, 160/190	8.00
Sugar, 160/30	7.00
Sugar, ftd., 160/31	7.00
Toast, w/cover, 160/123	75.00
Tom & Jerry footed punch bowl, 160/200	250.00
Tray, square covered sugar & creamer, 160/25/26	110.00
Tray, 7", for creamer/sugar, 160/29	8.00
Tray, 11", pastry, center handle, 160/68D	32.50
Tumbler, 2½ oz., whiskey, 160	9.50
Tumbler, 6 oz., ftd., juice, 1602	6.00
Tumbler, 6 oz., juice, 1600	7.00
Tumbler, 7 oz., old fashion, 160	9.00
Tumbler, 10 oz., ftd., water, 1602	9.00
Tumbler, 10 oz., water, 160	9.00
Tumbler, 12 oz., ftd., ice tea, 1602	12.00
Tumbler, 12 oz., ftd., tea, 1600	11.00
Tumbler, 12 oz., ice tea, 160	12.50
Tumbler, 14 oz., double old fashion, 160	20.00
Tumbler, 16 oz., 160	17.50
Vase, 6¼", ftd., 160/22	22.00
Vase, 6½", ftd., 160/110B	40.00
Vase, 7½", ftd., 160/22	30.00
Vase, 8", fan, 160/87F	65.00
Vase, 8½", flip, 160/143	45.00
Vase, 8½", ftd., 160/28	40.00
Vase, 10", cylinder, 160/192	50.00
Vase, 10½", hdld., urn, 160/186	100.00
Vase, 11", ftd., 160/21	55.00

CAPRICE, Cambridge Glass Company, 1940's – Early 1950's

Colors: crystal, blue, white, amber, amethyst, pink, emerald green, pink, cobalt blue, moonlight blue, white

Collectors of blue Caprice abound and although there have been four Doulton pitchers found in the last six months, all have been purchased at big prices for collections! Many blue Caprice items are not being found on the market at any price including 2½ oz. footed whiskies, 5 oz. moulded sherbets (both shown in the middle of the top photo on next page), clarets, finger bowls, and the moulded straight sided 9 and 12 oz. tumblers.

There are other hard to find items, but those listed above are the most difficult of a long list. Before I get letters again, let me point out that the footed bowl on the far right in the bottom photo of the next page is NOT Caprice. My collectors who furnish this pattern keep sneaking it by me at the photography session. When you photograph about 6,000 pieces for three different books in one grueling week long session, anything can - and does happen!

There are many collectors of crystal also, but they are helped by more reasonable prices. Of course, the punch bowl and candle reflectors shown at the top of page 41 are only found in crystal and are not priced cheaply.

Most of the pastel colored Caprice as shown in top photo is priced about the same or a little less than the blue. There are few collectors for any pastel color other than pink.

	Crystal	Blue		Crystal	Blue
Ashtray, 2¾", 3 ftd., shell, #213	6.00	10.00	Candlestick, 2½", ea., #67	12.00	22.00
* Ashtray, 3", #214	6.00	12.00	Candlestick, 2-lite, keyhole, 5",		
* Ashtray, 4", #215	7.00		#646	14.00	35.00
* Ashtray, 5", #216		17.50	Candlestick, 3-lite, #74................	25.00	45.00
Bonbon, 6", oval, ftd., #155..........	15.00	35.00	Candlestick, 5", ea. keyhole, #647	17.50	40.00
Bonbon, 6", sq., 2 hdld., #154.......	12.00	32.50	Candlestick, 7", ea. w/prism, #70 .	15.00	35.00
Bonbon, 6", sq., ftd., #133............	14.00	35.00	Candy, 6", 3 ftd. w/cover, #165	40.00	85.00
Bottle, 7 oz., bitters, #186	125.00	250.00	Candy, 6", w/cover (divided),		
Bowl, 2", 4 ftd., almond #95	12.00	35.00	#168	50.00	100.00
* Bowl, 5", 2 hdld., jelly, #151........	13.00	27.50	Celery & relish, 8½", 3 pt., #124....	17.50	37.50
Bowl, 8", 4 ftd., #49.....................	30.00	55.00	Cigarette box, w/cover, 3½" x 2¼",		
* Bowl, 8", 3 pt., relish, #124..........	17.50	32.50	#207	15.00	30.00
Bowl, 9½", crimped, 4 ftd., #52	27.50	65.00	Cigarette box, w/cover, 4½" x 3½",		
Bowl, 9", pickle, #102	17.50	47.50	#208	22.00	55.00
Bowl, 10", salad, 4 ftd., #57	32.50	67.50	Cigarette holder, 2" x 2¼",		
Bowl, 10", sq., 4 ftd., #58	30.00	65.00	triangular, #205	12.00	27.50
Bowl, 10½", crimped, 4 ftd.,			Cigarette holder, 3" x 3",		
#53	30.00	75.00	triangular, #204	20.00	40.00
Bowl, 11", crimped, 4 ftd., #60	32.00	75.00	Coaster, 3½", #13	12.00	22.00
* Bowl, 11", 2 hdld., oval, 4 ftd.,			Comport, 6", #130.......................	22.00	55.00
#65	30.00	65.00	Comport, 7", low ftd., #130...........	17.50	60.00
* Bowl, 12", 4 pt. relish, oval, #126.	60.00	135.00	Comport, 7", #136.......................	35.00	75.00
* Bowl, 12", relish, 3 pt.,			Cracker jar & cover, #202	150.00	300.00
rectangular, #125	40.00	100.00	* Creamer, large, #41.....................	10.00	17.50
Bowl, 12½", belled, 4 ftd., #62	30.00	70.00	* Creamer, medium, #38	8.00	15.00
Bowl, 12½", crimped, 4 ftd., #61 ..	32.50	75.00	* Creamer, ind., #40	10.00	20.00
Bowl, 13", crimped, 4 ftd., #66	32.50	75.00	Cup, #17	12.00	30.00
Bowl, 13½", 4 ftd., shallow			Decanter, w/stopper, 35 oz., #187.	100.00	250.00
cupped #82	35.00	77.50	Finger bowl & liner, #16................	25.00	75.00
Bridge set:			Ice bucket, #201..........................	45.00	125.00
*Cloverleaf, 6½", #173...............	20.00	65.00	Marmalade, w/cover, 6 oz., #89....	45.00	125.00
*Club, 6½", #170......................	20.00	65.00	* Mayonnaise, 6½", 3 pc. set, #129..	25.00	75.00
Diamond, 6½", #171	20.00	65.00	* Mayonnaise, 8", 3 pc. set, #106.....	40.00	80.00
*Heart, 6½", #169	20.00	75.00	Mustard, w/cover, 2 oz., #87........	35.00	100.00
*Spade, 6½", #172....................	20.00	60.00	* Oil, 3 oz., w/stopper, #101	22.00	57.50
* Butterdish, ¼ lb., #52	195.00		* Oil, 5 oz., w/stopper, #100	65.00	125.00
Cake plate, 13", ftd., #36	130.00	275.00	Pitcher, 32 oz., ball shape, #179 ...	75.00	265.00
Candle reflector...........................	150.00		Pitcher, 80 oz., ball shape, #183 ...	90.00	250.00

*Moulds owned by Summit Art Glass and many of these pieces have been reproduced.

CAPRICE, Cambridge Glass Company, 1940's – Early 1950's (continued)

	Crystal	Blue		Crystal	Blue
Pitcher, 90 oz., tall Doulton style, #178	700.00	4,000.00	Stem, 5 oz., low sherbet, #4	20.00	85.00
Plate, 6½", bread & butter, #21	10.00	20.00	* Stem, 7 oz., tall sherbet, #2	17.50	30.00
Plate, 6½", hdld., lemon, #152	11.00	20.00	Stem, 10 oz., water, #1	26.00	40.00
Plate, 7½", salad, #23	12.50	20.00	* Sugar, large, #41	10.00	15.00
Plate, 8½", #22	14.00	32.50	* Sugar, medium, #38	8.00	15.00
* Plate, 9½", dinner, #24	37.50	115.00	* Sugar, indiv., #40	10.00	19.00
Plate, 11", cabaret, 4 ftd., #32	22.00	45.00	* Tray, for sugar & creamer, #37	12.50	27.50
Plate, 11½", cabaret, #26	25.00	45.00	Tray, 9" oval, #42	18.00	40.00
Plate, 14", cabaret, 4 ftd., #33	27.50	55.00	* Tumbler, 2 oz., flat, #188	18.00	45.00
Plate, 14", 4 ftd., #28	27.50	55.00	Tumbler, 3 oz., ftd., #12	18.00	40.00
Plate, 16", #30	35.00	75.00	Tumbler, 5 oz., ftd., #11	20.00	42.50
Punch bowl, ftd.	1,950.00		Tumbler, 5 oz., flat, #180	18.00	40.00
* Salad dressing, 3 pc., ftd. & hdld., 2 spoons, #112	145.00	350.00	Tumbler, #300, 2½ oz., whiskey....	25.00	125.00
Saucer, #17	2.50	5.50	Tumbler, #300, 5 oz., ftd., juice	16.00	30.00
Salt & pepper, pr., ball, #91	37.50	75.00	Tumbler, #300, 10 oz.	18.00	36.00
* Salt & pepper, pr., flat, #96	22.00	40.00	Tumbler, #300, 12 oz.	18.00	35.00
Salt & pepper, indiv., ball, pr., #90	30.00	75.00	Tumbler, #301, blown, 4½ oz., low oyster cocktail	15.00	
Salt & pepper, indiv., flat, pr., #92	30.00	80.00	Tumbler, #301, blown, 5 oz., juice	13.00	
Salver, 13", 2 pc. (cake atop pedestal), #31	140.00	300.00	Tumbler, #301, blown, 12 oz., tea.	17.00	
Stem, #300, blown, 1 oz., cordial...	35.00	115.00	* Tumbler, 9 oz., straight side, #14 ..	30.00	75.00
Stem, #300, blown, 2½ oz., wine ..	25.00	55.00	* Tumbler, 10 oz., ftd., #10	18.00	35.00
Stem, #300, blown, 3 oz., cocktail	22.00	40.00	Tumbler, 12 oz., ftd., #9	22.00	40.00
Stem, #300, blown, 4½ oz., claret ...	45.00	150.00	* Tumbler, 12 oz., straight side, #15	35.00	65.00
Stem, #300, blown, 4½ oz., low oyster cocktail	18.00	35.00	Tumbler, #310, 5 oz., flat, juice.....	15.00	35.00
Stem, #300, blown, 5 oz., parfait ..	75.00	225.00	Tumbler, #310, 7 oz., flat, old fashion	30.00	90.00
Stem, #300, blown, 6 oz., low sherbet	10.00	14.00	Tumbler, #310, 10 oz., flat, table...	15.00	30.00
Stem, #300, blown, 6 oz., tall sherbet	12.00	21.50	Tumbler, #310, 11 oz., flat, tall, 4¹³⁄₁₆"	20.00	60.00
Stem, #300, blown, 9 oz. water.....	16.00	35.00	Tumbler, #310, 12 oz., flat, tea......	30.00	90.00
Stem, #301, blown, 1 oz., cordial .	35.00		Vase, 3½", #249	45.00	100.00
Stem, #301, blown, 2½ oz., wine ..	25.00		Vase, 4", #252	45.00	100.00
Stem, #301, blown, 3 oz., cocktail	20.00		Vase, 4½", #344, crimped	40.00	85.00
Stem, #301, blown, 4½ oz., claret .	30.00		Vase, 5", ivy bowl, #232	40.00	85.00
Stem, #301, blown, 6 oz., sherbet.	13.00		Vase, 5½", #345	40.00	85.00
Stem, #301, blown, 9 oz., water....	16.00		Vase, 6", #254.............................	55.00	120.00
* Stem, 3 oz., wine, #6	27.50	95.00	Vase, 6", #342.............................	45.00	85.00
* Stem, 3½ oz., cocktail, #3.............	24.00	45.00	Vase, 6½", #338, crimped	55.00	120.00
* Stem, 4½ oz., claret, #5	35.00	150.00	Vase, 7½", #346, crimped	60.00	130.00
Stem, 4½ oz., fruit cocktail, #7	27.50	65.00	Vase, 8½", #339...........................	45.00	100.00
			Vase, 8½", #343, crimped	65.00	150.00
			Vase, 9½" #340, crimped	75.00	225.00

*Moulds owned by Summit Art Glass and many of these pieces have been reproduced.

CARIBBEAN, Line #112, Duncan Miller Glass Company, 1936 – 1955

Colors: blue, crystal, amber, red

The demand for blue Caribbean far exceeds the supply. Notice that there are two styles of punch bowls. The curved in one is shown at the bottom of page 45, while the other flared top is shown opposite on page 44.

Many dinnerware pieces such as cups, saucers and plates have become scarce commodities. If more of this pattern does not start to show up, many collectors will start turning to other patterns to collect. Already many have begun to buy the crystal out of frustration in finding blue.

That 18" punch liner is very difficult to pack. It never fits any box and reminds me of trying to pack the console bowl in American Sweetheart.

	Crystal	Blue
Ashtray, 6", 4 indent	15.00	30.00
Bowl, 3¾" x 5", folded side, hdld.	15.00	30.00
Bowl, 4½", finger	13.00	27.50
Bowl, 5", fruit nappy (takes liner), hdld.	10.00	20.00
Bowl, 5" x 7", folded side, hdld.	15.00	30.00
Bowl, 6½", soup (takes liner)	12.50	27.50
Bowl, 7", hdld.	17.50	35.00
Bowl, 7¼", ftd., hdld., grapefruit	15.00	30.00
Bowl, 8½"	22.50	50.00
Bowl, 9", salad	25.00	55.00
Bowl, 9¼", veg., flared edge	22.50	50.00
Bowl, 9¼", veg., hdld.	22.50	50.00
Bowl, 9½", epergne, flared edge	30.00	65.00
Bowl, 10", 6¼ qt., punch	75.00	350.00
Bowl, 10", 6¼ qt. punch, flared top	75.00	400.00
Bowl, 10¾", oval, flower, hdld.	30.00	65.00
Bowl, 12", console, flared edge	35.00	75.00
Candelabrum, 4¾", 2-lite	30.00	60.00
Candlestick, 7¼", 1-lite, w/bl. prisms	35.00	125.00
Candy dish w/cover, 4" x 7"	35.00	85.00
Cheese/cracker crumbs, 3½" h., plate 11", hdld.	30.00	65.00
Cigarette holder, (stack ashtray top)	30.00	70.00
Cocktail shaker, 9", 33 oz.	60.00	150.00
Creamer	10.00	22.50
Cruet	25.00	65.00
Cup, tea	12.00	50.00
Cup, punch	5.00	17.50
Epergne, 4 pt., flower (12" bowl; 9½" bowl; 7¾" vase, 14" plate)	140.00	300.00
Ice bucket, 6½", hdld.	45.00	100.00
Ladle, punch	25.00	75.00
Mayonnaise, w/liner, 5¾", 2 pt., 2 spoons, hdld.	35.00	75.00
Mayonnaise, w/liner, 5¾", hdld., 1 spoon	30.00	65.00
Mustard, 4", w/slotted cover	30.00	60.00
Pitcher, 4¼", 9 oz., syrup	45.00	110.00
Pitcher, 4¾" 16 oz., milk	75.00	195.00
Pitcher, w/ice lip, 9", 72 oz., water	150.00	400.00
Plate, 6", hdld., fruit nappy liner	4.00	11.00
Plate 6¼", bread/butter	4.00	10.00
Plate, 7¼", rolled edge, soup liner	5.00	12.00
Plate, 7½", salad	8.00	17.50
Plate, 8", hdld., mayonnaise liner	5.00	12.00
Plate, 8½", luncheon	10.00	25.00
Plate, 10½", dinner	40.00	100.00
Plate, 11", hdld., cheese/cracker liner	15.00	35.00
Plate, 12", salad liner, rolled edge	17.50	40.00
Plate, 14"	15.00	40.00
Plate, 16", torte	25.00	60.00
Plate, 18", punch underliner	30.00	70.00
Relish, 6", round, 2 pt.	10.00	22.00

	Crystal	Blue
Relish, 9½", 4 pt., oblong	25.00	55.00
Relish, 9½", oblong	22.00	52.50
Relish, 12¾", 5 pt., rnd.	35.00	75.00
Relish, 12¾", 7 pt., rnd.	35.00	75.00
Salt dip, 2½"	7.00	15.00
Salt & pepper, 3", metal tops	30.00	65.00
Salt & pepper, 5", metal tops	35.00	75.00
Saucer	2.00	6.00
Server, 5¾", ctr. hdld.	11.50	40.00
Server, 6½", ctr. hdld.	20.00	45.00
Stem, 3", 1 oz., cordial	50.00	125.00
Stem, 3½", 3½ oz., ftd., ball stem, wine	20.00	35.00
Stem, 3⅝", 2½ oz., wine (egg cup shape)	22.50	32.50
Stem, 4", 6 oz., ftd., ball stem, champagne	12.00	25.00
Stem, 4¼", ftd., sherbet	6.00	15.00
Stem, 4¾", 3 oz., ftd., ball stem, wine	17.50	40.00
Stem, 5¾", 8 oz., ftd., ball stem	14.00	30.00
Sugar	9.00	20.00
Syrup, metal cut off top	60.00	125.00
Tray, 6¼", hand., mint, div.	10.00	22.00
Tray, 12¾", rnd.	17.50	40.00
Tumbler, 2¼", 2 oz., shot glass	20.00	45.00
Tumbler, 3½", 5 oz., flat	15.00	30.00
Tumbler, 5¼" 11½ oz., flat	15.00	30.00
Tumbler, 5½", 8½ oz., ftd.	17.50	35.00
Tumbler, 6½", 11 oz., ftd., ice tea	20.00	40.00
Vase, 5¾", ftd., ruffled edge	17.50	37.50
Vase, 7¼", ftd., flared edge, ball	22.00	45.00
Vase, 7½", ftd., flared edge, bulbous	25.00	50.00
Vase, 7¾", flared edge, epergne	25.00	50.00
Vase, 8", ftd., straight side	30.00	75.00
Vase, 9", ftd., ruffled top	35.00	135.00
Vase, 10", ftd.	35.00	110.00

CENTURY, Line #2630, Fostoria Glass Company

Colors: crystal

Stemware in Century has some big prices on the West Coast! In particular wines and footed iced teas are about fifty percent higher than in the East. However, on a whole in the west, prices for Elegant glassware are more reasonable than for Depression glassware.

Note that I have used some etched Fostoria patterns that are on the #2630 Century line in the pictures. There are two sized dinner plates as is the case in most of Fostoria's patterns. The larger plate is the harder to find. They were priced higher originally, and many people did without the larger plates.

The ice bucket has a metal handle and "ears" for the handle to fit. A similar item without a handle was called an 8½" oval vase by Fostoria and not an ice tub as I have seen it labeled recently.

There is some confusion between the candy and the covered preserve. The candy w/cover stands 7" tall, but the preserve w/cover only stands 6" tall.

	Crystal
Ashtray, 2¾"	5.00
Basket, 10¼" x 6½", wicker hdld.	60.00
Bowl, 4½", hdld.	9.00
Bowl, 5", fruit	12.00
Bowl, 6", cereal	20.00
Bowl, 6¼", snack, ftd.	12.50
Bowl, 7⅛", 3 ftd., triangular	14.00
Bowl, 7¼", bonbon, 3 ftd.	15.00
Bowl, 8", flared	22.00
Bowl, 8½", salad	22.00
Bowl, 9", lily pond	25.00
Bowl, 9½", hdld., serving bowl	25.00
Bowl, 9½", oval, serving bowl	25.00
Bowl, 10", oval, hdld.	25.00
Bowl, 10½", salad	25.00
Bowl, 10¾", ftd., flared	27.50
Bowl, 11, ftd., rolled edge	30.00
Bowl, 11¼", lily pond	30.00
Bowl, 12", flared	30.00
Butter, w/cover, ¼ lb.	30.00
Candy, w/cover, 7"	27.50
Candlestick, 4½"	12.00
Candlestick, 7", double	25.00
Candlestick, 7¾", triple	30.00
Comport, 2¾", cheese	12.00
Comport, 4⅜"	13.50
Cracker plate, 10¾"	30.00
Creamer, 4¼"	6.00
Creamer, individual	4.00
Cup, 6 oz., ftd.	9.00
Ice Bucket	45.00
Mayonnaise, 3 pc.	25.00
Mayonnaise, 4 pc., div. w/2 ladles	30.00
Mustard, w/spoon, cover	25.00
Oil, w/stopper, 5 oz.	40.00
Pickle, 8¾"	13.50
Pitcher, 6⅛", 16 oz.	45.00

	Crystal
Pitcher, 7⅛", 48 oz.	85.00
Plate, 6", bread/butter	3.00
Plate, 7½", salad	4.00
Plate, 7½", crescent salad	30.00
Plate, 8", party, w/indent for cup	20.00
Plate, 8½", luncheon	8.00
Plate, 9½", small dinner	17.50
Plate, 10", hdld., cake	18.00
Plate, 10½", dinner	25.00
Plate, 14", torte	20.00
Platter, 12"	45.00
Preserve, w/cover, 6"	22.00
Relish, 7⅜", 2 part	13.50
Relish, 11⅛", 3 part	20.00
Salt and pepper, 2⅜", individual, pr.	10.00
Salt and pepper, 3⅛", pr.	13.50
Salver, 12¼", ftd. (like cake stand)	45.00
Saucer	1.50
Stem, 3½ oz., cocktail, 4⅛"	13.00
Stem, 3½ oz., wine, 4½"	24.00
Stem, 4½ oz., oyster cocktail, 3¾"	14.00
Stem, 5½" oz., sherbet, 4½"	9.00
Stem, 10 oz., goblet, 5¾"	18.00
Sugar, 4", ftd.	6.00
Sugar, individual	4.00
Tid bit, 8⅛", 3 ftd., upturned edge	14.00
Tid bit, 10¼", 2 tier, metal hdld.	22.50
Tray, 4¼", for ind. salt/pepper	12.00
Tray, 7⅛", for ind. sug/cr	12.00
Tray, 9⅛", hdld., utility	22.00
Tray, 9½", hdld., muffin	25.00
Tray, 11½", center hdld.	20.00
Tumbler, 5 oz., ftd., juice, 4¾"	12.00
Tumbler, 12 oz., ftd., tea, 5⅞"	24.00
Vase, 6", bud	17.50
Vase, 7½", hdld.	55.00
Vase, 8½", oval	50.00

CHANTILLY, Cambridge Glass Company, Late 1940's – Early 1950's

Colors: crystal

The stemware line most often collected in Chantilly is #3625. As with other Cambridge patterns, there are a multitude of blanks and items that can be collected in this pattern.

Most of the items found with Rose Point can also be found with Chantilly. There is a more complete listing for the Rose Point since there are so many collectors of that pattern. If any collector of Chantilly has a major listing of available pieces, please contact me.

Be certain not to confuse this pattern with Elaine as many novice collectors seem to do.

	Crystal		Crystal
Bowl, 7", bonbon, 2 hdld., ftd.	16.00	Saucer	2.50
Bowl, 7", relish/pickle, 2 pt.	18.00	Stem, #3600, 1 oz., cordial	42.50
Bowl, 7", relish/pickle	18.00	Stem, #3600, 2½ oz., cocktail	24.00
Bowl, 9", celery/relish, 3 pt.	22.00	Stem #3600, 2½ oz., wine	29.00
Bowl, 10", 4 ftd., flared	30.00	Stem, #3600, 4½ oz., claret	30.00
Bowl, 11", tab hdld.	27.00	Stem, #3600, 4½ oz., low oyster cocktail	15.00
Bowl, 11½", tab hdld. ftd.	30.00	Stem, #3600, 7 oz., tall sherbet	17.50
Bowl, 12", celery/relish, 3 pt.	30.00	Stem, #3600, 7 oz., low sherbet	15.00
Bowl, 12", 4 ftd., flared	30.00	Stem, #3600, 10 oz., water	19.50
Bowl, 12", 4 ftd., oval	32.50	Stem, #3625, 1 oz., cordial	47.50
Bowl, 12", celery/relish, 5 pt.	30.00	Stem, #3625, 3 oz., cocktail	27.50
Butter, w/cover, round	125.00	Stem, #3625, 4½ oz., claret	30.00
Butter, ¼ lb.	195.00	Stem, #3625, 4½ oz., low oyster cocktail	16.00
Candlestick, 5"	17.50	Stem, #3625, 7 oz., low sherbet	16.00
Candlestick, 6", 2-lite, "fleur de lis"	30.00	Stem, #3625, 7 oz., tall sherbet	18.00
Candlestick, 6", 3-lite	35.00	Stem, #3625, 10 oz., water	25.00
Candy box, w/cover, ftd.	110.00	Stem, #3775, 1 oz., cordial	42.50
Candy box, w/cover, rnd.	52.50	Stem, #3775, 2½" oz., wine	27.00
Cocktail icer, 2 pc.	50.00	Stem, #3775, 3 oz., cocktail	25.00
Comport, 5½"	30.00	Stem, #3775, 4½ oz., claret	30.00
Comport, 5⅜", blown	35.00	Stem, #3775, 4½ oz., oyster cocktail	15.00
Creamer	14.50	Stem, #3775, 6 oz., low sherbet	15.00
Creamer, indiv., #3900, scalloped edge	11.00	Stem, #3775, 6 oz., tall sherbet	17.50
Cup	17.50	Stem, #3779, 1 oz., cordial	50.00
Decanter, ftd.	140.00	Stem, #3779, 2½ oz., wine	27.50
Decanter, ball	160.00	Stem, #3779, 3 oz., cocktail	25.00
Hat, small	125.00	Stem, #3779, 4½ oz., claret	30.00
Hat, large	175.00	Stem, #3779, 4½ oz., low oyster cocktail	15.00
Hurricane lamp, candlestick base	100.00	Stem, #3779, 6 oz., tall sherbet	17.50
Hurricane lamp, keyhole base w/prisms	130.00	Stem, #3779, 6 oz., low sherbet	15.00
Ice bucket, w/chrome handle	65.00	Stem, #3779, 9 oz., water	20.00
Marmalade & cover	55.00	Sugar	13.50
Mayonnaise, (sherbet type bowl w/ladle)	25.00	Sugar, indiv., #3900, scalloped edge	11.00
Mayonnaise, div. w/liner & 2 ladles	40.00	Tumbler, #3600, 5 oz., ftd., juice	14.00
Mayonnaise, w/liner & ladle	36.00	Tumbler, #3600, 12 oz., ftd., tea	18.00
Mustard & cover	45.00	Tumbler, #3625, 5 oz., ftd., juice	15.00
Oil, 6 oz., hdld., w/stopper	45.00	Tumbler, #3625, 10 oz., ftd., water	17.50
Pitcher, ball	120.00	Tumbler, #3625, 12 oz., ftd., tea	22.00
Pitcher, Doulton	225.00	Tumbler, #3775, 5 oz., ftd., juice	14.00
Pitcher, upright	165.00	Tumbler, #3775, 10 oz., ftd., water	15.00
Plate, crescent, salad	35.00	Tumbler, #3775, 12 oz., ftd., tea	18.00
Plate, 6½", bread/butter	6.50	Tumbler, #3779, 5 oz., ftd., juice	15.00
Plate, 8", salad	12.50	Tumbler, #3779, 12 oz., ftd., tea	18.00
Plate, 8", tab hdld., ftd., bonbon	15.00	Tumbler, 13 oz.	20.00
Plate, 10½", dinner	50.00	Vase, 5", globe	30.00
Plate, 12", 4 ftd., service	30.00	Vase, 6", high ftd., flower	22.00
Plate, 13", 4 ftd.	30.00	Vase, 8", high ftd., flower	30.00
Plate 13½", tab hdld., cake	31.50	Vase, 9", keyhole base	30.00
Plate, 14", torte	35.00	Vase, 10", bud	30.00
Salad dressing bottle	65.00	Vase, 11", ftd., flower	40.00
Salt & pepper, pr., flat	27.50	Vase, 11", ped. ftd., flower	45.00
Salt & pepper, footed	30.00	Vase, 12", keyhole base	50.00
Salt & pepper, handled	30.00	Vase, 13", ftd., flower	65.00

Note: See Pages 182-183 for stem identification.

CHEROKEE ROSE, Tiffin Glass Company, 1940's – 1950's

Colors: crystal

I find mostly stemware in this pattern. What I usually find is #17399 or the tear drop style which is shown on most of the stemware in the picture. The other stem #17403 is represented by the cordial nearest the creamer. There are several newly listed pieces this time; if you find any other items, let me know.

When collectors have asked me for this pattern, few have cared what stemware line I find since they are usually unaware that it comes on two different stems. I found that out several years ago, when I bought some water goblets for a customer, who informed me that those stems were not like what he had. Finally, he came back and purchased them, since he had searched for them so long.

There are still no reports of cups and saucers; so I doubt that they do exist at this point. It's a shame that a pattern that was made to compete with Cambridge's Rose Point which had three styles of cups and saucers has none.

	Crystal		Crystal
Bowl, 5", finger.	14.00	Stem, 2 oz., sherry	25.00
Bowl, 6", fruit or nut	16.00	Stem, 3½ oz., cocktail	17.00
Bowl, 7", salad	22.50	Stem, 3½ oz., wine	30.00
Bowl, 10", deep salad	35.00	Stem, 4 oz., claret	30.00
Bowl, 10½", celery, oblong	25.00	Stem, 4½ oz., parfait	35.00
Bowl, 12", crimped	35.00	Stem, 5½ oz., sherbet/champagne	16.00
Bowl, 12½" centerpiece, flared	35.00	Stem, 9 oz., water	23.50
Bowl, 13", centerpiece	40.00	Sugar	20.00
Cake plate, 12½", center hdld.	30.00	Table bell	40.00
Candlesticks, pr., double branch	60.00	Tumbler, 4½ oz., oyster cocktail	15.00
Comport, 6"	25.00	Tumbler, 5 oz., ftd., juice	16.00
Creamer	20.00	Tumbler, 8 oz., ftd., water	20.00
Mayonnaise, liner and ladle	40.00	Tumbler, 10½ oz., ftd., ice tea	25.00
Pitcher	250.00	Vase, 6", bud	22.00
Plate, 6", sherbet	5.00	Vase, 8", bud	30.00
Plate, 8", luncheon	12.00	Vase, 8½", tear drop	40.00
Plate, 13½", turned-up edge, lily	32.50	Vase, 9¼", tub	50.00
Plate, 14", sandwich	27.50	Vase, 10", bud	32.00
Relish, 6½", 3 pt.	22.00	Vase, 11", bud	38.00
Relish, 12½", 3 pt.	30.00	Vase, 11", urn	65.00
Stem, 1 oz., cordial	45.00	Vase, 12", flared	60.00

CHINTZ, (Plate Etching #338), Fostoria Glass Company

Colors: crystal

I have been told by several dealers that Fostoria Chintz sells as well as Rose Point. I find very little of it in my area except for stemware. It appears that the only Fostoria that was ever sold in Central Kentucky was American and none of the expensive, hard to find pieces were delivered here.

That oval divided bowl behind the sugar in the top photograph is the divided sauce boat. Note that many of the Chintz pieces are found on the #2496 blank (known as Baroque).

Crystal vases in Fostoria patterns are hard to find, so keep on the lookout for etched Fostoria vases in your travels.

	Crystal		Crystal
Bowl, #2496, 4⅝", tri-cornered	15.00	Plate, #2496, 9½", dinner	30.00
Bowl, #869, 4½", finger	35.00	Plate, #2496, 10", hdld., cake	40.00
Bowl, #2496, cream soup	35.00	Plate, #2496, 14", upturned edge	40.00
Bowl, #2496, 5", fruit	25.00	Plate, #2496, 16", torte, plain edge	65.00
Bowl, #2496, 5", hdld.	17.50	Platter, 12"	75.00
Bowl, #2496, 7⅝", bonbon	25.00	Relish, #2496, 6", 2 part, square	25.00
Bowl, #2496, 8½", hdld.	40.00	Relish, #2496, 10" x 7½", 3 part	30.00
Bowl, #2496, 9½", vegetable	60.00	Salad dressing bottle, #2083, 6½"	195.00
Bowl, #2484, 10", hdld.	50.00	Salt and pepper, #2496, 2¾", flat, pr.	65.00
Bowl, #2496, 10½" hdld.	50.00	Sauce boat, oval	65.00
Bowl, #2496, 12", flared	42.00	Sauce boat, oval, divided	50.00
Candlestick, #2496, 4"	12.00	Sauce boat liner, oval	20.00
Candlestick, #2496, 3½", double	25.00	Saucer, #2496	3.50
Candlestick, #2496, 5½"	22.00	Stem, #6026, 1 oz., cordial, 3⅞"	42.50
Candlestick, #2496, 6", triple	35.00	Stem, #6026, 4 oz., cocktail, 5"	22.50
Candy, w/cover, #2496, 3 part	90.00	Stem, #6026, 4 oz., oyster cocktail, 3⅜"	25.00
Celery, #2496, 11"	27.50	Stem, #6026, 4½ oz., claret-wine, 5⅜"	35.00
Comport, #2496, 3¼", cheese	22.00	Stem, #6026, 6 oz., low sherbet, 4⅜"	15.00
Comport, #2496, 4¾"	25.00	Stem, #6026, 6 oz., saucer champagne, 5½"	17.50
Cracker, #2496, 11", plate	37.50	Stem, #6026, 9 oz., water goblet, 7⅝"	27.50
Creamer, #2496, 3¾", ftd.	11.00	Sugar, #2496, 3½", ftd.	10.00
Creamer, #2496½, individual	20.00	Sugar, #2496½, individual	20.00
Cup, #2496, ftd.	17.00	Syrup, metal cut-off top	200.00
Ice bucket, #2496	95.00	Tid bit, #2496, 8¼", 3 ftd., upturned edge	25.00
Jelly, w/cover, #2496, 7½"	80.00	Tray, #2496½, 6½", for ind. sugar/creamer	15.00
Mayonnaise, #2496½, 3 piece	45.00	Tray, #2375, 11", center hdld.	30.00
Oil, w/stopper, #2496, 3½ oz.	80.00	Tumbler, #6026, 5 oz., juice, ftd.	20.00
Pickle, #2496, 8"	27.50	Tumbler, #6026, 9 oz., water or low goblet	22.00
Pitcher, #5000, 48 oz., ftd.	295.00	Tumbler, #6026, 13 oz., tea, ftd.	27.50
Plate, #2496, 6", bread/butter	8.00	Vase, #4108, 5"	65.00
Plate, #2496, 7½", salad	12.00	Vase, #4143, 6", ftd.	75.00
Plate, #2496, 8½", luncheon	17.50	Vase, #4143, 7½", ftd.	95.00

CHINTZ, #1401 (Empress Blank) and CHINTZ #3389 (Duquesne Blank) A.H. Heisey Co., 1931-1938

Colors: crystal, "Sahara" yellow, "Moongleam" green, "Flamingo" pink, and "Alexandrite" orchid

Finding new pieces to photograph in this pattern has proved difficult. The pieces with the encircled flowers is known as "formal" Chintz. Don't confuse this pattern with Fostoria's Chintz, and learn to specify the company name when you ask for Chintz. It was a popular name used by several companies as you can see.

	Crystal	Sahara
Bowl, finger, #4107	8.00	15.00
Bowl, 5½", ftd., preserve, hdld	15.00	27.00
Bowl, 6", ftd., mint	18.00	30.00
Bowl, 6", ftd., 2 hdld., jelly	15.00	30.00
Bowl, 7", triplex relish	16.00	33.00
Bowl, 7½", Nasturtium	16.00	30.00
Bowl, 8½", ftd., 2 hdld., floral	32.00	65.00
Bowl, 11", dolp. ft., floral	40.00	85.00
Bowl, 13", 2 pt., pickle & olive	15.00	25.00
Comport, 7", oval	40.00	75.00
Creamer, 3 dolp. ft.	20.00	42.50
Grapefruit, ftd., #3389, Duquesne	30.00	50.00
Ice bucket, ftd.	75.00	125.00
Mayonnaise, 5½", dolp. ft.	35.00	65.00
Oil, 4 oz.	60.00	125.00
Pitcher, 3 pint, dolp. ft.	115.00	200.00
Plate, 6", square, bread	6.00	15.00
Plate, 7", square, salad	8.00	18.00
Plate, 8", square, luncheon	10.00	22.00
Plate, 10½", square, dinner	35.00	75.00
Platter, 14", oval	30.00	65.00
Stem, #3389, Duquesne, 1 oz., cordial	100.00	195.00
Stem, #3389, 2½ oz., wine	17.50	42.50
Stem, #3389, 3 oz., cocktail	15.00	35.00
Stem, #3389, 4 oz., claret	20.00	45.00
Stem, #3389, 4 oz., oyster cocktail	10.00	20.00
Stem, #3389, 5 oz., parfait	14.00	30.00
Stem, #3389, 5 oz., saucer champagne	11.00	22.50
Stem, #3389, 5 oz., sherbet	8.00	17.50
Stem, #3389, 9 oz., water	15.00	30.00
Sugar, 3 dolp. ft.	20.00	42.50
Tray, 10", celery	14.00	27.50
Tray, 12", sq., ctr. hdld., sandwich	35.00	65.00
Tray, 13", celery	18.00	26.00
Tumbler, #3389, 5 oz., ftd., juice	11.00	22.00
Tumbler, #3389, 8 oz., soda	12.00	24.00
Tumbler, #3389, 10 oz., ftd., water	13.00	25.00
Tumbler, #3389, 12 oz., iced tea	14.00	27.50
Vase, 9", dolp. ft.	85.00	175.00

CLEO, Cambridge Glass Company, Introduced 1930

Colors: amber, blue, crystal, green, pink, yellow

Cleo is another of the "fun" patterns that I enjoy looking for in my travels. It amazes me how many different pieces were made in this pattern. However, it seems that all the unusual items always turn up in amber or pink instead of blue or green.

Note the little 1½" salt, 2½" individual almond and the wafer tray in pink on the top of page 57. There are some other unusual and hard to find pieces of Cleo in my new *Very Rare Glassware of the Depression Years, Second Series.*

	Blue	Pink/ Green/ Yellow/ Amber		Blue	Pink/ Green/ Yellow/ Amber
Almond, 2½", individual		60.00	Gravy boat, w/liner plate,		
Basket, 7", 2 hdld. (upturned			DECAGON	225.00	150.00
sides) DECAGON......................	30.00	20.00	Ice pail	95.00	60.00
Basket, 11", 2 hdld. (upturned			Ice tub	85.00	45.00
sides) DECAGON......................	50.00	30.00	Mayonnaise, w/liner and ladle,		
Bouillon cup, w/saucer, 2 hdld.,			DECAGON	95.00	45.00
DECAGON	35.00	25.00	Mayonnaise, ftd.	45.00	30.00
Bowl, 2 pt., relish	40.00	22.00	Oil, 6 oz., w/stopper, DECAGON		110.00
Bowl, 5½", fruit............................	22.00	15.00	Pitcher, 3½ pt., #38.....................		175.00
Bowl, 5½" 2 hdld., bonbon,			Pitcher, w/cover, 22 oz.		150.00
DECAGON	30.00	20.00	Pitcher, w/cover, 60 oz., #804.....		225.00
Bowl, 6", 4 ft., comport	50.00	35.00	Pitcher, w/cover, 62 oz., #955.....		225.00
Bowl, 6", cereal, DECAGON........	30.00	20.00	Pitcher, w/cover, 63 oz., #3077 ...		225.00
Bowl, 6½", 2 hdld., bonbon			Pitcher, w/cover, 68 oz., #937.....		250.00
DECAGON	35.00	22.00	Plate, 7"....................................	15.00	12.00
Bowl, 6½", cranberry	33.00	20.00	Plate, 7", 2 hdld., DECAGON......	20.00	14.00
Bowl, 7½", tab hdld., soup	40.00	30.00	Plate, 9½", dinner, DECAGON	85.00	60.00
Bowl, 8", miniature console........		90.00	Plate, 11", 2 hdld., DECAGON	110.00	30.00
Bowl, 8½".....................................	60.00	40.00	Platter, 12"..................................	150.00	100.00
Bowl, 8½" 2 hdld., DECAGON	60.00	40.00	Platter, 15"..................................	250.00	155.00
Bowl, 9", covered vegetable		100.00	Platter, w/cover, oval (toast)		300.00
Bowl, 9½", oval veg., DECAGON	75.00	40.00	Platter, asparagus, indented,		
Bowl, 9", pickle, DECAGON	60.00	25.00	w/sauce & spoon		275.00
Bowl, 10", 2 hdld., DECAGON....	65.00	35.00	Salt dip, 1½"		50.00
Bowl, 11", oval.............................	75.00	35.00	Saucer, DECAGON	5.00	3.00
Bowl, 11½", oval	75.00	35.00	Server, 12", ctr. hand.	65.00	35.00
Bowl, 12", console........................	65.00	35.00	Stem, #3077, 1 oz., cordial..........	135.00	100.00
Bowl, cream soup w/saucer,			Stem, #3077, 2½ oz., cocktail......	40.00	27.50
2 hdld., DECAGON	45.00	25.00	Stem, #3077, 3½ oz., wine	75.00	60.00
Bowl, finger w/liner, #3077	35.00	25.00	Stem, #3077, 6 oz., low sherbet ..	22.00	15.00
Bowl, finger w/liner, #3115	35.00	25.00	Stem, #3077, 6 oz., tall sherbet ...	30.00	17.50
Candlestick, 1-lite, 2 styles	35.00	22.00	Stem, #3115, 9 oz.		30.00
Candlestick, 2-lite.......................	75.00	35.00	Stem, #3115, 3½ oz., cocktail......		25.00
Candy box.....................................		65.00	Stem, #3115, 6 oz., fruit		15.00
Candy & cover, tall		125.00	Stem, #3115, 6 oz., low sherbet ..		13.00
Comport, 7", tall, #3115	75.00	40.00	Stem, #3115, 6 oz., tall sherbet ...		15.00
Creamer, DECAGON.....................	27.50	17.50	Stem, #3115, 9 oz.		.00
Creamer, ewer style		60.00	Sugar cube tray		100.00
Creamer, ftd.	30.00	20.00	Sugar, DECAGON	25.00	17.50
Cup, DECAGON	25.00	15.00	Sugar, ftd....................................	30.00	20.00
Decanter, w/stopper		195.00	Sugar sifter, ftd.		225.00

56

CLEO, Cambridge Glass Company, Introduced 1930 (continued)

	Blue	Pink/ Green/ Yellow/ Amber		Blue	Pink/ Green/ Yellow/ Amber
Syrup pitcher, drip cut................		145.00	Tumbler, #3022, 12 oz., ftd.	60.00	30.00
Syrup pitcher, glass lid		135.00	Tumbler, #3115, 2½ oz., ftd........		35.00
Toast & cover, round...................		325.00	Tumbler, #3115, 5 oz., ftd.		20.00
Tobacco humidor........................		300.00	Tumbler, #3115, 8 oz., ftd.		22.00
Tray, 12", handled serving...........		150.00	Tumbler, #3115, 10 oz., ftd.		25.00
Tray, 12", oval service			Tumbler, #3115, 12 oz., ftd.		30.00
DECAGON	125.00	100.00	Tumbler, 12 oz., flat...................		30.00
Tray, creamer & sugar		50.00	Vase, 5½"...................................		60.00
Tumbler, #3077, 2½ oz., ftd........	75.00	50.00	Vase, 9½"...................................		90.00
Tumbler, #3077, 5 oz., ftd.	30.00	20.00	Vase, 11"...................................		110.00
Tumbler, #3077, 8 oz., ftd.	35.00	25.00	Wafer tray		175.00
Tumbler, #3077, 10 oz., ftd.	35.00	25.00			

COLONY, Line #2412, Fostoria Glass Company, 1920's – 1970's

Colors: crystal; some yellow, blue, green, white amber

Colony evolved from an earlier Fostoria pattern called Queen Anne. The tall candlestick shown and many of the candelabra that you see similar to Colony are actually a part of this earlier Queen Anne pattern.

After I put the straight edged ice bucket in the first very rare book, they seemed to turn up in quantity. Now, the supply has been absorbed by collectors, and none are to be seen at shows. They are still difficult to find.

There are some new listings this time, and I have had reports of others that were not confirmed by pictures. The cream soups, 48 oz., ice lipped, pitcher and the 12" vase all remain scarce. Plates without scratched centers also plague collectors who want mint condition pieces. Otherwise this pattern was very durable.

	Crystal		Crystal
Ashtray, 3", round	7.00	Comport, cover, 6½"	30.00
Ashtray, 3½"	10.00	Creamer, 3¼" indiv.	6.00
Ashtray, 4½", round	12.50	Creamer, 3¾"	5.00
Ashtray, 6", round	15.00	Cup, 6 oz., ftd.	6.00
Bowl, 2¾" ftd., almond	13.00	Cup, punch	10.00
Bowl, 4½", rnd.	7.00	Ice bucket	50.00
Bowl, 4¾", finger	10.00	Ice bucket, plain edge	80.00
Bowl, 4¾", hdld.	8.00	Lamp, electric	125.00
Bowl, 5", bonbon	9.00	Mayonnaise, 3 pc.	32.50
Bowl, 5", cream soup	37.50	Oil w/stopper, 4½ oz.	35.00
Bowl, 5", hdld.	7.50	Pitcher, 16 oz., milk	65.00
Bowl, 5½", sq.	10.00	Pitcher, 48 oz., ice lip	175.00
Bowl, 5¾", high ft.	12.00	Pitcher, 2 qt., ice lip	85.00
Bowl, 5", rnd.	12.00	Plate, ctr. hdld., sandwich	27.50
Bowl, 6", rose	25.00	Plate, 6", bread & butter	4.00
Bowl, 7", bonbon, 3 ftd.	10.00	Plate, 6½", lemon, hdld.	12.00
Bowl, 7", olive, oblong	10.00	Plate, 7", salad	7.00
Bowl, 7¾", salad	20.00	Plate, 8", luncheon	9.00
Bowl, 8", cupped	30.00	Plate, 9", dinner	17.50
Bowl, 8", hdld.	30.00	Plate, 10", hdld., cake	20.00
Bowl, 9", rolled console	30.00	Plate, 12", ftd., salver	50.00
Bowl, 9½", pickle	10.00	Plate, 13", torte	25.00
Bowl, 9¾", salad	30.00	Plate, 15", torte	35.00
Bowl, 10", fruit	27.50	Plate, 18", torte	50.00
Bowl, 10½", low ft.	60.00	Platter, 12"	42.50
Bowl, 10½", high ft.	80.00	Relish, 10½", hdld., 3 part	20.00
Bowl, 10½", oval	26.00	Salt, 2½" indiv.	12.00
Bowl, 10½", oval, 2 part	30.00	Salt & pepper, pr., 3⅝"	12.50
Bowl, 11", oval, ftd.	32.50	Saucer	2.00
Bowl, 11", flared	32.50	Stem, 3⅜", 4 oz., oyster cocktail	10.00
Bowl, 11½", celery	28.00	Stem, 3⅝", 5 oz., sherbet	7.50
Bowl, 13", console	32.50	Stem, 4", 3½ oz., cocktail	10.00
Bowl, 13¼", punch, ftd.	295.00	Stem, 4¼", 3¼ oz., wine	20.00
Bowl, 14", fruit	35.00	Stem, 5¼", 9 oz., goblet	12.00
Butter dish, ¼ lb.	30.00	Sugar, 2¾", indiv.	5.50
Candlestick, 3½"	10.00	Sugar, 3½"	4.50
Candlestick, 6½", double	20.00	Tray for indiv. sugar/cream	10.00
Candlestick, 7"	15.00	Tumbler, 3⅝", 5 oz., juice	14.00
Candlestick, 7½", w/8 prisms	50.00	Tumbler, 3⅞", 9 oz., water	12.00
Candlestick, 9"	25.00	Tumbler, 4⅞", 12 oz., tea	20.00
Candlestick, 9¾", w/prisms	65.00	Tumbler, 4½", 5 oz., ftd.	11.00
Candlestick, 14½", w/10 prisms	110.00	Tumbler, 5¾", 12 oz., ftd.	14.00
Candy w/cover, 6½"	30.00	Vase, 6", bud, flared	14.00
Candy, w/cover, ftd., ½ lb.	55.00	Vase, 7", cupped	35.00
Cheese & cracker	45.00	Vase, 7½", flared	35.00
Cigarette box	35.00	Vase, 9", cornucopia	50.00
Comport, 4"	15.00	Vase, 12", straight	145.00

61

CRYSTOLITE, Blank #1503, A.H. Heisey & Co.

Colors: crystal, Zircon/Limelight, Sahara and rare in amber

Crystolite is the other pattern besides Colony that I put a heretofore rare piece in my book on Very Rare Glassware and it turned out not to be so rare. The 11", footed cake salver (cake stand) had not been seen at the National Heisey Antique Show in years. There were three the year my book came out and five the next year. This piece and the Colony ice bucket with the straight sided rim left the "rare" category for the time being. Maybe, it was that everyone started looking harder.

The swan handled pitcher, 6" basket, rye bottle and iced tea tumblers still remain elusive. Elusive does not describe the availability of the newly discovered 12" vase or the #1503 water goblet. Normally, Crystolite is found on the #5003 stem.

	Crystal		Crystal
Ashtray, 3½", square...	4.00	Ice tub, w/silver plate handle............................	75.00
Ashtray, 4½", square...	4.50	Jam jar, w/cover...	50.00
Ashtray, 5", w/book match holder.....................	25.00	Ladle, glass, punch..	25.00
Ashtray (coaster), 4", rnd.	6.00	Ladle, plastic..	7.50
Basket, 6", hdld.	375.00	Mayonnaise, 5½", shell, 3 ft.............................	32.00
Bonbon, 7", shell	17.00	Mayonnaise, 6", oval, hdld.	22.00
Bonbon, 7½", 2 hdld.	15.00	Mayonnaise ladle..	7.00
Bottle, 1 qt., rye, #107 stopper........................	175.00	Mustard & cover...	37.00
Bottle, 4 oz., bitters, w/short tube	80.00	Oil bottle, 3 oz.	40.00
Bottle, 4 oz., cologne w/#108 stopper	65.00	Oil bottle, w/stopper, 2 oz.	30.00
w/drip stop	145.00	Oval creamer, sugar, w/tray, set........................	47.50
Bottle, syrup w/drip & cut top...........................	60.00	Pitcher, ½ gallon, ice, blown............................	90.00
Bowl, 7½ quart, punch...	110.00	Pitcher, 2 quart swan, ice lip	800.00
Bowl, 2", indiv. swan nut (or ash tray)..............	15.00	Plate, 7", salad..	8.00
Bowl, 3", indiv. nut, hdld.	15.00	Plate, 7", shell..	12.00
Bowl, 4½", dessert (or nappy)...........................	6.00	Plate, 7", underliner for 1000 island dressing	
Bowl, 5", preserve	12.00	bowl	7.00
Bowl, 5", 1000 island dressing, ruffled top.......	18.00	Plate, 7½", coupe...	30.00
Bowl, 5½", dessert	8.00	Plate, 8", oval, mayonnaise liner	9.00
Bowl, 6", oval jelly, 4 ft.	13.00	Plate, 8½", salad...	15.00
Bowl, 6", preserve, 2 hdld.	13.00	Plate, 10½", service...	50.00
Bowl, 7", shell praline	30.00	Plate, 11", ftd., cake salver.............................	250.00
Bowl, 8", dessert (sauce)	15.00	Plate, 11", torte..	24.00
Bowl, 8", 2 pt. conserve, hdld.	16.00	Plate, 12", sand...	24.00
Bowl, 9", leaf pickle	17.00	Plate, 14", sand...	30.00
Bowl, 10", salad, rnd.	27.50	Plate, 14", torte..	30.00
Bowl, 11", w/attached mayonnaise (chip 'n dip)	75.00	Plate, 20", buffet or punch liner	42.00
Bowl, 12", gardenia, shallow	30.00	Puff box, w/cover, 4¾"	50.00
Bowl, 13", oval floral, deep	30.00	Salad dressing set, 3 pc.....................................	38.00
Candle block, 1-lite, sq.	12.00	Salt & pepper, pr..	30.00
Candle block, 1-lite, swirl.................................	12.00	Saucer	5.00
Candlestick, 1-lite, ftd..	12.00	Stem, 1 oz., cordial, wide optic, blown, #5003 ...	90.00
Candlestick, 1-lite, w/#4233, 5", vase	25.00	Stem, 3½ oz., cocktail, w.o., blown, #5003	25.00
Candlestick, 2-lite	20.00	Stem, 3½ oz., claret, w.o., blown, #5003	30.00
Candlestick, 2-lite, bobeche & 10 "D" prisms...	50.00	Stem, 3½ oz., oyster cocktail, w.o. blown, #5003 .	22.00
Candlestick sans vase, 3-lite..............................	17.00	Stem, 6 oz., sherbet/saucer champagne, #5003 ..	13.00
Candlestick w/#4233, 5", vase, 3-lite	30.00	Stem, 10 oz., water, #1503	250.00
Candy, 6½", swan	35.00	Stem, 10 oz., w.o., blown, #5003	22.00
Candy box, w/cover, 5½"	50.00	Sugar, indiv.	15.00
Candy box, w/cover, 7"	55.00	Syrup pitcher, drip cut	100.00
Cheese, 5½", ftd.	12.00	Tray, 5½", oval, liner indiv. creamer/sugar	35.00
Cigarette box, w/cover, 4"	15.00	Tray, 9", 4 pt., leaf relish	22.50
Cigarette box, w/cover, 4½"	17.00	Tray, 10", 5 pt., rnd. relish	35.00
Cigarette holder, ftd.	17.50	Tray, 12", 3 pt., relish	25.00
Cigarette holder, oval	12.00	Tray, 12", rect., celery.......................................	35.00
Cigarette holder, rnd.	10.00	Tray, 12", rect., celery/olive	35.00
Cigarette lighter..	10.00	Tumbler, 5 oz., ftd., juice, w.o., blown, #5003 ..	18.00
Coaster, 4"...	6.00	Tumbler, 8 oz., pressed, #5003	75.00
Cocktail shaker, 1 qt. w/#1 strainer; #86 stopper .	165.00	Tumbler, 10 oz., pressed	20.00
Comport, 5", fed., deep, #5003	25.00	Tumbler, 10 oz., iced tea, w.o., blown, #5003...	22.00
Creamer, indiv.	15.00	Tumbler, 12 oz., ftd., iced tea, w.o., blown #5003	24.00
Cup	15.00	Urn, 7", flower...	17.50
Cup, punch or custard	8.00	Vase, 3", short stem	17.50
Hurricane block, 1-lite, sq.	30.00	Vase, 6", ftd...	17.50
Hurricane block, w/#4061, 10" plain globe,		Vase, 12"	225.00
1-lite, sq.	85.00		

"DANCING GIRL," Sunrise Medallion #758, Morgantown Glass Works, Late 1920's – Early 1930's

Colors: pink, green, blue, crystal

The newly formed Morgantown Collectors' Guild has been at pains to broadcast the actual name of this pattern, Sunrise Medallion (etching #758).

There are several new pieces to show and several more items in my listing. A newly discovered piece is a green sugar bowl to go along with the only known blue creamer and sugar set that is pictured. Yes, I have seen it as I have all of the pieces and colors listed below. You will be able to see the green sugar in a future book.

The only cordials I have seen are crystal, but the owner thought they were "gold"; so I do not have one for my cordial collection. The only parfaits I have seen are the plain style stem.

One of the problems I have encountered over the years is listing pieces from catalogues that were supposedly made. Over twenty years of experience has taught me that listed in a catalogue and actually being made and existing today are two different things! When pieces and colors are actually proven to exist, then I will be able to list them for you.

The twisted stem items were #7642½ and the plain stems were #7630. Measurements in the catalogues were in ounces only. The twisted stem items are taller than their plain stem varieties. Measurements given below are from #7630 line.

The Morgantown Collectors' Guild's address is listed in the back of the book. If you would like more information about Morgantown Glass, please contact them!

	Crystal	Blue	Pink/ Green
Bowl, finger, ftd.		50.00	
Creamer		150.00	150.00
Cup	30.00	75.00	65.00
Parfait, 5 oz.	50.00	85.00	75.00
Pitcher		350.00	
Plate, 5⅞", sherbet	6.00	10.00	8.00
Plate, 7½", salad	10.00	20.00	15.00
Saucer	10.00	20.00	15.00
Stem, 1½ oz., cordial	65.00		
Stem, 2½ oz., wine	30.00	35.00	50.00
Stem, 2½", 3½ oz., oyster cocktail	22.50	35.00	30.00
Stem, 4¾", 7 oz., sherbet or champagne	25.00	40.00	30.00
Stem, 6⅛", cocktail	30.00	50.00	40.00
Stem, 7¾", 9 oz., water	35.00	60.00	45.00
Sugar		150.00	150.00
Tumbler, 2½ oz., ftd.	25.00		
Tumbler, 4¼", 5 oz., ftd.	15.00	45.00	30.00
Tumbler, 4¾", 9 oz., ftd.	20.00	50.00	35.00
Tumbler, 5½", 11 oz., ftd.	25.00	65.00	40.00
Vase, 10", slender, bud	40.00		75.00
Vase, 10", bulbous bottom			100.00

65

DECAGON, Cambridge Glass Company, 1930's

Colors: green, pink, red, cobalt blue, amber, Moonlight blue, black

This blank is more known for the etchings on it than it is by itself. Several of the stems pictured are etched, but Decagon has no etching at all. The Royal blue (cobalt) and Moonlight blue are the most collected colors although there are devotees of all the others. I still need a blue relish insert to replace the one broken during photography years ago if anybody comes across one.

	Pastel Colors	Red Blue		Pastel Colors	Red Blue
Basket, 7", 2 hdld. (upturned sides)	12.00	20.00	Mayonnaise, w/liner & ladle	18.00	30.00
Bowl, bouillon, w/liner	7.50	12.50	Oil, 6 oz., tall, w/hdld. & stopper	40.00	65.00
Bowl, cream soup, w/liner	10.00	22.00	Plate, 6¼", bread/butter	3.00	5.00
Bowl, 2½", indiv., almond	16.00	27.50	Plate, 7", 2 hdld.	9.00	15.00
Bowl, 3¾", flat rim, cranberry	10.00	14.00	Plate, 7½"	4.00	10.00
Bowl, 3½" belled, cranberry	9.00	14.00	Plate, 8½", salad	6.00	10.00
Bowl, 5½", 2 hdld., bonbon	10.00	17.00	Plate, 9½", dinner	15.00	25.00
Bowl, 5½", belled, fruit	5.50	10.00	Plate, 10", grill	8.00	14.00
Bowl, 5¾", flat rim, fruit	6.00	11.00	Plate, 10", service	8.50	16.00
Bowl, 6", belled, cereal	7.00	12.50	Plate, 12½", service	9.00	17.50
Bowl, 6", flat rim, cereal	8.00	12.00	Relish, 6 inserts	70.00	100.00
Bowl, 6", ftd., almond	20.00	35.00	Salt dip, 1½", ftd.	11.00	20.00
Bowl, 6¼", 2 hdld., bonbon	10.00	17.00	Sauce boat & plate	45.00	65.00
Bowl, 8½", flat rim, soup "plate"	8.00	15.00	Saucer	1.00	2.50
Bowl, 9", rnd., veg.	14.00	24.00	Server, center hdld.	12.00	20.00
Bowl, 9", 2 pt., relish	9.00	15.00	Stem, 1 oz., cordial	30.00	55.00
Bowl, 9½", oval, veg.	12.00	22.00	Stem, 3½ oz., cocktail	12.00	20.00
Bowl, 10", berry	12.00	20.00	Stem, 6 oz., low sherbet	9.00	15.00
Bowl, 10½", oval, veg.	16.00	27.50	Stem, 6 oz., high sherbet	10.00	20.00
Bowl, 11", rnd. veg.	17.00	30.00	Stem, 9 oz., water	15.00	30.00
Bowl, 11", 2 pt., relish	10.00	17.50	Sugar, lightning bolt handles	7.00	12.00
Comport, 5¾"	12.50	20.00	Sugar, ftd.	9.00	20.00
Comport, 6½", low ft.	15.00	25.00	Sugar, scalloped edge	9.00	20.00
Comport, 7", tall	20.00	30.00	Sugar, tall, lg. ft.	8.00	18.00
Creamer, ftd.	9.00	20.00	Tray, 8", 2 hdld., flat pickle	10.00	17.00
Creamer, scalloped edge	8.00	18.00	Tray, 9", pickle	10.00	17.50
Creamer, lightning bolt handles	7.00	12.00	Tray, 11", oval, service	8.00	15.00
Creamer, tall, lg. ft.	10.00	22.00	Tray, 11", celery	10.00	20.00
Cup	6.00	10.00	Tray, 12", center handled	15.00	25.00
French dressing bottle, "Oil/Vinegar"	50.00	80.00	Tray, 12", oval, service	10.00	20.00
Gravy boat, w/2 hdld. liner (like spouted cream soup)	55.00	85.00	Tray, 13", 2 hdld., service	20.00	30.00
Ice bucket	30.00	40.00	Tray, 15", oval, service	15.00	25.00
Ice tub	25.00	35.00	Tumbler, 2½ oz., ftd.	10.00	15.00
Mayonnaise, 2 hdld., w/2 hdld. liner and ladle	25.00	40.00	Tumbler, 5 oz., ftd.	10.00	16.00
			Tumbler, 8 oz., ftd.	12.00	22.00
			Tumbler, 10 oz., ftd.	15.00	25.00
			Tumbler, 12 oz., ftd.	20.00	35.00

"DEERWOOD" or "BIRCH TREE," U.S. Glass Company, Late 1920's – Early 1930's

Colors: light amber, green, pink, black, crystal

If you came to this picture from the Black Forest referral, it was because I again had no room for writing at that pattern. These two patterns are often confused, so look at the pattern shots of each. Deer and trees are the predominant pattern on Deerwood, whereas Black Forest pictures moose and trees. If you have trouble telling moose from deer, then you are in trouble with these two patterns.

I am now positive that Black Forest was made by Paden City, although no actual catalogue information backs that up. I recently found a blue ice tub the color of Paden City's blue which was the final puzzle piece as far as I was concerned.

Note the night set (pitcher and tumbler) in Black Forest. The tumbler has a molded band that will not allow it to drop down into the pitcher when turned upside down on it.

In Deerwood, note the crystal goblet with green stem. This is the only piece I have seen like that. I wonder if there are other pieces besides the water goblet!

	Amber	Green	Pink
Bowl, 10", straight edge			32.50
Bowl, 12", console		55.00	55.00
Cake plate, low pedestal			50.00
Candlestick, 2½"		35.00	
Candlestick, 4"			45.00
Candy dish, w/cover, 3 part, flat			75.00
Candy jar, w/cover, ftd. cone			85.00
Celery, 12"		50.00	
Cheese and cracker		65.00	
Comport, 10", low, ftd., flared			40.00
Creamer, 2 styles		40.00	40.00
Cup		60.00	60.00
Plate, 5½"		12.00	12.00
Plate, 7½", salad			20.00
Plate, 9½", dinner			40.00
Saucer		15.00	15.00
Server, center hdld.		40.00	40.00
Stem, 6 oz., sherbet, 4¾"		25.00	
Stem, 6 oz., cocktail, 5"		30.00	
Stem, 9 oz., water, 7"		35.00	
Sugar, 2 styles		40.00	40.00
Tumbler, 9 oz.	30.00	32.00	32.00
Tumbler, 12 oz., tea, 5½"	35.00		
Vase, 7", sweet pea, rolled edge			65.00
Vase, 10", ruffled top		85.00	75.00
Whipped cream pail, w/ladle		45.00	45.00

DIANE, Cambridge Glass Company, 1934 – Early 1950's

Colors: crystal; some pink, yellow, blue, Heatherbloom, Emerald green, amber, Crown Tuscan

Diane can be collected in crystal, but collecting a colored set is nearly impossible. Many collectors of crystal accent their sets with an occasional colored piece. The gold decorated Crown Tuscan pieces shown atop the next page are sought both by Diane collectors and by connoisseurs of the Crown Tuscan color. A few pieces of dark Emerald green, blue and Heatherbloom have surfaced; but I have been unable to find a saucer in Heatherbloom for my lonely cup or a bottom for my dark Emerald green candy lid.

Note the martini pitcher or cocktail beverage mixer in the top photo. One of these sold on the West Coast a few years ago for an exorbitant price. ($2000+)

There is a whole line of stems with Diane etching as shown in the pattern shot. These are known as Stradivari/Regency stems. Both names were used for this particular stem and the only other etching found on this stem is Portia.

Collectors take note of the hollow stem champagne, bitters bottle and cornucopia vase at the bottom of page 73. All of these items are rarely found in this etching.

	Crystal		Crystal
Basket, 6", 2 hdld., ftd.	16.00	Creamer, indiv. #3500 (pie crust edge)	14.00
Bottle, bitters	110.00	Creamer, indiv. #3900, scalloped edge	14.00
Bowl, #3106, finger, w/liner	25.00	Creamer, scroll handle, #3400	14.00
Bowl, #3122	25.00	Cup	20.00
Bowl, #3400, cream soup, w/liner	23.00	Decanter, ball	145.00
Bowl, 5", berry	20.00	Decanter, lg. ftd.	135.00
Bowl, 5¼" 2 hdld., bonbon	18.00	Decanter, short ft., cordial	165.00
Bowl, 6", 2 hdld., ftd., bonbon	17.00	Hurricane lamp, candlestick base	100.00
Bowl, 6", 2 pt., relish	18.00	Hurricane lamp, keyhole base w/prisms	175.00
Bowl, 6", cereal	23.00	Ice bucket, w/chrome hand	60.00
Bowl, 6½", 3 pt. relish	20.00	Mayonnaise, div., w/liner & ladles	38.00
Bowl, 7", 2 hdld., ftd., bonbon	22.00	Mayonnaise (sherbet type w/ladle)	27.50
Bowl, 7", 2 pt., relish	20.00	Mayonnaise, w/liner, ladle	25.00
Bowl, 7", relish or pickle	22.00	Oil, 6 oz., w/stopper	45.00
Bowl, 9", 3 pt., celery or relish	30.00	Pitcher, ball	110.00
Bowl, 9½", pickle (like corn)	22.00	Pitcher, Doulton	250.00
Bowl, 10", 4 ft., flared	40.00	Pitcher, martini	750.00
Bowl, 10", baker	40.00	Pitcher, upright	150.00
Bowl, 11", 2 hdld.	35.00	Plate, 6", 2 hdld., plate	7.00
Bowl, 11", 4 ftd.	40.00	Plate, 6", sq., bread/butter	5.00
Bowl, 11½" tab hdld., ftd.	40.00	Plate, 6½", bread/butter	5.00
Bowl, 12", 3 pt., celery & relish	32.50	Plate, 8", 2 hdld., ftd., bonbon	11.00
Bowl, 12", 4 ft.	40.00	Plate, 8", salad	10.00
Bowl, 12", 4 ft., flared	40.00	Plate, 8½"	11.00
Bowl, 12", 4 ft., oval	42.00	Plate, 10½", dinner	55.00
Bowl, 12", 4 ft., oval, w/"ears" hdld.	50.00	Plate, 12", 4 ft., service	35.00
Bowl, 12", 5 pt., celery & relish	32.50	Plate, 13", 4 ft., torte	35.00
Butter, rnd.	115.00	Plate, 13½", 2 hdld.	30.00
Cabinet flask	165.00	Plate, 14", torte	40.00
Candelabrum, 2-lite, keyhole	22.50	Platter, 13½"	65.00
Candelabrum, 3-lite, keyhole	30.00	Salt & pepper, ftd., w/glass tops, pr.	32.00
Candlestick, 1-lite, keyhole	17.50	Salt & pepper, pr., flat	28.00
Candlestick, 5"	17.50	Saucer	5.00
Candlestick, 6", 2-lite, "fleur-de-lis"	30.00	Stem, #1066, 1 oz., cordial	50.00
Candlestick, 6", 3-lite	35.00	Stem, #1066, 3 oz., cocktail	16.00
Candy box, w/cover, rnd.	70.00	Stem, #1066, 3 oz., wine	22.00
Cigarette urn	35.00	Stem, #1066, 3½ oz., tall cocktail	17.50
Cocktail shaker, glass top	100.00	Stem, #1066, 4½" oz., claret	25.00
Cocktail shaker, metal top	70.00	Stem, #1066, 5 oz., oyster/cocktail	12.00
Cocktail icer, 2 pc.	50.00	Stem, #1066, 7 oz., low sherbet	11.50
Comport, 5½"	25.00	Stem, #1066, 7 oz., tall sherbet	13.50
Comport, 5⅜", blown	35.00	Stem, #1066, 11 oz., water	15.00
Creamer	14.00	Stem, #3122, 1 oz., cordial	50.00

71

DIANE, Cambridge Glass Company, 1934 – Early 1950's (continued)

	Crystal
Stem, #3122, 2½ oz., wine	22.00
Stem, #3122, 3 oz., cocktail	14.00
Stem, #3122, 4½ oz., claret	25.00
Stem, #3122, 4½ oz., oyster/cocktail	15.00
Stem, #3122, 7 oz., low sherbet	11.00
Stem, #3122, 7 oz., tall sherbet	15.00
Stem, #3122, 9 oz., water goblet	20.00
Sugar, indiv., #3500 (pie crust edge)	13.00
Sugar, indiv., #3900, scalloped edge	13.00
Sugar, scroll handle, #3400	14.00
Tumbler, 2½ oz., sham bottom	30.00
Tumbler, 5 oz., ft., juice	27.00
Tumbler, 5 oz., sham bottom	30.00
Tumbler, 7 oz., old fashioned, w/sham bottom	30.00
Tumbler, 8 oz., ft.	22.00
Tumbler, 10 oz., sham bottom	30.00
Tumbler, 12 oz., sham bottom	32.00
Tumbler, 13 oz.	30.00
Tumbler, 14 oz., sham bottom	37.50
Tumbler, #1066, 3 oz.	16.00
Tumbler, #1066, 5 oz., juice	11.00

	Crystal
Tumbler, #1066, 9 oz., water	12.00
Tumbler, #1066, 12 oz., tea	18.00
Tumbler, #3106, 3 oz., ftd.	15.00
Tumbler, #3106, 5 oz., ftd., juice	13.00
Tumbler, #3106, 9 oz., ftd., water	11.00
Tumbler, #3106, 12 oz., ftd., tea	18.00
Tumbler, #3122, 2½ oz.	22.00
Tumbler, #3122, 5 oz., juice	13.00
Tumbler, #3122, 9 oz., water	15.00
Tumbler, #3122, 12 oz., tea	17.00
Tumbler, #3135, 2½ oz., ftd., bar	22.00
Tumbler, #3135, 10 oz., ftd., tumbler	14.00
Tumbler, #3135, 12 oz., ftd., tea	25.00
Vase, 5", globe	25.00
Vase, 6", high ft., flower	30.00
Vase, 8", high ft., flower	35.00
Vase, 9", keyhole base	40.00
Vase, 10", bud	32.50
Vase, 11", flower	50.00
Vase, 11", ped. ft., flower	55.00
Vase, 12", keyhole base	60.00
Vase, 13", flower	75.00

Note: See Page 182-183 for stem identification.

ELAINE, Cambridge Glass Company, 1934 – 1950's

Colors: crystal

I apologize for the picture quality of Elaine. The pattern just disappeared on the light blue and it was too late to correct it when I finally saw the photographs. Look at the gold encrusted bowl in the foreground to help you identify the pattern. New collectors often confuse this with Chantilly, so look closely at that pattern so you can tell these apart. (Chantilly has a thick scroll, whereas Elaine's is thin and delicate). At present there seem to be few collectors of Elaine, so this might be an elegant pattern to start collecting.

	Crystal
Basket, 6", 2 hdld. (upturned sides)	15.00
Bowl, #3104, finger, w/liner	20.00
Bowl, 5¼", 2 hdld., bonbon	13.00
Bowl, 6", 2 hdld., ftd., bonbon	16.00
Bowl, 6", 2 pt., relish	16.00
Bowl, 6½", 3 pt., relish	15.00
Bowl, 7", 2 pt., pickle or relish	16.00
Bowl, 7", ftd., tab hdld. bonbon	27.00
Bowl, 7", pickle or relish	18.00
Bowl, 9", 3 pt., celery & relish	20.00
Bowl, 9½", pickle (like corn dish)	22.00
Bowl, 10", 3 ftd., flared	30.00
Bowl, 11", tab hdld.	30.00
Bowl, 11½", ftd., tab hdld.	30.00
Bowl, 12", 3 pt., celery & relish	30.00
Bowl, 12", 4 ftd., flared	35.00
Bowl, 12", 4 ftd., oval, "ear" hdld.	40.00
Bowl, 12", 5 pt. celery & relish	37.50
Candlestick, 5"	17.50
Candlestick, 6", 2-lite	27.50
Candlestick, 6", 3-lite	35.00
Candy box, w/cover, rnd.	60.00
Cocktail icer, 2 pc.	50.00
Comport, 5½"	30.00
Comport, 5⅜", #3500 stem	39.00
Comport, 5⅜", blown	40.00
Creamer (several styles)	11.00
Creamer, indiv.	12.00
Cup	20.00
Decanter, lg., ftd.	150.00
Hurricane lamp, candlestick base	85.00
Hurricane lamp, keyhole ft., w/prisms	150.00
Ice bucket, w/chrome handle	60.00
Mayonnaise (cupped "sherbet" w/ladle)	22.00
Mayonnaise (div. bowl, liner, 2 ladles)	35.00
Mayonnaise, w/liner & ladle	25.00
Oil, 6 oz., hdld., w/stopper	45.00
Pitcher, ball	100.00
Pitcher, Doulton	250.00
Pitcher, upright	165.00
Plate, 6", 2 hdld.	10.00
Plate, 6½", bread/butter	6.50
Plate, 8", 2 hdld., ftd.	15.00
Plate, 8", salad	12.50
Plate, 8", tab hdld., bonbon	15.00
Plate, 10½", dinner	55.00
Plate, 11½" 2 hdld., ringed "Tally Ho" sand.	25.00
Plate, 12", 4 ftd., service	25.00
Plate, 13", 4 ftd., torte	30.00
Plate, 13½", tab hdld., cake	30.00
Plate, 14", torte	30.00
Salt & pepper, flat, pr.	27.50
Salt & pepper, ftd., pr.	30.00

	Crystal
Salt & pepper, hdld., pr.	35.00
Saucer	3.00
Stem, #1402, 1 oz., cordial	50.00
Stem, #1402, 3 oz., wine	25.00
Stem, #1402, 3½ oz., cocktail	20.00
Stem, #1402, 5 oz., claret	27.50
Stem, #1402, low sherbet	14.00
Stem, #1402, tall sherbet	15.00
Stem, #1402, goblet	20.00
Stem, #3104, (very tall stems), ¾ oz., brandy	100.00
Stem, #3104, 1 oz., cordial	100.00
Stem, #3104, 1 oz., pousse-cafe	100.00
Stem, #3104, 2 oz., sherry	80.00
Stem, #3104, 2½ oz., creme de menthe	80.00
Stem, #3104, 3 oz., wine	75.00
Stem, #3104, 3½ oz., cocktail	50.00
Stem, #3104, 4½ oz., claret	60.00
Stem, #3104, 5 oz., roemer	60.00
Stem, #3104, 5 oz., tall hock	60.00
Stem, #3104, 7 oz., tall sherbet	50.00
Stem, #3104, 9 oz., goblet	75.00
Stem, #3121, 1 oz., cordial	50.00
Stem, #3121, 3 oz., cocktail	22.00
Stem, #3121, 3½ oz., wine	27.50
Stem, #3121, 4½ oz., claret	27.50
Stem, #3121, 4½ oz., oyster cocktail	15.00
Stem, #3121, 5 oz., parfait, low stem	25.00
Stem, #3121, 6 oz., low sherbet	15.00
Stem, #3121, 6 oz., tall sherbet	17.50
Stem, #3121, 10 oz., water	21.00
Stem, #3500, 1 oz., cordial	50.00
Stem, #3500, 2½ oz., wine	25.00
Stem, #3500, 3 oz., cocktail	20.00
Stem, #3500, 4½ oz., claret	27.50
Stem, #3500, 4½ oz., oyster cocktail	14.00
Stem, #3500, 5 oz., parfait, low stem	23.00
Stem, #3500, 7 oz., low sherbet	13.00
Stem, #3500, 7 oz., tall sherbet	15.00
Stem, #3500, 10 oz., water	20.00
Sugar (several styles)	10.00
Sugar, indiv.	12.00
Tumbler, #1402, 9 oz., ftd., water	17.00
Tumbler, #1402, 12 oz., tea	20.00
Tumbler, #1402, 12 oz., tall ftd., tea	25.00
Tumbler, #3121, 5 oz., ftd., juice	19.00
Tumbler, #3121, 10 oz., ftd., water	20.00
Tumbler, #3121, 12 oz., ftd., tea	22.00
Tumbler, #3500, 5 oz., ftd., juice	17.00
Tumbler, #3500, 10 oz., ftd., water	18.00
Tumbler, #3500, 12 oz., ftd., tea	25.00
Vase, 6", ftd.	30.00
Vase, 8", ftd.	40.00
Vase, 9", keyhole, ftd.	38.00

Note: see Pages 182-183 for stem identification.

EMPRESS, Blank #1401, A.H. Heisey & Co.

Colors: crystal, "Flamingo" pink, "Sahara" yellow, "Moongleam" green, cobalt and "Alexandrite"; some Tangerine

A number of collectors are attracted to this pattern by the dolphin feet, but be careful not to have heart flutters when the prices are seen. This is one of the few patterns that I am aware of where tumblers approach the price of the pitcher.

	Crystal	Flam.	Sahara	Moon.	Cobalt	Alexan.
Ashtray.	30.00	60.00	85.00	175.00	200.00	125.00
Bonbon, 6"	10.00	20.00	25.00	30.00		
Bowl, cream soup	15.00	26.00	27.00	35.00		65.00
Bowl, cream soup, w/sq. liner	20.00	25.00	30.00	45.00		165.00
Bowl, frappe, w/center	20.00	45.00	60.00	75.00		
Bowl, nut, dolphin ftd., indiv.	15.00	22.00	26.00	32.00		80.00
Bowl, 4½", nappy	5.00	8.00	10.00	12.50		
Bowl, 5", preserve, 2 hdld.	12.00	18.00	22.00	27.50		
Bowl, 6", ftd., jelly, 2 hdld.	12.00	17.00	23.00	27.50		
Bowl, 6", dolp. ftd., mint	14.00	20.00	25.00	30.00		90.00
Bowl, 6", grapefruit, sq. top, grnd. bottom	9.00	12.50	15.00	22.50		
Bowl, 6½", oval, lemon, w/cover	35.00	65.00	75.00	90.00		
Bowl, 7", 3 pt., relish, triplex	12.50	25.00	27.50	37.50		
Bowl, 7", 3 pt., relish, ctr. hand.	20.00	45.00	50.00	75.00		
Bowl, 7½", dolp. ftd., nappy	25.00	60.00	65.00	75.00	275.00	325.00
Bowl, 7½", dolp. ftd., nasturtium	30.00	100.00	110.00	125.00	325.00	400.00
Bowl, 8", nappy	22.00	30.00	35.00	40.00		
Bowl, 8½", ftd., floral, 2 hdld	30.00	40.00	50.00	65.00		
Bowl, 9", floral, rolled edge	22.00	32.00	38.00	42.00		
Bowl, 9", floral, flared	30.00	70.00	75.00	90.00		
Bowl, 10", 2 hdld., oval dessert	30.00	45.00	60.00	65.00		
Bowl, 10", lion head, floral	250.00	550.00	550.00	700.00		
Bowl, 10", oval, veg.	27.00	35.00	45.00	55.00		
Bowl, 10", square, salad, 2 hdld.	30.00	40.00	55.00	65.00		
Bowl, 10", triplex, relish	20.00	45.00	55.00	65.00		
Bowl, 11", dolphin ftd., floral	32.00	65.00	75.00	90.00	400.00	450.00
Bowl, 13", pickle/olive, 2 pt.	15.00	18.00	20.00	27.50		
Bowl, 15", dolp. ftd., punch	400.00	700.00	800.00	900.00		
Candlestick, low, 4 ftd., w/2 hdld.	15.00	35.00	40.00	45.00		
Candlestick, 6", dolphin ftd.	50.00	75.00	85.00	125.00	250.00	
Candy, w/cover, 6", dolphin ftd.	40.00	95.00	100.00	135.00	340.00	
Comport, 6", ftd.	25.00	40.00	55.00	65.00		
Comport, 6", square	40.00	70.00	75.00	85.00		
Comport, 7", oval	35.00	60.00	66.00	75.00		
Compotier, 6", dolphin ftd.	70.00	130.00	170.00	195.00		
Creamer, dolphin ftd.	15.00	30.00	40.00	42.50		215.00
Creamer, indiv.	15.00	25.00	35.00	40.00		210.00
Cup	12.00	27.00	31.00	36.00		100.00
Cup, after dinner	15.00	40.00	50.00	60.00		
Cup, bouillon, 2 hdld.	16.00	28.00	30.00	33.00		
Cup, 4 oz., custard or punch	12.00	25.00	28.00	30.00		
Cup, #1401½, has rim as demi-cup	20.00	28.00	32.00	40.00		
Grapefruit, w/square liner	15.00	25.00	30.00	35.00		
Ice tub, w/metal handles	40.00	95.00	100.00	135.00		
Jug, 3 pint, ftd.	70.00	175.00	200.00	225.00		
Jug, flat				165.00		
Marmalade, w/cover, dolp. ftd.	40.00	70.00	80.00	95.00		
Mayonnaise, 5½", ftd.	20.00	35.00	45.00	55.00		165.00
Mustard, w/cover	30.00	60.00	65.00	75.00		
Oil bottle, 4 oz.	35.00	80.00	110.00	125.00		

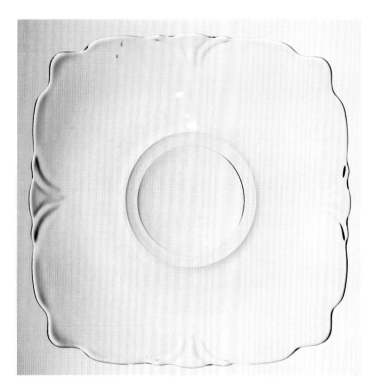

	Crystal	Flam.	Sahara	Moon.	Cobalt	Alexan.
Plate.	4.00	7.00	10.00	12.00		
Plate, cream soup liner	5.00	9.00	13.00	15.00		20.00
Plate, 4½"	5.00	6.00	6.00	8.00		
Plate, 6"	5.00	11.00	14.00	16.00		35.00
Plate, 6", square	5.00	10.00	13.00	15.00		25.00
Plate, 7"	8.00	12.00	15.00	17.00		40.00
Plate, 7", square	7.00	12.00	15.00	17.00	55.00	45.00
Plate, 8", square	10.00	18.00	22.00	35.00	65.00	60.00
Plate, 8"	9.00	16.00	20.00	24.00	65.00	60.00
Plate, 9"	12.00	25.00	35.00	40.00		
Plate, 10½"	40.00	100.00	100.00	125.00		
Plate, 10½", square	40.00	100.00	100.00	125.00		135.00
Plate, 12"	25.00	45.00	55.00	65.00		
Plate, 12", muffin, sides upturned	30.00	50.00	60.00	70.00		
Plate, 12", sandwich, 2 hdld.	25.00	35.00	40.00	50.00		165.00
Plate, 13", hors d'oeuvre, 2 hdld.	28.00	40.00	45.00	55.00		
Plate, 13", square, 2 hdld.	28.00	40.00	45.00	55.00		
Platter, 14"	25.00	35.00	40.00	47.50		
Salt & pepper, pr.	50.00	100.00	110.00	135.00		275.00
Saucer, square	3.00	8.00	14.00	16.00		22.50
Saucer, after dinner	2.00	7.00	10.00	10.00		
Saucer	3.00	8.00	14.00	16.00		
Stem, 2½ oz., oyster cocktail	15.00	20.00	25.00	30.00		
Stem, 4 oz., saucer champagne	20.00	35.00	40.00	60.00		
Stem, 4 oz., sherbet	15.00	22.00	28.00	35.00		
Stem, 9 oz., Empress stemware, unusual	30.00	55.00	65.00	75.00		
Sugar, indiv.	15.00	25.00	35.00	40.00		210.00
Sugar, dolphin ftd., 3 hdld.	10.00	22.00	25.00	27.00		210.00
Tray, condiment & liner for indiv. sugar/creamer	10.00	15.00	20.00	23.00		
Tray, 10", 3 pt., relish	18.00	25.00	30.00	35.00		
Tray, 10", 7 pt., hors d'oeuvre	25.00	45.00	50.00	75.00		
Tray, 10", celery	12.00	16.00	22.00	26.00		150.00
Tray, 12", ctr. hdld., sand.	30.00	48.00	57.00	65.00		
Tray, 12", sq. ctr. hdld., sand.	32.50	52.00	60.00	67.50		
Tray, 13", celery	16.00	20.00	24.00	30.00		
Tray, 16", 4 pt., buffet relish	30.00	50.00	75.00	86.00		
Tumbler, 8 oz., dolp. ftd., unusual	75.00	125.00	150.00	160.00		
Tumbler, 8 oz., grnd. bottom	15.00	30.00	35.00	39.50		
Tumbler, 12 oz., tea, grnd. bottom	18.00	32.00	40.00	45.00		
Vase, 8", flared	45.00	80.00	90.00	105.00		
Vase, 9", ftd.	60.00	100.00	110.00	150.00		625.00

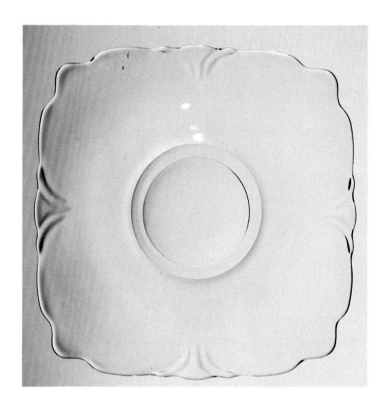

FAIRFAX NO. 2375, Fostoria Glass Company, 1927 – 1944

Colors: blue, orchid, amber, rose, green, topaz; some ruby and black

Fairfax is the Fostoria blank on which many of the most popular Fostoria etchings are found, notably June, Versailles and Trojan. Most collectors do not get as excited about this No. 2375 line without an etching. It is the Azure blue that is the most collected color even in the non-etched line.

The blue pitchers show the differences in Fostoria's blue. The light blue was called Azure; the more vivid color was called Blue. This Blue was an early color and used in only the first dinnerware lines and the popular American pattern.

Note the Azure flower vase with frog in front of the pitcher. This piece is found rarely and the frog even less often than its holder.

Fairfax collectors have a choice of stems. In the photo of blues at the top is stem and tumbler line #2375 which is usually used for Versailles and June etchings. The other stem line #5299 is shown in the bottom picture; this is more commonly found in yellow with the Trojan etch. Some collectors are mixing the stem lines; but tumblers are difficult to mix because of their different shapes. The #5299 tumblers are more cone shaped; the #2375 tumblers are rounded.

The pink picture at the bottom of page 82 also shows the differences in Fostoria's purple colors (Orchid and Wisteria). Orchid is on the left in the form of an ashtray, cup, saucer and plates while Wisteria is shown by the cordials on the right. The 12" bread tray is only listed in 1927 catalogues and is rare. It is shaped like a large sauce boat plate.

Due to confusion among collectors and dealers alike, I have shown the various Fostoria stems on page 83 so that differences in shapes can be seen. The claret and high sherbets are major concerns. Each is 6" high. Note the claret is shaped like the wine; and the parfait is taller than the juice!

	Rose, Blue, Orchid	Amber	Green, Topaz		Rose, Blue, Orchid	Amber	Green, Topaz
Ashtray, 2½"	15.00	7.50	10.00	Pickle, 8½"	18.00	7.00	9.00
Ashtray, 4"	17.50	10.00	12.50	Pitcher, #5000	175.00	110.00	120.00
Ashtray, 5½"	20.00	13.00	17.50	Plate, canape	15.00	10.00	10.00
Baker, 9", oval	25.00	15.00	20.00	Plate, whipped cream	11.00	8.00	9.00
Baker, 10½", oval	35.00	20.00	22.50	Plate, 6", bread/butter	3.00	2.00	2.50
Bonbon	12.50	9.00	10.00	Plate, 7½", salad	5.00	3.00	3.50
Bottle, salad dressing	125.00	60.00	70.00	Plate, 7½", cream soup			
Bouillon, ftd.	11.00	7.00	8.00	or mayonnaise liner	5.00	3.00	3.50
Bowl, 9", lemon, 2 hdld.	9.00	6.00	7.00	Plate, 8¾", salad	10.00	4.50	5.00
Bowl, sweetmeat	15.00	10.00	12.00	Plate, 9½", luncheon	15.00	6.00	7.00
Bowl, 5", fruit	12.00	5.00	6.00	Plate, 10¼", dinner	35.00	15.00	22.00
Bowl, 6", cereal	20.00	9.00	11.00	Plate, 10¼", grill	30.00	12.00	20.00
Bowl, 7", soup	25.00	12.00	14.00	Plate, 10", cake	17.50	13.00	15.00
Bowl, 8", rnd., nappy	27.50	13.00	14.00	Plate, 12", bread, oval	40.00	25.00	27.50
Bowl, lg., hdld., dessert	22.00	10.00	12.00	Plate, 13", chop	17.50	14.00	15.00
Bowl, 12"	22.00	15.00	18.00	Platter, 10½", oval	30.00	17.00	19.00
Bowl, 12", centerpiece	25.00	17.50	20.00	Platter, 12", oval	35.00	20.00	22.50
Bowl, 13", oval, centerpiece	30.00	20.00	22.50	Platter, 15", oval	60.00	27.00	32.00
Bowl, 15", centerpiece	35.00	20.00	24.00	Relish, 3 part, 8½"	10.00	7.00	8.00
Butter dish, w/cover	125.00	80.00	90.00	Relish, 11½"	15.00	10.00	12.00
Candlestick, flattened top	15.00	10.00	10.00	Sauce boat	40.00	20.00	25.00
Candlestick, 3"	12.50	9.00	10.00	Sauce boat liner	12.00	9.00	10.00
Celery, 11½"	20.00	12.00	14.00	Saucer, after dinner	6.00	4.00	5.00
Cheese & cracker set (2 styles)	35.00	20.00	22.50	Saucer	4.00	2.50	3.00
Comport, 5"	15.00	15.00	17.00	Shaker, ftd., pr.	55.00	30.00	35.00
Comport, 7"	25.00	10.00	12.00	Shaker, indiv., ftd., pr.		20.00	25.00
Cream soup, ftd.	15.00	9.00	8.00	Stem, 4", ¾ oz., cordial	50.00	25.00	35.00
Creamer, flat		10.00	12.00	Stem, 4¼", 6 oz., low sherbet	18.00	9.00	11.00
Creamer, ftd.	11.00	7.00	9.00	Stem, 5¼", 3 oz., cocktail	24.00	12.00	18.00
Creamer, tea	17.50	7.00	9.00	Stem, 5½", 3 oz., wine	30.00	18.00	22.50
Cup, after dinner	20.00	10.00	12.50	Stem, 6", 4 oz., claret	35.00	25.00	25.00
Cup, flat		4.00	6.00	Stem, 6", 6 oz., high sherbet	20.00	10.00	12.50
Cup, ftd.	8.00	6.00	7.00	Stem, 8¼", 10 oz., water	30.00	16.00	20.00
Flower holder, oval,				Sugar, flat	27.50	10.00	12.00
window box	50.00	20.00	30.00	Sugar, ftd.	10.00	6.00	8.00
Grapefruit	25.00	15.00	20.00	Sugar cover	30.00	20.00	22.50
Grapefruit liner	20.00	12.00	15.00	Sugar pail	40.00	25.00	28.00
Ice bucket	50.00	30.00	35.00	Sugar, tea	17.50	6.00	8.00
Ice bowl	15.00	12.00	10.00	Tray, 11", ctr. hdld.	20.00	12.00	15.00
Ice bowl liner	20.00	12.00	* 10.00	Tumbler, 2½ oz., ftd.	18.00	10.00	12.00
Mayonnaise	15.00	9.00	10.00	Tumbler, 4½", 5 oz., ftd.	18.00	10.00	11.00
Mayonnaise ladle	35.00	20.00	25.00	Tumbler, 5¼", 9 oz., ftd.	20.00	12.00	13.00
Mayonnaise liner, 7"	5.00	3.00	3.50	Tumbler, 6", 12 oz., ftd.	25.00	13.50	18.00
Nut cup, blown	25.00	15.00	20.00	Vase, 8" (2 styles)	60.00	35.00	45.00
Oil, ftd.	105.00	80.00	90.00	Whipped cream pail	40.00	25.00	28.00

See page 83 for stem identification.　　　　　　　　　　　　　　　　　　　　　　　* Green $20.00

FOSTORIA STEMS AND SHAPES

Top Row: Left to Right
1. Water, 10 oz., 8¼"
2. Claret, 4 oz., 6"
3. Wine, 3 oz., 5½"
4. Cordial, ¾ oz., 4"
5. Sherbet, low, 6 oz., 4¼"
6. Cocktail, 3 oz., 5¼"
7. Sherbet, high, 6 oz., 6"

Bottom Row: Left to Right
1. Grapefruit and liner
2. Ice tea tumbler, 12 oz., 6"
3. Water tumbler, 9 oz., 5¼"
4. Parfait, 6 oz., 5¼"
5. Juice tumbler, 5 oz., 4½"
6. Oyster cocktail, 5½ oz.
7. Bar tumbler, 2½ oz.

FLANDERS, Tiffin Glass Company, Mid 1910's – Mid 1930's

Colors: crystal, pink, yellow

The listing for Flanders continues to grow. Several exciting pieces have been found in crystal and yellow. Shakers have turned up in both colors and you can see a crystal one here. The Chinese hurricane lamp has been found in crystal. An example of this style can be seen on the bottom of page 87 in Fuchsia.

Although I have only seen one style footed creamer and sugar, another style has been reported. The flat sugar and creamer were made very early and remain quite rare. Round plates are line #8800 and each size plate has a different number. Scalloped ones are line #5831 for the purists who worry about little details.

Some other pieces shown for the first time include the handled parfait, Dahlia style vase, 6" comport and covered candy. The green footed tumbler with pink top must have been a regular issued line as I have also seen a saucer champagne.

Some stems are crystal, while others are the same color as the bowl. This phenomenon seems to occur in lines from all glass companies.

	Crystal	Pink	Yellow		Crystal	Pink	Yellow
Bowl, finger, w/liner	17.00	35.00	24.00	Plate, 10¼", dinner	25.00	50.00	40.00
Bowl, 2 hdld., bonbon	15.00	30.00	20.00	Relish, 3 pt.	25.00	45.00	35.00
Bowl, 12", flanged rim,				Salt & pepper, pr.	60.00		100.00
console	25.00	45.00	35.00	Saucer	5.00	10.00	8.00
Candlestick, 2 styles	30.00	60.00	40.00	Stem, ftd., whiskey	30.00	60.00	45.00
Candy jar, w/cover, flat	60.00	110.00	90.00	Stem, claret	40.00	75.00	60.00
Candy jar, w/cover, ftd.	75.00	195.00	145.00	Stem, cordial	40.00	75.00	55.00
Celery, 11"	20.00	40.00	30.00	Stem, cocktail	15.00	30.00	25.00
Cheese & cracker	30.00	65.00	55.00	Stem, oyster cocktail	12.00	25.00	18.00
Comport, 3½"	25.00	50.00	35.00	Stem, parfait	30.00	60.00	45.00
Comport, 6"	50.00	100.00	75.00	Stem, saucer champagne	15.00	25.00	18.00
Creamer, flat	40.00	95.00	62.50	Stem, sherbet	10.00	20.00	15.00
Creamer, ftd.	35.00	85.00	50.00	Stem, water	15.00	35.00	25.00
Cup, 2 styles	25.00	50.00	35.00	Stem, wine	25.00	50.00	35.00
Decanter	100.00	250.00	200.00	Sugar, flat	40.00	95.00	62.50
Grapefruit, w/liner	30.00	60.00	40.00	Sugar, ftd.	35.00	85.00	50.00
Hurricane lamp, Chinese				Tumbler, 2½ oz., ftd.	30.00	60.00	40.00
style	125.00			Tumbler, 9 oz., ftd., water	12.00	25.00	20.00
Mayonnaise, w/liner	30.00	75.00	50.00	Tumbler, 10 oz., ftd.	15.00	30.00	25.00
Nut cup, ftd., blown	30.00	50.00	40.00	Tumbler, 12 oz., ftd., tea	20.00	35.00	27.50
Oil bottle & stopper	100.00	225.00	145.00	Vase, bud	25.00	50.00	40.00
Parfait, hdld.	50.00	125.00	75.00	Vase, ftd.	75.00	150.00	100.00
Pitcher & cover	200.00	350.00	275.00	Vase, Dahalia style	75.00	200.00	150.00
Plate, 6"	4.00	12.00	9.00	Vase, fan	50.00	125.00	75.00
Plate, 8"	9.00	15.00	12.50				

FUCHSIA, Tiffin Glass Company, Late 1930's – Early 1940's

Colors: crystal

There are at least sixteen new listings for this pattern! If you have seen a cup and saucer, let me know. I believe this is another of Tiffin's patterns without one. Most of the new listings are shown. The large shade over the candle is known as a Chinese hurricane.

	Crystal		Crystal
Bowl, finger, w/liner	25.00	Plate, 14½", salad liner	30.00
Bowl, 2 hdld., bonbon	18.00	Relish, 5 part	35.00
Bowl, 11½", salad	35.00	Saucer	7.50
Bowl, 12", crimped	35.00	Stem, cordial	35.00
Bowl, 12", flanged rim, console	30.00	Stem, cocktail	17.00
Candlestick, double, w/pointed center	40.00	Stem, oyster cocktail	14.00
Candlestick, double, w/fan center	45.00	Stem, parfait	25.00
Candlestick, single	22.00	Stem, saucer champagne	15.00
Celery, 11"	25.00	Stem, saucer champagne, hollow stem	30.00
Comport, 6"	30.00	Stem, sherbet	12.00
Creamer, flat	22.50	Stem, water	25.00
Creamer, ftd.	20.00	Stem, wine	30.00
Creamer, individual	20.00	Sugar, flat	22.50
Cup	37.50	Sugar, ftd.	16.50
Hurricane, Chinese style	75.00	Sugar, individual	25.00
Icer, with insert	65.00	Tray, sugar/creamer	17.50
Mayonnaise, w/liner	40.00	Tumbler, 2 oz., bar	35.00
Pitcher & cover	275.00	Tumbler, 5 oz., ftd., juice	18.00
Plate, 3-ftd.	20.00	Tumbler, 9 oz., ftd., water	15.00
Plate, 6"	6.00	Tumbler, 12 oz., ftd., tea	30.00
Plate, 8"	15.00	Vase, bud	35.00
Plate, 10", dinner	37.50	Vase, urn, 2 hdld.	95.00

GLORIA, (etching 1746), Cambridge Glass 3400 Line Dinnerware, Introduced 1930

Colors: crystal, yellow, pink, green, emerald green, amber, Heatherbloom

Gloria is most often confused with Tiffin's Flanders by novice collectors. See the pattern shots for comparison of the two patterns. They are easily distinguished once you see them side by side.

Sets can be collected in crystal and yellow with work, but any other color will take infinite patience and beaucoup money. Heatherbloom and blue will cost up to 50% more than the prices below for color. I have never been able to find a saucer for my Heatherbloom cup in this pattern. My favorite color in Gloria is the dark Emerald green, but I do not see enough of it in my travels to seriously collect it.

A cobalt blue, gold encrusted vase is pictured in my new Very Rare Glassware book. It's a beauty!

	Crystal	Green, Pink/ Yellow		Crystal	Green, Pink/ Yellow
Basket, 6", 2 hdld. (sides up)	13.00	25.00	Comport, 5", 4 ftd.	17.00	37.50
Bowl, 3", indiv. nut, 4 ftd.	30.00	50.00	Comport, 6", 4 ftd.	19.00	35.00
Bowl, 3½", cranberry, 4 ftd.	15.00	35.00	Comport, 7", low	30.00	45.00
Bowl, 5", ftd., crimped edge, bonbon	14.00	22.00	Comport, 7", tall	35.00	65.00
Bowl, 5", sq. fruit, "saucer"	7.00	14.00	Comport, 9½", tall, 2 hdld., ftd. bowl	65.00	125.00
Bowl, 5½", bonbon, 2 hdld.	14.00	21.00	Creamer, ftd.	11.00	17.50
Bowl, 5½", bonbon, ftd.	12.00	19.00	Creamer, tall, ftd.	11.00	20.00
Bowl, 5½", flattened, ftd., bonbon	12.00	18.00	Cup, rnd. or sq.	15.00	25.00
Bowl, 5½", fruit, "saucer"	7.50	15.00	Cup, 4 ftd., sq.	20.00	50.00
Bowl, 6", rnd., cereal	9.00	20.00	Cup, after dinner (demitasse), rnd.		
Bowl, 6", sq., cereal	9.00	18.00	or sq.	35.00	65.00
Bowl, 8", 2 pt., 2 hdld., relish	15.00	23.00	Fruit cocktail, 6 oz., ftd. (3 styles)	9.00	15.00
Bowl, 8", 3 pt., 3 hdld., relish	20.00	34.00	Ice pail, metal handle w/tongs	37.50	75.00
Bowl, 8¾", 2 hdld., figure, "8" pickle	17.50	30.00	Icer, w/insert	50.00	65.00
Bowl, 8¾", 2 pt., 2 hdld., figure "8"			Mayonnaise, w/liner & ladle,		
relish	20.00	32.00	(4 ftd. bowl)	35.00	55.00
Bowl, 9", salad, tab hdld.	20.00	50.00	Oil, w/stopper; tall, ftd., hdld.	75.00	150.00
Bowl, 9½", 2 hdld., veg.	55.00	80.00	Oyster cocktail, #3035, 4½ oz.	10.00	15.00
Bowl, 10", oblong, tab hdld., "baker"	32.00	70.00	Oyster cocktail, 4½ oz., low stem	10.00	15.00
Bowl, 10", 2 hdld.	32.00	70.00	Pitcher, 67 oz., middle indent	110.00	235.00
Bowl, 11", 2 hdld., fruit	30.00	55.00	Pitcher, 80 oz., ball	125.00	225.00
Bowl, 12", 4 ftd., console	25.00	50.00	Pitcher, w/cover, 64 oz.	110.00	250.00
Bowl, 12", 4 ftd., flared rim	22.00	50.00	Plate, 6", 2 hdld.	8.00	13.50
Bowl, 12", 4 ftd., oval	30.00	65.00	Plate, 6", bread/butter	6.00	9.00
Bowl, 12", 5 pt., celery & relish	25.00	45.00	Plate, 7½", tea	8.00	12.00
Bowl, 13", flared rim	25.00	50.00	Plate, 8½"	9.00	14.00
Bowl, cream soup, w/rnd. liner	15.00	32.00	Plate, 9½", dinner	45.00	65.00
Bowl, cream soup, w/sq. saucer	15.00	32.00	Plate, 10", tab hdld. salad	15.00	30.00
Bowl, finger, flared edge, w/rnd. plate	14.00	26.00	Plate, 11", 2 hdld.	15.00	25.00
Bowl, finger, ftd.	12.00	27.50	Plate, 11", sq., ftd. cake	45.00	100.00
Bowl, finger, w/rnd. plate	15.00	30.00	Plate, 11½", tab hdld., sandwich	17.50	38.00
Butter, w/cover, 2 hdld.	110.00	250.00	Plate, 14", chop or salad	35.00	65.00
Candlestick, 6", ea.	17.50	32.50	Plate, sq., bread/butter	6.00	9.00
Candy box, w/cover, 4 ftd. w/tab hdld.	45.00	95.00	Plate, sq., dinner	45.00	65.00
Cheese compote w/11½" cracker plate,			Plate, sq., salad	7.00	12.00
tab hdld.	25.00	55.00	Plate, sq., service	22.00	45.00
Cocktail shaker, grnd. stopper, spout			Platter, 11½"	45.00	95.00
(like pitcher)	70.00	175.00	Salt & pepper, pr., short	25.00	55.00
Comport, 4", fruit cocktail	10.00	20.00	Salt & pepper, pr., w/glass top, tall	27.50	70.00

	Crystal	Green Pink/ Yellow		Crystal	Green Pink/ Yellow
Salt & pepper, ftd., metal tops..............	32.50	62.50	Tray, 4 pt., ctr. hdld., relish.................	30.00	45.00
Saucer, rnd...	2.00	4.00	Tray, 9", pickle, tab hdld.	15.00	25.00
Saucer, rnd. after dinner	4.00	10.00	Tumbler, #3035, 5 oz., high ftd.	11.00	20.00
Saucer, sq., after dinner (demitasse)....	4.00	10.00	Tumbler, #3035, 10 oz., high ftd.	12.00	22.00
Saucer, sq.	2.00	3.00	Tumbler, #3035, 12 oz., high ftd.	17.00	25.00
Stem, #3035, 2½ oz., wine	20.00	35.00	Tumbler, #3115, 5 oz., ftd., juice	12.00	20.00
Stem, #3035, 3 oz., cocktail	17.50	28.00	Tumbler, #3115, 8 oz., ftd.	12.00	20.00
Stem, #3035, 3½ oz., cocktail..............	17.00	27.00	Tumbler, #3115, 10 oz., ftd.	13.00	21.00
Stem, #3035, 4½ oz., claret	25.00	40.00	Tumbler, #3115, 12 oz., ftd.	17.00	25.00
Stem, #3035, 6 oz., low sherbet	10.00	15.00	Tumbler, #3120, 2½" oz., ftd. (used		
Stem, #3035, 6 oz., tall sherbet	11.00	17.50	w/cocktail shaker)	15.00	30.00
Stem, #3035, 9 oz., water	15.00	30.00	Tumbler, #3120, 5 oz., ftd.	12.00	20.00
Stem, #3035, 3½ oz., cocktail..............	17.00	28.00	Tumbler, #3120, 10 oz., ftd.	12.00	20.00
Stem, #3115, 9 oz., goblet	13.00	26.00	Tumbler, #3120, 12 oz., ftd.	17.00	25.00
Stem, #3120, 1 oz., cordial..................	45.00	100.00	Tumbler, #3120, 2½ oz., ftd. (used		
Stem, #3120, 4½" oz., claret	25.00	40.00	w/shaker)	15.00	30.00
Stem, #3120, 6 oz., low sherbet	10.00	15.00	Tumbler, #3130, 5 oz., ftd.	12.00	20.00
Stem, #3120, 6 oz., tall sherbet............	11.00	16.00	Tumbler, #3130, 10 oz., ftd.	13.00	20.00
Stem, #3120, 9 oz., water	15.00	25.00	Tumbler, #3130, 12 oz., ftd.	15.00	25.00
Stem, #3130, 2½ oz., wine	20.00	35.00	Tumbler, #3135, 5 oz., juice	12.00	20.00
Stem, #3130, 6 oz., low sherbet	10.00	15.00	Tumbler, #3135, 10 oz., water..............	12.00	20.00
Stem, #3130, 6 oz., tall sherbet............	11.00	16.00	Tumbler, #3135, 12 oz., tea	17.00	25.00
Stem, #3130, 8 oz., water	15.00	25.00	Tumbler, 12 oz., flat, (2 styles), one		
Stem, #3135, 1 oz., cordial..................	50.00	100.00	indent side to match 67 oz. pitcher.	14.00	25.00
Stem, #3135, 6 oz., low sherbet	11.00	15.00	Vase, 9", oval, 4 indent.........................	45.00	100.00
Stem, #3135, 6 oz., tall sherbet............	12.00	16.00	Vase, 10", keyhole base	37.50	90.00
Stem, #3135, 8 oz., water	15.00	26.00	Vase, 10", squarish top	35.00	80.00
Sugar, ftd...	11.00	18.00	Vase, 11"...	40.00	80.00
Sugar, tall, ftd.	11.00	19.00	Vase, 11", neck indent	45.00	85.00
Sugar shaker, w/glass top.....................	100.00	225.00	Vase, 12", keyhole base, flared rim	45.00	100.00
Syrup, tall, ftd......................................	50.00	95.00	Vase, 12", squarish top	45.00	80.00
Tray, 11", ctr. hdld., sandwich	20.00	35.00	Vase, 14", keyhole base, flared rim	55.00	125.00
Tray, 2 pt., ctr. hdld., relish.................	22.00	35.00			

Note: See Pages 182-183 for stem identification.

GREEK KEY, A.H. Heisey & Co.

Colors: crystal; "Flamingo" pink punch bowl and cups only

	Crystal		Crystal
Bowl, finger	20.00	Pitcher, 1 pint	70.00
Bowl, jelly, w/cover, 2 hdld. ftd	145.00	Pitcher, 1 quart	75.00
Bowl, indiv., ftd., almond	25.00	Pitcher, 3 pint	100.00
Bowl, 4", nappy	20.00	Pitcher, ½ gal.	125.00
Bowl, 4", shallow, low ft., jelly	20.00	Oil bottle, 2 oz., squat, w/#8 stopper	65.00
Bowl, 4½", nappy	20.00	Oil bottle, 2 oz., w/#6 stopper	70.00
Bowl, 4½", scalloped, nappy	17.50	Oil bottle, 4 oz., squat, w/#8 stopper	75.00
Bowl, 4½", shallow, low ft., jelly	16.00	Oil bottle, 4 oz., w/#6 stopper	80.00
Bowl, 5", ftd., almond	35.00	Oil bottle, 6 oz., w/#6 stopper	90.00
Bowl, 5", ftd., almond, w/cover	90.00	Oil bottle, 6 oz., squat, w/#8 stopper	90.00
Bowl, 5", hdld., jelly	35.00	Plate, 4½"	10.00
Bowl, 5", low ft., jelly, w/cover	40.00	Plate, 5"	11.00
Bowl, 5", nappy	22.50	Plate, 5½"	11.00
Bowl, 5½", nappy	25.00	Plate, 6"	12.00
Bowl, 5½", shallow nappy, ftd.	55.00	Plate, 6½"	12.00
Bowl, 6", nappy	25.00	Plate, 7"	13.00
Bowl, 6", shallow nappy	27.50	Plate, 8"	15.00
Bowl, 6½", nappy	30.00	Plate, 9"	20.00
Bowl, 7", low ft., straight side	35.00	Plate, 10"	55.00
Bowl, 7", nappy	32.00	Plate, 16", orange bowl liner	60.00
Bowl, 8", low ft., straight side	40.00	Puff box, #1, w/cover	75.00
Bowl, 8", nappy	37.50	Puff box, #3, w/cover	85.00
Bowl, 8", scalloped nappy	42.00	Salt & pepper, pr.	85.00
Bowl, 8", shallow, low ft.	45.00	Sherbet, 4½ oz., ftd., straight rim	12.50
Bowl, 8½", shallow nappy	45.00	Sherbet, 4½ oz., ftd., flared rim	12.50
Bowl, 9", flat banana split	25.00	Sherbet, 4½ oz., high ft., shallow	12.50
Bowl, 9", ftd. banana split	22.50	Sherbet, 4½" oz., ftd., shallow	12.50
Bowl, 9", low ft., straight side	45.00	Sherbet, 4½ oz., ftd., cupped rim	12.50
Bowl, 9", nappy	40.00	Sherbet, 6 oz., low ft.	13.00
Bowl, 9", shallow, low ft.	45.00	Spooner, lg.	75.00
Bowl, 9½", shallow nappy	45.00	Spooner, 4½", (or straw jar)	75.00
Bowl, 10", shallow, low ft.	50.00	Stem, ¾ oz., cordial	175.00
Bowl, 11", shallow nappy	50.00	Stem, 2 oz., wine	150.00
Bowl, 12", orange bowl	55.00	Stem, 2 oz., sherry	140.00
Bowl, 12", punch, ftd.	175.00	Stem, 3 oz., cocktail	25.00
(Flamingo)	750.00	Stem, 3½ oz., burgundy	110.00
Bowl, 14", orange, flared rim	65.00	Stem, 4½ oz., saucer champagne	110.00
Bowl, 14½", orange, flared rim	76.50	Stem, 4½ oz., claret	120.00
Bowl, 15", punch, ftd.	165.00	Stem, 7 oz.	75.00
Bowl, 18", punch, shallow	165.00	Stem, 9 oz.	125.00
Butter, indiv. (plate)	15.00	Stem, 9 oz., low ft.	85.00
Butter/jelly, 2 hdld., w/cover	175.00	Straw jar, w/cover	300.00
Candy, w/cover, ½ lb.	135.00	Sugar	25.00
Candy, w/cover, 1 lb.	140.00	Sugar, oval, hotel	30.00
Candy, w/cover, 2 lb.	195.00	Sugar, rnd., hotel	27.50
Cheese & cracker set, 10"	75.00	Sugar & creamer, oval, individual	67.50
Compote, 5"	50.00	Tray, 9", oval celery	17.50
Compote, 5", w/cover	75.00	Tray, 12", oval celery	20.00
Creamer	25.00	Tray, 12½", French roll	55.00
Creamer, oval, hotel	30.00	Tray, 13", oblong	60.00
Creamer, rnd., hotel	27.50	Tray, 15", oblong	62.50
Cup, 4½ oz., punch	15.00	Tumbler, 2½ oz., (or toothpick)	285.00
Coaster	12.00	Tumbler, 5 oz., flared rim	20.00
(Flamingo)	30.00	Tumbler, 5 oz., straight side	20.00
Egg cup, 5 oz.	60.00	Tumbler, 5½ oz., water	20.00
Hair receiver	65.00	Tumbler, 7 oz., flared rim	22.00
Ice tub, lg., tab hdld.	75.00	Tumbler, 7 oz., straight side	25.00
Ice tub, sm., tab hdld.	60.00	Tumbler, 8 oz., w/straight, flared, cupped,	
Ice tub, w/cover, hotel	85.00	shallow	30.00
Ice tub, w/cover, 5", individual w/5" plate	85.00	Tumbler, 10 oz., flared rim	33.00
Jar, 1 qt., crushed fruit, w/cover	200.00	Tumbler, 10 oz., straight wide	33.00
Jar, 2 qt., crushed fruit, w/cover	250.00	Tumbler, 12 oz., flared rim	35.00
Jar, lg. cover, horseradish	67.50	Tumbler, 12 oz., straight side	35.00
Jar, sm. cover, horseradish	57.50	Tumbler, 13 oz., straight side	35.00
Jar, tall celery	62.00	Tumbler, 13 oz., flared rim	38.00
Jar, w/knob cover, pickle	110.00	Water bottle	165.00

IMPERIAL HUNT SCENE, #718, Cambridge Glass Company, Late 1920's – 1930's

Colors: amber, black, crystal, Emerald green, green, pink

If your desire is to collect a pattern with an array of stems and tumblers - this is the one. I have difficulty in finding anything other than stems to photograph.

About six months ago, I had an exciting letter and photograph of a black, gold encrusted humidor from a reader. The picture was almost good enough to use for the book. On a recent trip to The Green River Depression Glass Club show, I was able to purchase another one. There is even a metal attachment to the lid to let the cigars breathe (or so I was told). Being a non-smoker all my life, I am not too familiar with such intricacies.

Black and dark Emerald green will fetch 15% to 25% higher prices than those listed.

	Crystal	Colors
Bowl, 6", cereal.	10.00	20.00
Bowl, 8".	30.00	50.00
Bowl, 8½", 3 pt.	25.00	40.00
Candlestick, 2-lite, keyhole.	15.00	30.00
Candlestick, 3-lite, keyhole.	25.00	50.00
Comport, 5½", #3085		30.00
Creamer, ftd.	15.00	30.00
Decanter		225.00
Finger bowl, w/plate, #3085		30.00
Humidor, tobacco		350.00
Ice bucket.	40.00	75.00
Ice tub.	35.00	70.00
Mayonnaise, w/liner.	30.00	50.00
Pitcher, w/cover, 63 oz., #3085.		225.00
Pitcher, w/cover, 76 oz., #711.	125.00	200.00
Plate, 8".	12.00	22.00
Stem, 1 oz., cordial, #1402.	50.00	
Stem, 2½ oz., wine, #1402.	40.00	
Stem, 3 oz., cocktail, #1402.	40.00	
Stem, 6 oz., tomato, #1402.	40.00	
Stem, 6½ oz., sherbet, #1402.	35.00	
Stem, 7½ oz., sherbet, #1402.	40.00	
Stem, 10 oz., water, #1402.	40.00	
Stem, 14 oz., #1402.	50.00	
Stem, 18 oz., #1402.	60.00	
Stem, 1 oz., cordial, #3085.		125.00
Stem, 2½ oz., cocktail, #3085.		35.00
Stem, 2½ oz., wine, #3085.		50.00
Stem, 4½ oz., claret, #3085.		60.00
Stem, 5½ oz., parfait, #3085.		55.00
Stem, 6 oz., low sherbet, #3085.		20.00
Stem, 6 oz., high sherbet, #3085.		25.00
Stem, 9 oz., water, #3085.		40.00
Sugar, ftd.	15.00	30.00
Tumbler, 2½ oz., flat, #1402.	17.00	
Tumbler, 5 oz., flat, #1402.	16.00	
Tumbler, 7 oz., flat, #1402.	20.00	
Tumbler, 10 oz., flat, #1402.	23.00	
Tumbler, 10 oz., flat, tall, #1402.	25.00	
Tumbler, 15 oz., flat, #1402.	35.00	
Tumbler, 2½ oz., ftd., #3085.		20.00
Tumbler, 5 oz., ftd., #3085.		20.00
Tumbler, 8 oz., ftd., #3085.		22.50
Tumbler, 10 oz., ftd., #3085.		25.00
Tumbler, 12 oz., ftd., #3085.		30.00

IPSWICH, Blank #1405, A.H. Heisey & Co.

Colors: crystal, "Flamingo" pink, "Sahara" yellow, "Moongleam" green, cobalt and "Alexandrite"

If you find any colored piece of Ipswich **other than those listed below**, it was made at Imperial and not Heisey. Even if it is marked Heisey, it was still manufactured at Imperial. Mostly, I get letters on Alexandrite candy jars which is Imperial's Heather color.

The only piece of Ipswich made in Alexandrite is the goblet. If you have any problems in determining whether a piece you have is Alexandrite or not, look in the back of this book on pages 184-185. We have been able to show this color more consistently than any other book ever has. You can also take an Alexandrite piece outside in natural light where it will look pinkish and then near a fluorescent bulb where it will change to a bluish look.

Note the candle vase in green which goes on the top of the candlestick centerpiece. Has anyone got the bottom?

	Crystal	Pink	Sahara	Green	Cobalt	Alexan
Bowl, finger w/underplate	20.00	45.00	40.00	45.00		
Bowl, 11", ftd., floral	35.00				325.00	
Candlestick, 6", 1-lite	75.00	205.00	160.00	200.00	350.00	
Candlestick centerpiece, ftd., vase, "A" prisms	95.00	275.00	275.00	350.00	500.00	
Candy jar, ½ lb., w/cover	45.00	195.00	250.00	300.00		
Cocktail shaker, 1 quart, strainer #86 stopper	160.00	300.00	300.00	525.00		
Creamer	17.00	47.50	37.50	42.50		
Stem, 4 oz., oyster cocktail	8.00					
Stem, 5 oz., saucer champagne	12.50					
Stem, 10 oz., goblet	18.00					750.00
Stem, 12 oz., schoppen	27.50					
Pitcher, ½ gal.	125.00	250.00	350.00	750.00		
Oil bottle, 2 oz., ftd., #86 stopper	75.00	185.00	150.00	200.00		
Plate, 7", square	15.00	20.00	22.00	26.00		
Plate, 8", square	16.00	22.50	25.00	30.00		
Sherbet, 4 oz.	7.00	17.50	22.50	30.00		
Sugar	17.00	42.50	37.50	42.50		
Tumbler, 5 oz., ftd.	10.00	35.00	30.00	35.00		
Tumbler, 8 oz., ftd.	10.00	34.00	30.00	35.00		
Tumbler, 10 oz., cupped rim	12.50	40.00	35.00	40.00		
Tumbler, 10 oz., straight rim	12.50	40.00	35.00	40.00		
Tumbler, 12 oz., ftd.	15.00	50.00	45.00	50.00		

97

JUNE, Fostoria Glass Company, 1928 – 1944

Colors: crystal, "Azure" blue, "Topaz" yellow, "Rose" pink

There is not enough room in this book to list all the line numbers for the items in June in the space I have allotted. If you will refer to Versailles, I have listed all the Fostoria line numbers for each piece. Since these are virtually the same listings, you can use the item number listings from Versailles if you need such information. There is some other Fostoria information under Versailles you need to read! I will try to allow enough space for that next time. I have sacrificed writing space to show you more glass.

Yes, I know the fleur-de-lis knob is missing on the blue candy, but for $10.00 I could not pass it by! **Prices for pink June are now listed with the blue!**

	Crystal	Rose, Blue	Topaz		Crystal	Rose, Blue	Topaz
Ashtray	23.00	45.00	32.00	Ice dish liner (tomato, crab, fruit)	5.00	20.00	10.00
Bottle, salad dressing, #2083 or #2375	165.00	400.00	275.00	Mayonnaise, w/liner	22.50	45.00	37.50
Bowl, baker, 9", oval	35.00	85.00	65.00	Oil, ftd	165.00	450.00	275.00
Bowl, baker, 10", oval	40.00	95.00	75.00	Oyster cocktail, 5½ oz.	16.00	35.00	25.00
Bowl, bonbon	12.50	27.50	20.00	Parfait, 5¼"	25.00	85.00	50.00
Bowl, bouillon, ftd.	12.00	30.00	20.00	Pitcher	195.00	450.00	300.00
Bowl, finger, w/liner	32.50	45.00	25.00	Plate, canape	10.00	18.00	15.00
Bowl, mint, 3-ftd., 4½"	10.00	25.00	15.00	Plate, lemon	14.00	25.00	18.00
Bowl, 5", mint	11.00	22.00	18.00	Plate, 6", bread/butter	4.50	12.00	6.00
Bowl, 6", cereal	15.00	35.00	25.00	Plate, 6", finger bowl liner	4.50	8.00	6.00
Bowl, 6", nappy, 3-ftd., jelly	10.00	25.00	18.00	Plate, 7½", salad	5.00	9.00	8.00
Bowl, 7", soup	25.00	75.00	75.00	Plate, 7½, cream soup	4.00	12.00	7.50
Bowl, lg., dessert, hdld.	25.00	85.00	45.00	Plate, 8¾", luncheon	6.00	15.00	10.00
Bowl, 10"	30.00	95.00	55.00	Plate, 9½", sm. dinner	8.00	20.00	15.00
Bowl, 10", Grecian	30.00	75.00	50.00	Plate, 10", grill	30.00	75.00	60.00
Bowl, 11", centerpiece	25.00	60.00	40.00	Plate, 10", cake, hdld (no indent)	20.00	50.00	37.50
Bowl, 12", centerpiece, several types	25.00	75.00	45.00	Plate, 10", cheese with indent, hdld.	20.00	50.00	37.50
Bowl, 13", oval centerpiece, w/flower frog	35.00	100.00	55.00	Plate, 10¼", dinner	35.00	75.00	50.00
Candlestick, 2"	10.00	25.00	20.00	Plate, 13", chop	22.00	50.00	35.00
Candlestick, 3"	12.00	25.00	18.00	Plate, 14", torte			50.00
Candlestick, 3", Grecian	15.00	30.00	25.00	Platter, 12"	22.00	75.00	45.00
Candlestick, 5"	15.00	35.00	25.00	Platter, 15"	30.00	150.00	90.00
Candy, w/cover, 3 pt.		225.00		Relish, 8½", 3-part	14.00	27.00	21.00
Candy, w/cover, ½ lb., ¼ lb.			135.00	Sauce boat	35.00	275.00	85.00
Celery, 11½"	25.00	60.00	35.00	Sauce boat liner	12.00	75.00	25.00
Cheese & cracker set, #2368 or #2375	25.00	85.00	45.00	Saucer, after dinner	6.00	10.00	8.00
Comport, 5", #2400	18.00	40.00	27.50	Saucer	4.00	7.50	5.00
Comport, 6", #5298 or #5299	20.00	65.00	30.00	Shaker, ftd., pr	60.00	150.00	100.00
Comport, 7", #2375	22.00	75.00	35.00	Sherbet, high, 6", 6 oz.	17.50	32.00	25.00
Comport, 8", #2400	30.00	85.00	40.00	Sherbet, low, 4¼", 6 oz.	15.00	25.00	20.00
Cream soup, ftd.	12.00	35.00	30.00	Sugar, ftd., straight or scalloped top	12.00	25.00	20.00
Creamer, ftd.	12.00	25.00	17.50	Sugar cover	45.00	175.00	120.00
Creamer, tea	17.50	50.00	37.50	Sugar pail	65.00	195.00	130.00
Cup, after dinner	20.00	65.00	35.00	Sugar, tea	17.50	50.00	37.50
Cup, ftd.	15.00	30.00	22.00	Sweetmeat	14.00	30.00	18.00
Decanter	400.00		400.00	Tray, service and lemon			250.00
Goblet, claret, 6", 4 oz.	30.00	95.00	60.00	Tray, 11", ctr. hdld.	20.00	45.00	35.00
Goblet, cocktail, 5¼", 3 oz.	20.00	40.00	32.50	Tumbler, 2½ oz., ftd.	20.00	50.00	35.00
Goblet, cordial, 4", ¾ oz.	40.00	95.00	65.00	Tumbler, 5 oz., 4½", ftd.	15.00	30.00	22.50
Goblet, water, 8¼", 10 oz.	21.00	35.00	30.00	Tumbler, 9 oz., 5¼", ftd.	15.00	35.00	21.50
Goblet, wine, 5½", 3 oz.	22.00	80.00	45.00	Tumbler, 12 oz., 6", ftd.	17.50	45.00	27.50
Grapefruit	25.00	85.00	60.00	Vase, 8", 2 styles	60.00	195.00	135.00
Grapefruit liner	20.00	70.00	40.00	Vase, 8½", fan, ftd.	60.00	165.00	100.00
Ice bucket	47.50	100.00	75.00	Whipped cream bowl	10.00	20.00	14.00
Ice dish	21.00	45.00	37.50	Whipped cream pail	65.00	195.00	115.00

Note: See stemware identification on page 83.

KASHMIR, Fostoria Glass Company, 1930 – 1934

Colors: "Topaz" yellow, green; some blue

Kashmir is another of the patterns I can only find a piece here and there. Rarely do I see a lot of it for sale at one time except for yellow which few people seem to notice. Both styles of after dinner cups are shown in the picture of blue. Notice that I have found very little green in my travels. For those of you who like blue and want a challenging set to put together, this may be it. I warn you, you will find it infrequently!

	Yellow, Green	Blue		Yellow, Green	Blue
Ashtray	25.00	30.00	Plate, 9" luncheon	9.00	12.00
Bowl, cream soup	22.00	25.00	Plate, 10", dinner	35.00	45.00
Bowl, finger	15.00	20.00	Plate, 10", grill	30.00	50.00
Bowl, 5", fruit	13.00	15.00	Plate, cake, 10"	35.00	
Bowl, 6", cereal	22.00	25.00	Salt & pepper, pr.	90.00	125.00
Bowl, 7", soup	25.00	30.00	Sandwich, center hdld.	35.00	40.00
Bowl, 8½", pickle	20.00	25.00	Sauce boat, w/liner	75.00	100.00
Bowl, 9", baker	37.50	45.00	Saucer, rnd.	5.00	6.00
Bowl, 10"	40.00	45.00	Saucer, after dinner, sq.	5.00	
Bowl, 12", centerpiece	40.00	50.00	Saucer, after dinner, rnd.	6.00	6.00
Candlestick, 2"	15.00	17.50	Stem, ¾ oz., cordial	85.00	100.00
Candlestick, 3"	20.00	25.00	Stem, 2½ oz., ftd.	25.00	30.00
Candlestick, 5"	22.50	27.50	Stem, 2 oz., ftd., whiskey	25.00	30.00
Candlestick, 9½"	40.00	50.00	Stem, 2½ oz., wine	32.00	35.00
Candy, w/cover	75.00	95.00	Stem, 3 oz., cocktail	22.00	25.00
Cheese and cracker set	65.00	85.00	Stem, 3½ oz., ftd., cocktail	22.00	25.00
Comport, 6"	35.00	45.00	Stem, 4 oz., claret	30.00	40.00
Creamer, ftd.	17.50	20.00	Stem, 4½ oz., oyster cocktail	16.00	18.00
Cup	15.00	20.00	Stem, 5½ oz., parfait	30.00	40.00
Cup, after dinner, flat	25.00		Stem, 5 oz., ftd., juice	15.00	25.00
Cup, after dinner, ftd.	25.00	35.00	Stem, 5 oz., low sherbet	13.00	20.00
Grapefruit	40.00		Stem, 6 oz., high sherbet	17.50	22.50
Grapefruit liner	30.00		Stem, 9 oz., water	20.00	35.00
Ice bucket	65.00	85.00	Stem, 10 oz., ftd., water	22.00	30.00
Oil, ftd.	250.00	350.00	Stem, 11 oz.	22.50	
Pitcher, ftd.	250.00	350.00	Stem, 12 oz., ftd.	25.00	35.00
Plate, 6", bread & butter	5.00	6.00	Stem, 13 oz., ftd., tea	25.00	
Plate, 7", salad, rnd.	6.00	7.00	Stem, 16 oz., ftd., tea	30.00	
Plate, 7", salad, sq.	6.00	7.00	Sugar, ftd.	15.00	20.00
Plate, 8", salad	8.00	10.00	Vase, 8"	85.00	100.00

Note: See stemware identification on page 83.

LARIAT, Blank #1540, A.H. Heisey & Co.

Colors: crystal; rare in black and amber

Notice the salt and pepper shakers and the swung vase. Both of these are hard to find. There is a special surprise for Lariat collectors in the new edition of my Very Rare Glassware book!

	Crystal		Crystal
Ashtray, 4"	8.00	Oil bottle, 4 oz., hdld., w/#133 stopper	75.00
Basket, 7½", bonbon	95.00	Oil bottle, 6 oz., oval	55.00
Basket, 8½", ftd.	165.00	Plate, 6", finger bowl liner	5.00
Basket, 10", ftd.	195.00	Plate, 7", salad	7.00
Bowl, 7 quart, punch	110.00	Plate, 8", salad	9.00
Bowl, 4", nut	14.00	Plate, 11", cookie	22.00
Bowl, 7", 2 pt., relish	17.00	Plate, 12", demi-torte, rolled edge	22.50
Bowl, 7", nappy	13.00	Plate, 13", deviled egg	135.00
Bowl, 8", flat, nougat	15.00	Plate, 14", 2 hdld., sandwich	35.00
Bowl, 9½", camellia	22.00	Plate, 21", buffet	60.00
Bowl, 10", hdld., celery	30.00	Platter, 15", oval	30.00
Bowl, 10½", 2 hdld., salad	30.00	Salt & pepper, pr.	195.00
Bowl, 10½", salad	30.00	Saucer	5.00
Bowl, 11", 2 hdld., oblong, relish	22.00	Stem, 1 oz., cordial, double loop	175.00
Bowl, 12", floral or fruit	18.00	Stem, 1 oz., cordial blown	145.00
Bowl, 13", celery	20.00	Stem, 2½ oz., wine, blown	22.00
Bowl, 13", gardenia	22.00	Stem, 3½ oz., cocktail, pressed	11.00
Bowl, 13", oval, floral	27.00	Stem, 3½ oz., cocktail, blown	11.00
Candlestick, 1-lite	12.00	Stem, 3½ oz., wine, pressed	11.00
Candlestick, 2-lite	20.00	Stem, 4 oz., claret, blown	20.00
Candlestick, 3-lite	30.00	Stem, 4¼ oz., oyster cocktail or fruit	11.00
Candy box, w/cover	37.50	Stem, 4½ oz., oyster cocktail, blown	11.00
Candy, w/cover, 7"	42.50	Stem, 5½ oz., sherbet/saucer champagne	
Cheese, 5", ftd., w/cover	37.50	blown	12.00
Cheese dish, w/cover, 8"	45.00	Stem, 6 oz., low sherbet	7.50
Cigarette box	22.50	Stem, 6 oz., sherbet/saucer champagne,	
Coaster, 4"	7.50	pressed	10.00
Compote, 10", w/cover	65.00	Stem, 9 oz., pressed	16.00
Creamer	12.50	Stem, 10 oz., blown	16.00
Creamer & sugar, w/tray, indiv.	37.50	Sugar	12.00
Cup	12.00	Tray for sugar & creamer	15.00
Cup, punch	5.25	Tumbler, 5 oz., ftd., juice	11.00
Ice tub	75.00	Tumbler, 5 oz., ftd., juice, blown	11.00
Jar, w/cover, 12", urn	150.00	Tumbler, 12 oz., ftd., ice tea	18.00
Lamp & globe, 7", black-out	95.00	Tumbler, 12 oz., ftd., ice tea, blown	18.00
Lamp & globe, 8", candle	85.00	Vase, 7", ftd., fan	32.00
Mayonnaise, 5" bowl, 7" plate	32.50	Vase, swung	125.00

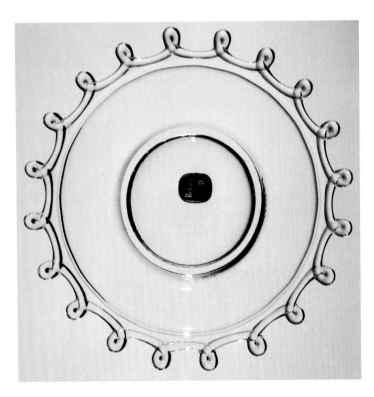

LODESTAR, Pattern #1632, A.H. Heisey & Co.

Color: Dawn

This Heisey pattern is only called Lodestar in the Dawn color. If you find pieces in crystal, the pattern name becomes Satellite and the prices are entirely different than for this rarer Heisey color. Note the star-like design in each base design.

Ashtray	65.00
Bowl, 4½", sauce dish, #1626	35.00
Bowl, 5", mayonnaise	55.00
Bowl, 6¾", #1565	45.00
Bowl, 8"	40.00
Bowl, 11", crimped	95.00
Bowl, 12", deep floral	75.00
Candleblock, 2¾" tall, 1-lite star, #1543, pr.	275.00
Candlestick, 2" tall, 1-lite centerpiece, pr.	95.00
Candlestick, 5¾" tall, 2-lite, pr.	600.00
Candy jar, w/cover, 5"	135.00
Celery, 10"	60.00
Creamer	50.00
Creamer, w/handle	85.00
Jar, w/cover, 8", #1626	140.00
Pitcher, 1 qt., #1626	140.00
Plate, 8½"	65.00
Plate, 14"	85.00
Relish, 7½", 3 pt.	55.00
Salt and pepper, pr., #1485	250.00
Sugar	50.00
Sugar, w/handles	85.00
Tumbler, 6 oz., juice	35.00
Vase, 8", #1626	140.00
Vase, 8", crimped, #1626	175.00

MINUET, Etching 1530, QUEEN ANN Blank, #1509; TOUJOURS Blank, #1511; SYMPHONE Blank, #5010, et. al.; 1939 – 1950's

Colors: crystal

That Universal cocktail icer with liner on the right behind the footed tumbler is one of the few I have seen.

The pattern shot is of a 2-lite Toujours candlestick. The Minuet pattern really stands out on this and the Toujours centerpiece vase. Finding either of these makes you lucky!

	Crystal		Crystal
Bell, dinner	55.00	Plate, 7", salad	12.00
Bowl, finger, #3309	18.00	Plate, 7", salad, #1511 TOUJOURS	14.00
Bowl, 6", ftd., mint	16.00	Plate, 8", luncheon	18.00
Bowl, 6", ftd., 2 hdld., jelly	20.00	Plate, 8", luncheon, #1511 TOUJOURS	20.00
Bowl, 6½", salad dressings	27.50	Plate, 10½", service	50.00
Bowl, 7", salad dressings	30.00	Plate, 12", rnd., 2 hdld., sandwich	50.00
Bowl, 7", triplex, relish	27.50	Plate, 13", floral, salver, #1511 TOUJOURS	45.00
Bowl, 7½", sauce, ftd.	30.00	Plate, 14", torte, #1511 TOUJOURS	45.00
Bowl, 9½", 3 pt., "5 o'clock" relish	40.00	Plate, 15", sand., #1511 TOUJOURS	60.00
Bowl, 10", salad, #1511 TOUJOURS	50.00	Plate, 16", snack rack, w/#1477 2-lite candle	95.00
Bowl, 11", 3 pt., "5 o'clock" relish	50.00	Salt & pepper, pr. (#10)	75.00
Bowl, 11", ftd., floral	50.00	Saucer	5.00
Bowl, 12", oval, floral, #1511 TOUJOURS	50.00	Stem, #5010, SYMPHONE, 1 oz., cordial	135.00
Bowl, 12", oval, #1514	50.00	Stem, #5010, 2½ oz., wine	70.00
Bowl, 13", floral, #1511 TOUJOURS	45.00	Stem, #5010, 3½ oz., cocktail	40.00
Bowl, 13", pickle & olive	32.50	Stem, #5010, 4 oz., claret	40.00
Bowl, 13½", shallow salad	40.00	Stem, #5010, 4½ oz., oyster cocktail	30.00
Candelabrum, 1-lite w/prisms	125.00	Stem, #5010, 6 oz., saucer champagne	30.00
Candelabrum, 2-lite, bobeche & prisms	150.00	Stem, #5010, 6 oz., sherbet	18.00
Candlestick, 1-lite, #112	25.00	Stem, #5010, 9 oz., water	35.00
Candlestick, 2-lite, #1511 TOUJOURS	175.00	Sugar, indiv., #1511 TOUJOURS	35.00
Candlestick, 3-lite, #142 CASCADE	85.00	Sugar, indiv., #1509 QUEEN ANN	30.00
Candlestick, 5", 2-lite, #134 TRIDENT	75.00	Sugar dolp. ft., #1509 QUEEN ANN	37.50
Centerpiece vase & prisms #1511 TOUJOURS	350.00	Sugar, #1511 TOUJOURS	30.00
Cocktail icer, w/liner #3304 UNIVERSAL	60.00	Tray, 12", celery, #1511 TOUJOURS	30.00
Comport, 5½", #5010	35.00	Tray, 15", social hour	55.00
Comport, 7½", #1511 TOUJOURS	80.00	Tray for indiv. sugar & creamer	17.50
Creamer, #1511 TOUJOURS	30.00	Tumbler, #5010, 5 oz., fruit juice	25.00
Creamer, dolp. ft.	37.50	Tumbler, #5010, 9 oz., low ftd., water	30.00
Creamer, indiv., #1509 QUEEN ANN	30.00	Tumbler, #5010, 12 oz., tea	40.00
Creamer, indiv., #1511 TOUJOURS	35.00	Tumbler, #2351, 12 oz., tea	40.00
Cup	30.00	Vase, 5", #5013	35.00
Ice bucket, dolp. ft.	135.00	Vase, 5½", ftd., #1511 TOUJOURS	50.00
Marmalade, w/cover, #1511 TOUJOURS (apple shape)	85.00	Vase, 6", urn, #5012	60.00
Mayonnaise, 5½", dolp. ft.	40.00	Vase, 7½", urn, #5012	65.00
Mayonnaise, ftd., #1511 TOUJOURS	40.00	Vase, 8", #4196	65.00
Pitcher, 73 oz., #4164	195.00	Vase, 9", urn, #5012	75.00
Plate, 7", mayonnaise liner	12.00	Vase, 10", #4192	75.00
		Vase, 10", #4192, SATURN optic	95.00

MT. VERNON, Cambridge Glass Company, late 1920's – 1940's

Colors: amber, crystal, red, blue, Heatherbloom, emerald green (light and dark); rare in violet

The range of colors in Mt. Vernon gives collectors a wide choice. Large sets can be accumulated in only amber and crystal. Carmen, Royal Blue and Heatherbloom are eagerly acquired, but are difficult to assemble as sets. Note the Violet sherbet shown as it is seldom seen!

	Amber/Crystal		Amber/Crystal
Ashtray, 3½", #63	7.50	Honey jar, w/cover (marmalade), #74	30.00
Ashtray, 4", #68	11.00	Ice bucket, w/tongs, #92	30.00
Ashtray, 6" x 4½", oval, #71	11.00	Lamp, 9" hurricane, #1607	65.00
Bonbon, 7", ftd., #10	12.50	Mayonnaise, divided, 2 spoons, #107	25.00
Bottle bitters, 2½ oz., #62	50.00	Mug, 14 oz., stein, #84	27.50
Bottle, 7 oz., sq., toilet, #18	60.00	Mustard, w/cover, 2½ oz., #28	22.00
Bowl, finger, #23	10.00	Pickle, 6", 1 hdld., #78	12.00
Bowl, 4½", ivy ball or rose, ftd., #12	27.50	Pitcher, 50 oz., #90	75.00
Bowl, 5¼", fruit, #6	10.00	Pitcher, 66 oz., #13	80.00
Bowl, 6", cereal, #32	12.00	Pitcher, 80 oz., ball, #95	90.00
Bowl, 6", preserve, #76	12.00	Pitcher, 86 oz., #91	100.00
Bowl, 6½", rose, #106	18.00	Plate, finger bowl liner, #23	4.00
Bowl, 8", pickle, #65	15.00	Plate, 6", bread & butter, #4	3.00
Bowl, 8½", 4 pt., 2 hdld., sweetmeat, #105	27.50	Plate, 6⅜", bread & butter, #19	4.00
Bowl, 10", 2 hdld., #39	20.00	Plate, 8½", salad, #5	7.00
Bowl, 10½", deep, #43	25.00	Plate, 10½", dinner, #40	25.00
Bowl, 10½", salad, #120	25.00	Plate, 11½", hdld., #37	20.00
Bowl, 11", oval, 4 ftd., #136	27.50	Relish, 6", 2 pt., 2 hdld., #106	12.00
Bowl, 11", oval, #135	25.00	Relish, 8", 2 pt., hdld., #101	17.50
Bowl, 11½", belled, #128	25.00	Relish, 8", 3 pt., 3 hdld., #103	20.00
Bowl, 11½", shallow, #126	25.00	Relish, 11", 3 part, #200	25.00
Bowl, 11½", shallow cupped, #61	25.00	Relish, 12", 2 part, #80	27.50
Bowl, 12", flanged, rolled edge, #129	30.00	Relish, 12", 5 part, #104	27.50
Bowl, 12", oblong, crimped, #118	30.00	Salt, indiv., #24	7.00
Bowl, 12", rolled edge, crimped, #117	30.00	Salt, oval, 2 hdld., #102	12.00
Bowl, 12½", flanged, rolled edge, #45	30.00	Salt & pepper, pr., #28	22.50
Bowl, 12½", flared, #121	32.00	Salt & pepper, pr., short, #88	20.00
Bowl, 12½", flared, #44	32.00	Salt & pepper, tall, #89	25.00
Bowl, 13", shallow, crimped, #116	35.00	Salt dip, #24	8.50
Box, 3", w/cover, round, #16	22.00	Sauce boat & ladle, tab hdld., #30-445	55.00
Box, 4", w/cover, sq., #17	25.00	Saucer, #7	7.50
Box, 4½", w/cover, ftd., round, #15	30.00	Stem, 3 oz., wine, #27	12.50
Butter tub, w/cover, #73	60.00	Stem, 3½ oz., cocktail, #26	9.00
Cake stand, 10½" ftd., #150	35.00	Stem, 4 oz., oyster cocktail, #41	9.00
Candelabrum, 13½", #38	40.00	Stem, 4½ oz., claret, #25	12.50
Candlestick, 4", #130	10.00	Stem, 4½ oz., low sherbet, #42	7.50
Candlestick, 5", 2-lite, #110	15.00	Stem, 6½ oz., tall sherbet, #2	9.00
Candlestick, 8", #35	20.00	Stem, 10 oz., water, #1	12.50
Candy, w/cover, 1 lb., ftd., #9	40.00	Sugar, ftd., #8	10.00
Celery, 10½", #79	15.00	Sugar, indiv., #4	12.00
Celery, 11", #98	17.50	Sugar, #86	10.00
Celery, 12", #79	20.00	Tray, for indiv., sugar & creamer, #4	10.00
Cigarette box, 6", w/cover, oval, #69	25.00	Tumbler, 1 oz., ftd., cordial, #87	20.00
Cigarette holder, #66	15.00	Tumbler, 2 oz., whiskey, #55	10.00
Coaster, 3", plain, #60	5.00	Tumbler, 3 oz., ftd., juice, #22	9.00
Coaster, 3", ribbed, #70	5.00	Tumbler, 5 oz., #56	12.00
Cocktail icer, 2 pc., #85	22.50	Tumbler, 5 oz., ftd., #21	12.00
Cologne, 2½ oz., w/stopper, #1340	30.00	Tumbler, 7 oz., old fashion, #57	14.00
Comport, 4½", #33	12.00	Tumbler, 10 oz., ftd., water, #3	15.00
Comport, 5½", 2 hdld., #77	15.00	Tumbler, 10 oz., table, #51	12.00
Comport, 6", #34	15.00	Tumbler, 10 oz., tall, #58	12.00
Comport, 6½", #97	17.50	Tumbler, 12 oz., barrel shape, #13	15.00
Comport, 6½", belled, #96	20.00	Tumbler, 12 oz., ftd., tea, #20	16.00
Comport, 7½" #11	25.00	Tumbler, 14 oz., barrel shape, #14	20.00
Comport, 8", #81	25.00	Tumbler, 14 oz., tall, #59	20.00
Comport, 9", oval, 2 hdld., #100	27.50	Urn, w/cover (same as candy), #9	45.00
Comport, 9½", #99	27.50	Vase, 5", #42	15.00
Creamer, ftd., #8	10.00	Vase, 6", crimped, #119	20.00
Creamer, indiv., #4	10.00	Vase, 6", ftd., #50	25.00
Creamer, #86	10.00	Vase, 6½", squat, #107	27.50
Cup, #7	6.50	Vase, 7", #58	30.00
Decanter, 11 oz., #47	50.00	Vase, 7", ftd., #54	35.00
Decanter, 40 oz., w/stopper, #52	65.00	Vase, 10", ftd., #46	50.00

NAVARRE, (Plate Etching #327) Fostoria Glass Company, 1937-1980

Colors: crystal; all other colors found made very late

As of now, I am going to stick to pricing the older pieces of Navarre. Colors in pink, blue and green were all made in the 1970's as were additional pieces not originally made. The later pieces included carafes, roemer wines, brandies.

Most of these are signed "Fostoria" although some only carried a sticker. I am showing a few of these pieces to make you aware of this. Some of the Depression era glass shows do not allow this glass to be sold since it is so recently manufactured.

Navarre is extremely popular on the West Coast. Prices there are much higher as is the case of Fostoria's Chintz. Sometimes it takes a while for Eastern prices to catch up, since there is a more abundant supply here.

	Crystal		Crystal
Bell, dinner	30.00	Plate, #2440, 7½", salad	12.50
Bowl, #2496, 4", square, hdld.	10.00	Plate, #2440, 8½", luncheon	15.00
Bowl, #2496, 4⅜", hdld.	11.00	Plate, #2440, 9½", dinner	35.00
Bowl, #869, 4½", finger	35.00	Plate, #2496, 10", hdld., cake	45.00
Bowl, #2496, 4⅝", tri-cornered	14.00	Plate, #2440, 10½" oval cake	45.00
Bowl, #2496, 5", hdld., ftd.	14.00	Plate, #2496, 14", torte	40.00
Bowl, #2496, 6", square, sweetmeat	16.00	Plate, #2464, 16", torte	75.00
Bowl, #2496, 6¼", 3 ftd., nut	17.50	Relish, #2496, 6", 2 part, square	25.00
Bowl, #2496, 7⅜", ftd., bonbon	25.00	Relish, #2496, 10" x 7½", 3 part	35.00
Bowl, #2496, 10", oval, floating garden	45.00	Relish, #2496, 10", 4 part	50.00
Bowl, #2496, 10½", hdld., ftd.	50.00	Relish, #2419, 13¼", 5 part	75.00
Bowl, #2470 ½, 10½", ftd.	50.00	Salt & pepper, #2364, 3¼", flat, pr.	50.00
Bowl, #2496, 12", flared	55.00	Salt & pepper, #2375, 3½", ftd., pr.	85.00
Bowl, #2545, 12½", oval, "Flame"	50.00	Salad dressing bottle, #2083, 6½"	215.00
Candlestick, #2496, 4"	17.50	Sauce dish, #2496, div. mayo., 6½"	35.00
Candlestick, #2496, 4½", double	30.00	Sauce dish, #2496, 6½" x 5¼"	90.00
Candlestick, #2472, 5", double	40.00	Sauce dish liner, #2496, 8" oval	20.00
Candlestick, #2496, 5½"	25.00	Saucer, #2440	3.50
Candlestick, #2496, 6", triple	40.00	Syrup, #2586, metal cut-off top, 5½"	225.00
Candlestick, #2545, 6¾", double, "Flame"	45.00	Stem, #6106, 1 oz., cordial, 3⅞"	35.00
Candlestick, #2482, 6¾", triple	40.00	Stem, #6106, 3¼ oz., wine, 5½"	30.00
Candy, w/cover, #2496, 3 part	95.00	Stem, #6106, 3½ oz., cocktail, 6"	22.50
Celery, #2440, 9"	25.00	Stem, #6106, 4 oz., oyster cocktail, 3⅝"	25.00
Celery, #2496, 11"	35.00	Stem, #6106, 4½ oz., claret, 6½"	35.00
Comport, #2496, 3¼", cheese	25.00	Stem, #6106, 6 oz., low sherbet, 4⅜"	22.00
Comport, #2400, 4½"	27.50	Stem, #6106, 6 oz., saucer champagne,	
Comport, #2496, 4¾"	27.50	5⅝"	20.00
Cracker, #2496, 11" plate	40.00	Stem, #6106, 10 oz., water, 7⅝"	25.00
Creamer, #2440, 4¼", ftd.	12.00	Sugar, #2440, 3⅝", ftd.	10.00
Creamer, #2496, individual	15.00	Sugar, #2496, individual	15.00
Cup, #2440	15.00	Tid bit, #2496, 8¼", 3 ftd., turned up edge	20.00
Ice bucket, #2496, 4⅜" high	75.00	Tray, #2496½", for ind. sugar/creamer	20.00
Ice bucket, #2375, 6" high	125.00	Tumbler, #6106, 5 oz., ftd., juice, 4⅝"	20.00
Mayonnaise, #2375, 3 piece	65.00	Tumbler, #6106, 10 oz., ftd., water, 5⅜"	17.50
Mayonnaise, #2496½, 3 piece	65.00	Tumbler, #6106, 13 oz., ftd., tea, 5⅞"	22.50
Pickle, #2496, 8"	25.00	Vase, #4108, 5"	65.00
Pickle, #2440, 8½"	27.50	Vase, #4121, 5"	70.00
Pitcher, #5000, 48 oz., ftd.	295.00	Vase, #4128, 5"	70.00
Plate, #2440, 6", bread/butter	9.00	Vase, #2470, 10", ftd.	125.00

OCTAGON, Blank #1231 – Ribbed; also Blank 500 and Blank 1229, A.H. Heisey & Co.

Colors: crystal, "Flamingo" pink, "Sahara" yellow, "Moongleam" green, "Hawthorne" orchid, "Marigold," a deep, amber/yellow and "Dawn"

Octagon is one of those Heisey patterns that everyone recognizes, since it is almost always marked; but few collectors buy it. True, it is one of the plainer patterns, but it does come in a multitude of colors! The piece in the price guide that jumps out at you is the Dawn colored tray. Otherwise, it is priced reasonably and is usually just sitting around waiting for a new home.

	Crystal	Flam.	Sahara	Moon.	Hawth.	Marigold
Basket, 5", #500.	60.00	100.00	115.00	115.00	150.00	
Bonbon, 6", sides up, #1229	5.00	8.00	10.00	12.00	15.00	
Bowl, cream soup, 2 hdld.	10.00	18.00	22.50	30.00	35.00	
Bowl, 5½", jelly, #1229	5.00	8.00	10.00	12.00	15.00	
Bowl, 6", mint, #1229	5.00	8.00	10.00	12.00	15.00	
Bowl, 6", #500	12.00	17.00	19.00	20.00	25.00	
Bowl, 6½", grapefruit	9.00	17.00	19.00	18.00	30.00	
Bowl, 8", ftd., #1229	12.00	17.00	20.00	24.00	28.00	
Bowl, 9", vegetable	10.00	18.00	20.00	25.00	45.00	
Candlestick, 3", 1-lite	7.00	17.50	22.00	26.00	37.50	
Cheese dish, 6", 2 hdld., #1229	5.00	8.00	11.00	13.00	16.00	
Creamer #500	5.00	12.50	16.00	17.00	22.00	
Creamer, hotel	7.00	13.00	15.00	19.00	25.00	
Cup, after dinner	8.00	22.50	25.00	30.00	40.00	
Dish, frozen dessert, #500	7.00	12.00	15.00	15.00	25.00	45.00
Ice tub, #500	26.00	60.00	80.00	85.00	95.00	135.00
Mayonnaise, 5½", ftd., #1229	10.00	14.00	16.00	18.00	22.50	
Plate, cream soup liner	3.00	5.00	7.00	9.00	12.00	
Plate, 6"	4.00	6.00	8.00	10.00	12.00	
Plate, 7", bread	5.00	7.00	9.00	11.00	13.00	
Plate, 8", luncheon	6.00	8.00	10.00	12.00	14.00	
Plate, 9", soup	10.00	14.00	19.00	27.50	27.00	
Plate, 10", sand., #1229	13.00	18.00	22.00	25.00	30.00	
Plate, 10", muffin, #1229	16.00	22.00	26.00	32.00	35.00	
Plate, 10½"	16.00	22.00	27.00	30.00	32.00	
Plate, 10½", ctr. hdld., sandwich	21.00	30.00	37.50	45.00	55.00	
Plate, 12", muffin, #1229	20.00	27.00	30.00	34.00	40.00	
Plate, 13", hors d'oeuvre, #1229	15.00	25.00	28.00	35.00	45.00	
Plate, 14"	22.00	25.00	30.00	30.00	35.00	
Platter, 12¾"	25.00	35.00	40.00	45.00	52.50	
Saucer, after dinner	2.00	5.00	6.00	6.00	12.00	
Sugar #500	5.00	12.00	16.00	17.00	22.00	
Sugar, hotel	7.00	12.00	15.00	18.00	27.50	
Tray, 6", oblong, #500	5.00	12.00	16.00	17.00	22.00	
Tray, 9", celery	7.00	15.00	18.00	20.00	25.00	
Tray, 12", celery	12.00	25.00	27.00	30.00	35.00	**(Dawn)**
Tray, 12", 4 pt., #500	25.00	65.00	75.00	85.00	85.00	300.00

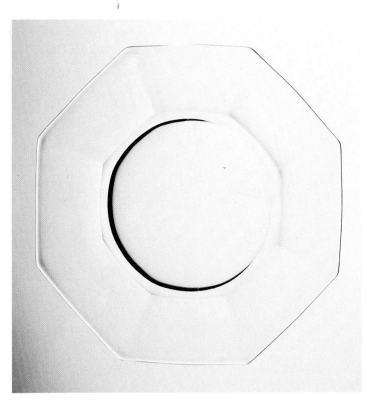

113

OLD COLONY, Empress Blank #1401; Caracassone Blank #3390; and Old Dominion Blank #3380,
A.H. Heisey & Co., 1930 – 1939

Colors: crystal, "Flamingo" pink, "Sahara" yellow, "Moongleam" green, "Marigold," a deep, amber/yellow, and cobalt

	Crystal	Flam.	Sahara	Moon.	Marigold
Bouillon cup, 2 hdld., ftd.	12.50	18.00	20.00	24.00	
Bowl, finger, #4075	5.50	10.00	11.00	14.00	18.00
Bowl, ftd., finger, #3390	5.50	16.00	21.00	27.50	
Bowl, 4½", nappy	7.00	10.00	12.50	15.00	
Bowl, 5", ftd., 2 hdld.	12.50	17.50	22.50	27.50	
Bowl, 6", ftd., 2 hdld., jelly	15.00	20.00	25.00	32.50	
Bowl, 6", dolp. ftd., mint	16.00	22.00	27.50	35.00	
Bowl, 7", triplex, dish	15.00	22.00	25.00	28.00	
Bowl, 7½", dolp. ftd., nappy	22.00	60.00	65.00	75.00	
Bowl, 8", nappy	25.00	35.00	40.00	42.50	
Bowl, 8½", ftd., floral, 2 hdld.	32.00	47.00	57.50	67.50	
Bowl, 9", 3 hdld.	36.00	75.00	90.00	95.00	
Bowl, 10", rnd., 2 hdld., salad	32.00	47.50	57.50	65.00	
Bowl, 10", sq., salad, 2 hdld.	30.00	45.00	55.00	65.00	
Bowl, 10", oval, dessert, 2 hdld.	30.00	40.00	50.00	62.50	
Bowl, 10", oval, veg.	30.00	34.00	42.00	50.00	
Bowl, 11", floral, dolp. ft.	32.00	70.00	80.00	95.00	
Bowl, 13", ftd., flared	30.00	35.00	40.00	45.00	
Bowl, 13", 2 pt., pickle & olive	12.50	20.00	22.50	27.50	
Cigarette holder, #3390 (Cobalt $100.00)	16.00	47.50	42.50	55.00	
Comport, 7", oval, ftd.	40.00	75.00	80.00	85.00	
Comport, 7", ftd., #3368	30.00	57.50	62.50	85.00	95.00
Cream soup, 2 hdld.	12.00	20.00	22.00	27.00	
Creamer, dolp. ft.	17.50	32.00	45.00	50.00	
Creamer, indiv.	15.00	30.00	40.00	37.50	
Cup, after dinner	12.00	25.00	35.00	50.00	
Cup	10.00	26.00	32.00	38.00	
Decanter, 1 pt.	150.00	300.00	275.00	525.00	
Flagon, 12 oz., #3390	25.00	55.00	55.00	85.00	
Grapefruit, 6"	15.00	23.00	30.00	35.00	
Grapefruit, ftd., #3380	10.00	16.00	18.00	20.00	30.00
Ice tub, dolp. ft.	42.50	110.00	115.00	135.00	
Mayonnaise, 5½", dolp. ft.	36.00	55.00	70.00	80.00	
Oil, 4 oz., ftd.	42.50	70.00	105.00	120.00	
Pitcher, 3 pt., #3390	90.00	245.00	210.00	400.00	
Pitcher, 3 pt., dolp. ft.	85.00	195.00	200.00	210.00	
Plate, bouillon	5.00	8.00	12.00	15.00	
Plate, cream soup	5.00	8.00	12.00	15.00	
Plate, 4½", rnd.	3.00	6.00	7.00	8.00	
Plate, 6", rnd.	6.00	12.00	15.00	18.00	
Plate, 6", sq.	6.00	12.00	15.00	18.00	
Plate, 7", rnd.	8.00	14.00	18.00	20.00	
Plate, 7", sq.	8.00	14.00	18.00	20.00	
Plate, 8", rnd.	10.00	17.00	22.00	27.00	
Plate, 8", sq.	10.00	17.00	22.00	27.00	
Plate, 9", rnd.	15.00	22.00	25.00	28.00	
Plate, 10½", rnd.	28.50	60.00	70.00	75.00	
Plate, 10½", sq.	27.50	50.00	65.00	70.00	
Plate, 12", rnd.	31.00	57.50	70.00	75.00	
Plate, 12", 2 hdld., rnd., muffin	31.00	57.50	70.00	75.00	
Plate, 12", 2 hdld., rnd., sand.	31.00	57.50	70.00	75.00	
Plate, 13", 2 hdld., sq., sand.	35.00	40.00	45.00	50.00	
Plate, 13", 2 hdld., sq., muffin	35.00	40.00	45.00	50.00	
Platter, 14", oval	25.00	35.00	40.00	45.00	
Salt & pepper, pr.	52.50	80.00	110.00	130.00	
Saucer, sq.	4.00	8.00	10.00	10.00	
Saucer, rnd.	4.00	8.00	10.00	10.00	
Stem, #3380, 1 oz., cordial	75.00	135.00	135.00	155.00	375.00
Stem, #3380, 2½ oz., wine	18.00	40.00	35.00	50.00	75.00
Stem, #3380, 3 oz., cocktail	13.00	34.00	25.00	40.00	60.00
Stem, #3380, 4 oz., oyster/cocktail	8.00	13.00	15.00	17.00	25.00
Stem, #3380, 4 oz., claret	20.00	50.00	40.00	55.00	65.00
Stem, #3380, 5 oz., parfait	10.00	15.00	15.00	17.00	40.00
Stem, #3380, 6 oz., champagne	8.00	13.00	15.00	17.00	25.00
Stem, #3380, 6 oz., sherbet	6.00	11.00	13.00	15.00	25.00

	Crystal	Flam.	Sahara	Moon.	Marigold
Stem, #3380, 10 oz., short soda	7.00	18.00	15.00	22.00	30.00
Stem, #3380, 10 oz., tall soda		21.00	18.00	25.00	32.50
Stem, #3390, 1 oz., cordial..	50.00	130.00	125.00	165.00	
Stem, #3390, 2½ oz., wine..	12.00	20.00	27.50	35.00	
Stem, #3390, 3 oz., cocktail	7.00	15.00	20.00	25.00	
Stem, #3390, 3 oz., oyster/cocktail	7.00	15.00	20.00	25.00	
Stem, #3390, 4 oz., claret	12.00	22.50	27.50	32.50	
Stem, #3390, 6 oz., champagne..	10.00	20.00	25.00	30.00	
Stem, #3390, 6 oz., sherbet	10.00	20.00	25.00	30.00	
Stem, #3390, 11 oz., low water	8.00	20.00	25.00	30.00	
Stem, #3390, 11 oz., tall water	10.00	22.00	27.00	32.00	
Sugar, dolp. ft.	17.50	30.00	45.00	50.00	
Sugar, indiv.	12.50	27.50	32.50	35.00	
Tray, 10", celery	14.00	20.00	25.00	30.00	
Tray, 12", ctr. hdld., sand..	35.00	65.00	75.00	85.00	
Tray, 12", ctr. hdld., sq...	35.00	65.00	75.00	85.00	
Tray, 13", celery	17.00	20.00	26.00	30.00	
Tray, 13", 2 hdld., hors d'oeuvre	30.00	36.00	45.00	55.00	
Tumbler, dolp. ft.	90.00	135.00	165.00	195.00	
Tumbler, #3380, 1 oz., ftd., bar	22.00	37.50	42.50	52.50	55.00
Tumbler, #3380, 2 oz., ftd., bar	12.00	20.00	20.00	25.00	35.00
Tumbler, #3380, 5 oz., ftd., bar	7.00	12.00	12.00	17.00	25.00
Tumbler, #3380, 8 oz., ftd., soda	10.00	21.00	18.00	25.00	32.50
Tumbler, #3380, 10 oz., ftd., soda	12.00	23.00	20.00	25.00	32.50
Tumbler, #3380, 12 oz., ftd., tea	13.00	25.00	22.00	27.00	35.00
Tumbler, #3390, 2 oz., ftd.	7.00	18.00	22.50	28.00	
Tumbler, #3390, 5 oz., ftd., juice......................................	7.00	15.00	20.00	25.00	
Tumbler, #3390, 8 oz., ftd., soda	10.00	22.00	25.00	30.00	
Tumbler, #3390, 12 oz., ftd., tea.......................................	12.00	24.00	27.00	30.00	
Vase, 9", ftd.	75.00	130.00	150.00	175.00	

OLD SANDWICH, Blank #1404, A.H. Heisey & Co.

Colors: crystal, "Flamingo" pink, "Sahara" yellow, "Moongleam" green, cobalt

	Crystal	Flam.	Sahara	Moon.	Cobalt
Ashtray, individual...	5.00	25.00	23.00	26.00	32.00
Beer mug, 12 oz..	30.00	200.00	210.00	400.00	300.00
Beer mug, 14 oz..	35.00	200.00	225.00	425.00	325.00
Beer mug, 18 oz..	40.00	225.00	250.00	450.00	375.00
Bottle, catsup, w/#3 stopper (like lg. cruet)...............	30.00	75.00	90.00	95.00	
Bowl, finger..	9.00	12.00	15.00	18.00	
Bowl, ftd., popcorn, cupped.................................	35.00	50.00	60.00	67.50	
Bowl, 11", rnd., ftd., floral................................	25.00	40.00	50.00	60.00	
Bowl, 12", oval, ftd., floral................................	27.00	50.00	60.00	70.00	
Candlestick, 6"	30.00	55.00	65.00	75.00	235.00
Cigarette holder...	27.50	35.00	40.00	45.00	
Comport, 6"	37.50	85.00	90.00	95.00	
Creamer, oval	7.00	20.00	22.00	25.00	
Creamer, 12 oz...	32.00	165.00	170.00	175.00	300.00
Creamer, 14 oz...	35.00	175.00	180.00	185.00	
Creamer, 18 oz...	40.00	185.00	190.00	195.00	
Cup	40.00	65.00	65.00	65.00	
Decanter, 1 pint, w/#98 stopper	75.00	185.00	200.00	225.00	425.00
Floral block, #22	15.00	25.00	30.00	35.00	
Oil bottle, 2½ oz., #85 stopper	65.00	90.00	95.00	100.00	
Parfait, 4½ oz...	10.00	15.00	20.00	25.00	
Pilsner, 8 oz...	14.00	28.00	32.00	38.00	
Pilsner, 10 oz..	16.00	32.00	37.00	42.00	
Pitcher, ½ gallon, ice lip	75.00	155.00	165.00	180.00	
Pitcher, ½ gallon, reg.	70.00	150.00	160.00	175.00	
Plate, 6", sq., grnd. bottom................................	4.00	8.00	10.00	13.00	
Plate, 7", sq...	5.00	10.00	13.00	15.00	
Plate, 8", sq...	7.00	12.00	15.00	17.00	
Salt & pepper, pr.	40.00	65.00	75.00	85.00	
Saucer...	10.00	15.00	15.00	15.00	
Stem, 2½ oz., wine..	12.00	24.00	32.00	38.00	
Stem, 3 oz., cocktail..	9.00	15.00	18.00	20.00	
Stem, 4 oz., claret...	10.00	20.00	23.00	27.50	150.00
Stem, 4 oz., oyster cocktail.................................	5.00	10.00	12.00	15.00	
Stem, 4 oz., sherbet...	6.00	12.00	15.00	18.00	
Stem, 5 oz., saucer champagne	9.00	27.50	28.00	32.00	
Stem, 10 oz., low ft...	9.00	25.00	30.00	35.00	
Sugar, oval..	8.00	20.00	22.00	25.00	
Sundae, 6 oz...	5.00	10.00	15.00	20.00	
Tumbler, 1½ oz., bar, grnd. bottom..........................	12.00	35.00	40.00	50.00	
Tumbler, 5 oz., juice..	5.00	13.00	17.50	22.00	
Tumbler, 6½ oz., toddy......................................	8.00	16.00	20.00	22.00	
Tumbler, 8 oz., grnd. bottom, cupped & straight rim ..	9.00	17.00	22.00	27.50	
Tumbler, 10 oz.	10.00	17.00	22.00	27.50	
Tumbler, 10 oz., low ft......................................	10.00	17.00	22.00	27.50	
Tumbler, 12 oz., ftd., iced tea	12.00	22.00	30.00	40.00	
Tumbler, 12 oz., iced tea....................................	12.00	22.00	30.00	40.00	

ORCHID, (Etching 1507) ON WAVERLY BLANK 1519, A.H. Heisey & Co. 1940-1957

Colors: crystal

Orchid continues to be one of the hottest selling Heisey patterns. I decided to individually "show" a few of the harder to find pieces this time. These include the Universal #3304 cocktail icer, Cabochon ¼ pound butter dish and the Fern #1495 mayonnaise and liner. Each of these items are extremely hard to find and very desirable to own.

The pint size cocktail shaker is harder to find that its quart size counterpart. The oval sherry decanter is pictured between these two at the top of page 121.

	Crystal
Ashtray, 3".	27.50
Basket, 8½", LARIAT	400.00
Bell, dinner, #5022 or #5025	125.00
Bottle, 8 oz., French dressings	145.00
Bowl, finger, #3309 or #5025	55.00
Bowl, 4½", nappy, QUEEN ANN	37.50
Bowl, 5½", ftd., mint	32.00
Bowl, 6", jelly, 2 hdld.	30.00
Bowl, 6", oval, lemon, w/cover, WAVERLY	750.00
Bowl, 6½", ftd., honey; cheese, QUEEN ANN	32.50
Bowl, 6½", ftd., jelly	32.50
Bowl, 6½", 2 pt., oval, dressings	47.50
Bowl, 7", lily	42.50
Bowl, 7", salad	42.50
Bowl, 7", 3 pt., rnd., relish	42.50
Bowl, 7", ftd., honey; cheese	47.50
Bowl, 7", ftd., jelly	40.00
Bowl, 7", ftd., oval, nut	55.00
Bowl, 8", mint, ftd., QUEEN ANN	57.50
Bowl, 8", nappy, QUEEN ANN	55.00
Bowl, 8", 2 pt., oval, dressings	47.50
Bowl, 8", pt., rnd., relish	57.50
Bowl, 8½", flared, QUEEN ANN	55.00
Bowl, 8½", floral, 2 hdld., ftd., QUEEN ANN	57.50
Bowl, 9", 4 pt., rnd., relish	60.00
Bowl, 9", ftd., fruit or salad	85.00
Bowl, 9", gardenia, QUEEN ANN	55.00
Bowl, 9", salad	60.00
Bowl, 9½", crimped floral	55.00
Bowl, 9½" epergne	395.00
Bowl, 10", crimped	62.50
Bowl, 10", deep salad	75.00
Bowl, 10", gardenia	65.00
Bowl, 10½", ftd., floral	85.00
Bowl, 11", shallow, rolled edge	67.50
Bowl, 11", 3 ftd., floral, seahorse ft.	135.00
Bowl, 11", 3 pt., oblong, relish	67.50
Bowl, 11", 4 ftd., oval	80.00
Bowl, 11", flared	55.00
Bowl, 11", floral	55.00

	Crystal
Bowl, 11", ftd., floral	95.00
Bowl, 12", crimped, floral	60.00
Bowl, 13", floral	65.00
Bowl, 13", crimped, floral	60.00
Bowl, 13", gardenia	65.00
Butter, w/cover, ¼ lb., CABOCHON	275.00
Butter, w/cover, 6"	165.00
Candleholder, 6", deep epernette	295.00
Candlestick, 1-lite, MERCURY	32.00
Candlestick, 1-lite, QUEEN ANN w/prisms	115.00
Candlestick, 2-lite, FLAME	135.00
Candlestick, 5", 2-lite, TRIDENT	50.00
Candlestick, 3-lite, CASCADE	72.50
Candlestick, 3-lite, WAVERLY	87.50
Candy box, w/cover, 6", low ft.	145.00
Candy, w/cover, 5", high ft.	160.00
Candy, w/cover, 6", bow knot finial	160.00
Cheese (comport) & cracker (11½") plate	110.00
Cheese & cracker, 14" plate	130.00
Chocolate, w/cover, 5"	175.00
Cigarette box, w/cover, 4", PURITAN	110.00
Cigarette holder, #4035	57.50
Cigarette holder, w/cover	125.00
Cocktail icer, w/liner, UNIVERSAL, #3304	165.00
Cocktail shaker, pt., #4225	250.00
Cocktail shaker, qt., #4036 or #4225	195.00
Comport, 5½", blown	87.50
Comport, 6", low ft.	40.00
Comport, 6½", low ft.	42.50
Comport, 7", ftd., oval	115.00
Creamer, individual	20.00
Creamer, ftd.	25.00
Cup, WAVERLY or QUEEN ANN	45.00
Decanter, oval, sherry, pt.	185.00
Decanter, pt., ftd. #4036	300.00
Decanter, pt., #4036½	225.00
Ice bucket, ftd., QUEEN ANN	235.00
Ice bucket, 2 hdld., WAVERLY	250.00
Marmalade, w/cover	90.00
Mayonnaise and liner, #1495, FERN	195.00

119

ORCHID, (Etching 1507) ON WAVERLY BLANK 11519, A.H. Heisey & Co. 1940-1957

	Crystal
Mayonnaise, 5½", 1 hdl.	40.00
Mayonnaise, 5½", ftd.	40.00
Mayonnaise, 5½", 1 hdl., div.	42.50
Mayonnaise, 6½", 1 hdl.	50.00
Mayonnaise, 6½", 1 hdl., div.	52.50
Mustard, w/cover, QUEEN ANN	125.00
Oil, 3 oz., ftd.	155.00
Pitcher, 73 oz.	400.00
Pitcher, 64 oz., ice tankard	475.00
Plate, 6"	12.50
Plate, 7", mayonnaise	15.00
Plate, 7", salad	15.50
Plate, 8", salad	20.00
Plate, 10½", dinner	115.00
Plate, 11", demi-torte	50.00
Plate, 11", sandwich	50.00
Plate, 12", ftd., salver	215.00
Plate, 13½", ftd., cake or salver	265.00
Plate, 14", torte, rolled edge	52.50
Plate, 14", torte	50.00
Plate, 14", sandwich	80.00
Plate, 15½", QUEEN ANN	95.00
Salt & pepper, pr.	60.00
Salt & pepper, ftd., pr.	65.00
Saucer, WAVERLY or QUEEN ANN	7.50
Stem, #5022 or #5025, 1 oz., cordial	135.00

	Crystal
Stem, #5022 or #5025, 2 oz., sherry	95.00
Stem, #5022 or #5025, 3 oz., wine	65.00
Stem, #5022 or #5025, 4 oz., oyster cocktail	37.50
Stem, #5025, 4 oz., cocktail	40.00
Stem, #5022 or #5025, 4½ oz., claret	60.00
Stem, #5022 or #5025, 6 oz., saucer champagne	30.00
Stem, #5022 or #5025, 6 oz., sherbet	25.00
Stem, #5022 or #5025, 10 oz., low water goblet	35.00
Sugar, individual	20.00
Sugar, ftd.	25.00
Toast, w/dome	250.00
Tray, indiv., creamer/sugar, QUEEN ANN	75.00
Tray, 12", celery	45.00
Tray, 13", celery	47.50
Tumbler, #5022 or #5025, 5 oz., fruit	50.00
Tumbler, #5022 or #5025, 12 oz., iced tea	60.00
Vase, 4", ftd., violet	75.00
Vase, 6", crimped top	110.00
Vase, 7", ftd., fan	75.00
Vase, 7", ftd.	85.00
Vase, 8", ftd., bud	165.00
Vase, 8", sq., ftd., bud	165.00
Vase, 10", sq., ftd., bud	175.00
Vase, 14"	600.00

PLANTATION, Blank #1567, A.H. Heisey & Co.

Colors: crystal; rare in amber

	Crystal		Crystal
Ashtray, 3½"..	17.50	Cup, punch	20.00
Bowl, 9 qt., Dr. Johnson, punch....................	300.00	Marmalade, w/cover	60.00
Bowl, 5", nappy	15.00	Mayonnaise, 4½", rolled ft.	45.00
Bowl, 5½", nappy	15.00	Mayonnaise, 5¼", w/liner	25.00
Bowl, 6½", 2 hdld., jelly..........................	18.00	Oil bottle, 3 oz., w/#125 stopper	75.00
Bowl, 6½", flared, jelly	18.00	Pitcher, ½ gallon, ice lip, blown	110.00
Bowl, 6½", ftd., honey, cupped...................	30.00	Plate, coupe (rare)	225.00
Bowl, 8", 4 pt., rnd., relish	25.00	Plate, 7", salad	10.00
Bowl, 8½", 2 pt., dressing........................	22.50	Plate, 8", salad	12.00
Bowl, 9", salad	30.00	Plate, 10½", demi-torte	20.00
Bowl, 9½", crimped, fruit or flower.............	30.00	Plate, 13", ftd., cake salver	95.00
Bowl, 9½", gardenia..............................	25.00	Plate, 14", sandwich..........................	40.00
Bowl, 11", 3 part, relish..........................	25.00	Plate, 18", buffet	50.00
Bowl, 11½", ftd., gardenia	40.00	Plate, 18", punch bowl liner	85.00
Bowl, 12", crimped, fruit or flower..............	45.00	Salt & pepper, pr...............................	40.00
Bowl, 13", celery.................................	25.00	Saucer	5.00
Bowl, 13", 2 part, celery	30.00	Stem, 1 oz., cordial...........................	90.00
Bowl, 13", 5 part, oval relish....................	40.00	Stem, 3 oz., wine, blown......................	40.00
Bowl, 13", gardenia	35.00	Stem, 3½ oz., cocktail, pressed	22.00
Butter, ¼ lb., oblong, w/cover	75.00	Stem, 4 oz., fruit/oyster cocktail..............	16.00
Butter, 5", rnd., (or cov. candy)................	75.00	Stem, 4½ oz., claret, blown	25.00
Candelabrum, w/two #1503 bobeche & 10		Stem, 4½ oz., claret, pressed..................	25.00
"A" prisms	150.00	Stem, 4½ oz., oyster cocktail, blown	20.00
Candle block, hurricane type.....................	100.00	Stem, 6½ oz., sherbet/saucer champagne,	
Candle block, 1-lite	85.00	blown	20.00
Candle holder, 5", ftd., epergne	100.00	Stem, 10 oz., pressed..........................	20.00
Candlestick, 1-lite	75.00	Stem, 10 oz., blown	20.00
Candlestick, 2-lite	45.00	Sugar, ftd.	15.50
Candlestick, 3-lite	85.00	Syrup bottle, w/drip, cut top	65.00
Candy box, w/cover, 7"	115.00	Tray, 8½", condiment/sugar & creamer	20.00
Candy, w/cover, 5", tall, ftd.....................	165.00	Tumbler, 5 oz., ftd., juice, pressed..............	25.00
Cheese, w/cover, 5", ftd..........................	85.00	Tumbler, 5 oz., ftd., juice, blown	25.00
Coaster, 4".......................................	12.00	Tumbler, 10 oz., pressed	30.00
Comport, 5".......................................	25.00	Tumbler, 12 oz., ftd., iced tea, pressed	30.00
Comport, 5", w/cover, deep.......................	60.00	Tumbler, 12 oz., ftd., iced tea, blown	30.00
Creamer, ftd.	16.00	Vase, 5", ftd., flared	40.00
Cup..	12.00	Vase, 9", ftd., flared	50.00

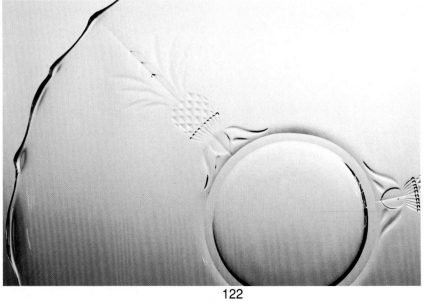

PLEAT & PANEL, Blank #1170, A.H. Heisey & Co.

Colors: crystal, "Flamingo" pink, "Moongleam" green

	Crystal	Flam.	Moongleam
Bowl, 4", chow chow	5.00	8.00	10.00
Bowl, 4½", nappy	5.00	8.00	9.00
Bowl, 5", 2 hdld., bouillon	6.00	10.00	12.00
Bowl, 5", 2 hdld., jelly	6.00	10.00	12.00
Bowl, 5", lemon, w/cover	10.00	20.00	22.00
Bowl, 6½", grapefruit/cereal	5.00	10.00	12.00
Bowl, 8", nappy	10.00	15.00	17.00
Bowl, 9", oval, vegetable	11.00	20.00	22.00
Cheese & cracker set, 10½", tray, w/compote	20.00	35.00	40.00
Compotier, w/cover, 5", hi. ftd.	25.00	50.00	60.00
Creamer, hotel	5.00	10.00	15.00
Cup	5.00	10.00	15.00
Marmalade, 4¾"	7.00	12.00	17.00
Oil bottle, 3 oz., w/pressed stopper	17.00	35.00	40.00
Pitcher, 3 pint, ice lip	35.00	65.00	75.00
Pitcher, 3 pint	35.00	65.00	75.00
Plate, 6"	3.00	6.00	8.00
Plate, 6¾", bouillon underliner	3.00	6.00	8.00
Plate, 7", bread	4.00	7.00	9.00
Plate, 8", luncheon	5.00	10.00	12.00
Plate, 10¾", dinner	10.00	30.00	35.00
Plate, 14", sandwich	15.00	25.00	30.00
Platter, 12", oval	17.00	30.00	35.00
Saucer	3.00	5.00	6.00
Sherbet, 5 oz., footed	4.00	7.00	8.00
Stem, 5 oz., saucer champagne	5.00	10.00	12.00
Stem, 7½ oz., low foot	9.00	15.00	20.00
Stem, 8 oz.	12.00	20.00	25.00
Sugar w/lid, hotel	7.00	17.00	22.00
Tray, 10", compartmented spice	15.00	30.00	35.00
Tumbler, 8 oz., ground bottom	8.00	12.00	15.00
Tumbler, 12 oz., tea, ground bottom	9.00	15.00	18.00
Vase, 8"	25.00	40.00	45.00

125

PORTIA, Cambridge Glass Company, 1932 – Early 1950's

Colors: crystal, yellow, Heatherbloom, green, amber

	Crystal
Basket, 2 hdld. (upturned sides)	16.00
Basket, 7", 1 hdld.	150.00
Bowl, 3½", cranberry	16.00
Bowl, 3½" sq., cranberry	15.00
Bowl, 5¼", 2 hdld., bonbon	15.00
Bowl, 6", 2 pt., relish	16.00
Bowl, 6", ftd., 2 hdld., bonbon	16.00
Bowl, 6", grapefruit or oyster	12.50
Bowl, 6½", 3 pt., relish	15.00
Bowl, 7", 2 pt., relish	16.00
Bowl, 7", ftd., bonbon, tab hdld.	20.00
Bowl, 7", pickle or relish	18.00
Bowl, 9", 3 pt., celery & relish, tab hdld.	25.00
Bowl, 9½", ftd., pickle (like corn bowl)	20.00
Bowl, 10", flared, 4 ftd.	30.00
Bowl, 11", 2 pt., 2 hdld., "figure 8" relish	27.50
Bowl, 11", 2 hdld	30.00
Bowl, 12", 3 pt., celery & relish, tab hdld.	30.00
Bowl, 12", 5 pt., celery & relish	32.50
Bowl, 12", flared, 4 ftd.	32.50
Bowl, 12", oval, 4 ftd., "ears" handles	40.00
Bowl, finger, w/liner #3124	22.00
Bowl, seafood (fruit cocktail w/liner)	25.00
Candlestick, 5"	17.50
Candlestick, 6", 2-lite, "fleur de lis"	27.50
Candlestick, 6", 3-lite	40.00
Candy box, w/cover, rnd.	60.00
Cigarette holder, urn shape	37.50
Cocktail icer, 2 pt.	40.00
Cocktail shaker, w/stopper	75.00
Cocktail shaker, 80 oz., hdld. ball w/chrome top	85.00
Cologne, 2 oz., hdld. ball w/stopper	65.00
Comport, 5½"	27.50
Comport, 5⅜", blown	35.00
Creamer, hdld. ball	17.50
Creamer, indiv.	11.50
Cup, ftd. sq.	18.00
Decanter, 29 oz. ftd., sherry, w/stopper	145.00
Hurricane lamp, candlestick base	135.00
Hurricane lamp, keyhole base, w/prisms	100.00
Ice bucket, w/chrome handle	55.00
Ivy ball, 5¼"	25.00
Mayonnaise, div. bowl, w/liner & 2 ladles	40.00
Mayonnaise, w/liner & ladle	35.00
Oil, 6 oz., loop hdld., w/stopper	50.00
Oil, 6 oz., hdld. ball, w/stopper	55.00
Pitcher, ball	110.00
Pitcher, Doulton	250.00
Plate, 6", 2 hdld.	15.00
Plate, 6½", bread/butter	7.50
Plate, 8", salad	12.50
Plate, 8", ftd., 2 hdld	17.50
Plate, 8", ftd., bonbon, tab hdld.	20.00
Plate, 8½", sq.	15.00
Plate, 10½", dinner	55.00
Plate, 13", 4 ftd., torte	30.00
Plate, 13½", 2 hdld., cake	27.50
Plate, 14", torte	35.00
Puff box, 3½", ball shape, w/lid	65.00
Salt & pepper, pr., flat	25.00

	Crystal
Saucer, sq. or rnd.	3.00
Set: 3 pc. Frappe (bowl, 2 plain inserts)	35.00
Stem, #3121, 1 oz., cordial	50.00
Stem, #3121, 1 oz., low ftd., brandy	32.00
Stem, #3121, 2½ oz., wine	22.50
Stem, #3121, 3 oz., cocktail	20.00
Stem, #3121, 4½ oz., claret	30.00
Stem, #3121, 4½ oz., oyster cocktail	15.00
Stem, #3121, 5 oz., parfait	22.00
Stem, #3121, 6 oz., low sherbet	13.50
Stem, #3121, 6 oz., tall sherbet	15.00
Stem, #3121, 10 oz., goblet	20.00
Stem, #3124, 3 oz., cocktail	15.00
Stem, #3124, 3 oz., wine	20.00
Stem, #3124, 4½ oz., claret	19.00
Stem, #3124, 7 oz., low sherbet	14.00
Stem, #3124, 7 oz., tall sherbet	15.00
Stem, #3124, 10 oz., goblet	18.00
Stem, #3126, 1 oz., cordial	50.00
Stem, #3126, 1 oz., low ft., brandy	30.00
Stem, #3126, 2½ oz., wine	23.00
Stem, #3126, 3 oz., cocktail	17.50
Stem, #3126, 4½ oz., claret	30.00
Stem, #3126, 4½ oz., low ft., oyster cocktail	12.50
Stem, #3126, 7 oz., low sherbet	14.00
Stem, #3126, 7 oz., tall sherbet	15.00
Stem, #3126, 9 oz., goblet	18.00
Stem, #3130, 1 oz., cordial	50.00
Stem, #3130, 2½ oz., wine	23.00
Stem, #3130, 3 oz., cocktail	17.50
Stem, #3130, 4½ oz., claret	30.00
Stem, #3130, 4½ oz., fruit/oyster cocktail	15.00
Stem, #3130, 7 oz., low sherbet	14.00
Stem, #3130, 7 oz., tall sherbet	15.00
Stem, #3130, 9 oz., goblet	21.00
Sugar, ftd., hdld. ball	17.50
Sugar, indiv.	11.50
Tray, 11", celery	22.50
Tumbler, #3121, 2½ oz., bar	20.00
Tumbler, #3121, 5 oz., ftd., juice	16.00
Tumbler, #3121, 10 oz., ftd., water	16.50
Tumbler, #3121, 12 oz., ftd., tea	22.00
Tumbler, #3124, 3 oz.	13.00
Tumbler, #3124, 5 oz., juice	12.50
Tumbler, #3124, 10 oz., water	15.00
Tumbler, #3124, 12 oz., tea	18.00
Tumbler, #3126, 2½ oz.	18.00
Tumbler, #3126, 5 oz., juice	14.00
Tumbler, #3126, 10 oz., water	15.00
Tumbler, #3126, 12 oz., tea	18.00
Tumbler, #3130, 5 oz., juice	16.00
Tumbler, #3130, 10 oz., water	15.00
Tumbler, #3130, 12 oz., tea	20.00
Tumbler, 12 oz., "roly-poly"	20.00
Vase, 5", globe	30.00
Vase, 6", ftd.	35.00
Vase, 8", ftd.	45.00
Vase, 9", keyhole ft.	55.00
Vase, 10", bud	35.00
Vase, 11", flower	45.00
Vase, 11", pedestal ft.	50.00
Vase, 12", keyhole ft.	65.00
Vase, 13", flower	75.00

PROVINCIAL, Blank #1506, A.H. Heisey & Co.

Colors: crystal, "Limelight" green

	Crystal	Limelight Green
Ashtray, 3" square	12.50	
Bonbon dish, 7", 2 hdld., upturned sides	11.00	37.50
Bowl, 5 quart, punch	75.00	
Bowl, individual, nut/jelly	21.00	27.50
Bowl, 4½", nappy	11.00	30.00
Bowl, 5", 2 hdld., nut/jelly	12.00	
Bowl, 5½", nappy	12.00	40.00
Bowl, 5½", round, hdld., nappy	15.00	
Bowl, 5½", tri-corner, hdld., nappy	20.00	55.00
Bowl, 10", 4 part, relish	40.00	195.00
Bowl, 12", floral	40.00	
Bowl, 13", gardenia	35.00	
Box, 5½", footed, candy, w/cover	95.00	350.00
Butter dish, w/cover	85.00	
Candle, 1-lite, block	20.00	
Candle, 3-lite	45.00	
Candle, 3-lite, #4233, 5", vase	60.00	
Cigarette lighter	25.00	
Coaster, 4"	5.00	
Creamer, footed	15.00	95.00
Creamer & sugar, w/tray, individual	40.00	
Cup, punch	10.00	
Mayonnaise, 7" (plate, ladle, bowl)	35.00	150.00
Mustard	20.00	
Oil bottle, 4 oz., #1 stopper	45.00	
Plate, 5", footed, cheese	10.00	
Plate, 7", 2 hdld., snack	12.00	
Plate, 7", bread	10.00	
Plate, 8", luncheon	15.00	50.00
Plate, 14", torte	27.50	
Plate, 18", buffet	37.50	165.00
Salt & pepper, pr.	25.00	
Stem, 3½ oz., oyster cocktail	9.00	
Stem, 3½ oz., wine	19.00	
Stem, 5 oz., sherbet/champagne	10.00	
Stem, 10 oz.	20.00	
Sugar, footed	15.00	90.00
Tray, 13", oval, celery	22.00	
Tumbler, 5 oz., footed, juice	10.00	45.00
Tumbler, 8 oz.	12.00	
Tumbler, 9 oz., footed	14.00	65.00
Tumbler, 12 oz., footed, iced tea	15.00	75.00
Tumbler, 13", flat, ice tea	17.00	
Vase, 3½", violet	15.00	85.00
Vase, 4", pansy	15.00	
Vase, 6", sweet pea	25.00	

Colors: crystal, "Sahara," "Zircon," rare

	Crystal		Crystal
Ashtray, round	4.25	Mustard, w/cover	40.00
Ashtray, square	3.25	Oil bottle, 3 oz., w/#103 stopper	50.00
Ashtray, 4", round	11.00	Pitcher, ½ gallon	125.00
Ashtray, 6", square	16.00	Pitcher, ½ gallon, ice lip	145.00
Ashtrays, bridge set (heart, diamond, spade, club)	30.00	Plate, oval, hors d'oeuvres	25.00
Basket, bonbon	11.00	Plate, 2 hdld., ice tub liner	15.00
Bottle, rock & rye, w/#104 stopper	90.00	Plate, 6", round	5.00
Bottle, 4 oz., cologne	85.00	Plate, 6", scalloped	5.00
Bottle, 5 oz., bitters, w/tube	65.00	Plate, 6", square	5.00
Bowl, indiv., nut	7.25	Plate, 7", square	6.00
Bowl, oval, indiv., jelly	12.50	Plate, 8", round	7.00
Bowl, indiv., nut, 2 part	10.50	Plate, 8", square	7.00
Bowl, 4½", nappy, bell or cupped	7.00	Plate, 13½", sandwich	25.00
Bowl, 4½", nappy, scalloped	7.00	Plate, 13½", ftd., torte	25.00
Bowl, 5", lemon, w/cover	20.00	Plate, 14", salver	60.00
Bowl, 5", nappy, straight	6.50	Salt & pepper, pr.	30.00
Bowl, 5", nappy, square	6.50	Salt dip, indiv.	13.00
Bowl, 6", 2 hdld., divided, jelly	12.75	Saucer	3.00
Bowl, 6", 2 hdld., jelly	12.75	Soda, 12 oz., cupped or flared	25.00
Bowl, 7", 2 part, oval, relish	12.75	Stem, cocktail, pressed	20.00
Bowl, 8", centerpiece	22.00	Stem, claret, pressed	25.00
Bowl, 8", nappy, square	27.50	Stem, oyster cocktail, pressed	14.00
Bowl, 9", nappy, square	27.50	Stem, sherbet, pressed	10.00
Bowl, 9", salad	30.00	Stem, saucer champagne, pressed	11.00
Bowl, 10", flared, fruit	35.00	Stem, wine, pressed	30.00
Bowl, 10", floral	35.00	Stem, 1 oz., cordial, blown	125.00
Bowl, 11", centerpiece	35.00	Stem, 2 oz., sherry, blown	60.00
Bowl, 11", punch	90.00	Stem, 2½ oz., wine, blown	50.00
Bowl, 11½", floral	35.00	Stem, 3½ oz., cocktail, blown	27.50
Bowl, 12", oval, floral	40.00	Stem, 4 oz., claret, blown	30.00
Bowl, 12", flared, fruit	40.00	Stem, 4 oz., oyster cocktail, blown	16.00
Bowl, 13", cone, floral	40.00	Stem, 5 oz., saucer champagne, blown	17.50
Bowl, 14", oblong, floral	50.00	Stem, 5 oz., sherbet, blown	12.50
Bowl, 14", oblong, swan hdld., floral	110.00	Stem, 8 oz., luncheon, low stem	13.00
Box, 8", floral	25.00	Stem, 8 oz., tall stem	18.00
Candle block, 3"	18.00	Sugar	15.00
Candle vase, 6"	18.00	Sugar, indiv.	10.00
Candlestick, 2", 1-lite	14.00	Tray, for indiv. sugar & creamer	10.00
Candlestick, 2-lite, bobeche & "A" prisms	50.00	Tray, 10½", oblong	25.00
Candlestick, 7", w/bobeche & "A" prisms	95.00	Tray, 11", 3 part, relish	30.00
Cheese, 6", 2 hdld.	7.25	Tray, 12", celery & olive, divided	25.00
Cigarette box, w/cover, oval	25.00	Tray, 12", celery	22.50
Cigarette box, w/cover, 6"	10.00	Tumbler, 2½ oz., bar, pressed	20.00
Cigarette holder, oval, w/2 comp. ashtrays	35.00	Tumbler, 5 oz., juice, blown	18.00
Cigarette holder, round	6.00	Tumbler, 5 oz., soda, ftd., pressed	15.00
Cigarette holder, square	6.00	Tumbler, 8 oz., (#1469¾), pressed	16.00
Cigarette holder, w/cover	15.00	Tumbler, 8 oz., old fashioned, pressed	18.00
Coaster or cocktail rest	3.00	Tumbler, 8 oz., soda, blown	17.00
Cocktail shaker, 1 qt., w/#1 strainer & #86 stopper	165.00	Tumbler, 10 oz., (#1469¾), pressed	14.00
Comport, 6", low ft., flared	16.00	Tumbler, 12 oz., ftd., soda, pressed	20.00
Comport, 6", low ft., w/cover	30.00	Tumbler, 12 oz., soda, (#1469¾) pressed	25.00
Creamer	15.00	Tumbler, 13 oz., iced tea, blown	18.00
Creamer, indiv.	10.00	Vase, #1 indiv., cuspidor shape	25.00
Cup	10.00	Vase, #2 indiv., cupped top	22.00
Cup, beverage	12.00	Vase, #3 indiv., flared rim	27.50
Cup, punch	10.00	Vase, #4 indiv., fan out top	25.00
Decanter, 1 pint, w/#95 stopper	95.00	Vase, #5 indiv., scalloped top	25.00
Ice tub, 2 hdld.	45.00	Vase, 3½"	22.00
Marmalade, w/cover	40.00	Vase, 6" (also flared)	17.50
Mayonnaise	35.00	Vase, 8"	22.00
		Vase, 8", triangular (#1469¾)	22.00

ROSALIE, or #731, Cambridge Glass Company, Late 1920's – 1930's

Colors: blue, green, Heatherbloom, pink, red, amber, bluebell, crystal, topaz

Rosalie is another of the patterns which makes you wonder what will turn up next. Look at the variety of colors that this pattern has! Pink, green and maybe amber sets could be collected, but finding enough of the other colors for a set would be an enormous task.

I would like to point out the center handled tray in green in the bottom photo. Not only does it have Rosalie etching on the inside, but it has Apple-Blossom around the edge! It is truly an unusual piece of Cambridge.

	Blue Pink Green	Amber		Blue Pink Green	Amber
Bottle, French dressing	95.00	65.00	Gravy, double, w/platter	125.00	65.00
Bowl, bouillon, 2 hdld.	20.00	15.00	Ice bucket or pail	65.00	45.00
Bowl, cream soup	20.00	15.00	Icer, w/liner	40.00	
Bowl, finger, w/liner	30.00	20.00	Ice tub	55.00	35.00
Bowl, finger, ftd., w/liner	32.50	25.00	Marmalade	75.00	60.00
Bowl, 3½", cranberry	20.00	15.00	Mayonnaise, ftd., w/liner	45.00	25.00
Bowl, 3⅝", w/cover, 3 pt.	40.00	25.00	Nut, 2½", ftd.	45.00	30.00
Bowl, 5½", fruit	15.00	10.00	Pitcher, 62 oz., #955	195.00	135.00
Bowl, 5½", 2 hdld., bonbon	20.00	12.00	Plate, 6¾", bread/butter	7.00	5.00
Bowl, 6¼", 2 hdld., bonbon	22.50	15.00	Plate, 7", 2 hdld.	15.00	7.00
Bowl, 7", basket, 2 hdld.	250.00	150.00	Plate, 7½", salad	10.00	6.00
Bowl, 8½", soup	30.00	20.00	Plate, 8⅜"	15.00	10.00
Bowl, 8½", 2 hdld.	25.00	15.00	Plate, 9½", dinner	55.00	30.00
Bowl, 8½", w/cover, 3 pt.	45.00	30.00	Plate, 11", 2 hdld.	30.00	20.00
Bowl, 10"	37.50	25.00	Platter, 12"	65.00	35.00
Bowl, 10", 2 hdld.	39.00	27.00	Platter, 15"	85.00	45.00
Bowl, 11"	40.00	25.00	Relish, 9", 2 pt.	25.00	15.00
Bowl, 11", basket, 2 hdld.	45.00	35.00	Relish, 11", 2 pt.	35.00	20.00
Bowl, 11½"	65.00	45.00	Salt dip, 1½", ftd.	25.00	10.00
Bowl, 12", decagon	95.00	75.00	Saucer	3.00	2.00
Bowl, 13", console	40.00		Stem, 1 oz., cordial, #3077	75.00	40.00
Bowl, 14", decagon	190.00	145.00	Stem, 3½ oz., cocktail, #3077	20.00	15.00
Bowl, 15", oval console	50.00	35.00	Stem, 6 oz., low sherbet, #3077	15.00	12.00
Bowl, 15", oval, flanged	60.00	40.00	Stem, 6 oz., high sherbet, #3077	18.00	14.00
Bowl, 15½", oval	65.00	40.00	Stem, 9 oz., water goblet, #3077	25.00	20.00
Candlestick, 4", 2 styles	30.00	20.00	Stem, 10 oz., goblet, #801	30.00	20.00
Candlestick, 5", keyhole	35.00	25.00	Sugar, ftd.	16.00	13.00
Candlestick, 6", 3-lite keyhole	50.00	30.00	Sugar shaker	195.00	145.00
Candy and cover, 6"	85.00	50.00	Tray for sugar shaker/creamer	30.00	20.00
Celery, 11"	35.00	20.00	Tray, ctr. hdld., for sugar/creamer	20.00	14.00
Cheese & cracker, 11" plate	50.00	35.00	Tray, 11", ctr. hdld.	30.00	20.00
Comport, 5½", 2 hdld.	30.00	15.00	Tumbler, 2½ oz., ftd., #3077	25.00	15.00
Comport, 5¾"	30.00	15.00	Tumbler, 5 oz., ftd., #3077	22.00	18.00
Comport, 6", ftd., almond	40.00	25.00	Tumbler, 8 oz., ftd. #3077	25.00	16.00
Comport, 6½", low ft.	40.00	25.00	Tumbler, 10 oz., ftd., #3077	27.00	20.00
Comport, 6½", high ft.	40.00	25.00	Tumbler, 12 oz., ftd., #3077	30.00	22.00
Comport, 6¾"	45.00	30.00	Vase, 5½", ftd.	35.00	22.00
Creamer, ftd.	17.00	12.00	Vase, 6"	45.00	30.00
Creamer, ftd., tall	22.50	15.00	Vase, 6½", ftd.	65.00	35.00
Cup	20.00	15.00			

ROSE, Etching #1515, on WAVERLY Blank #11519, A.H. Heisey & Co., 1949 – 1957

Colors: crystal

Heisey's Rose pattern is a close second to Orchid in collector demand. I can finally show you a dinner plate. It arrived late and was photographed just in time to include it in this edition.

	Crystal
Ashtray, 3"	37.50
Bell, dinner, #5072	125.00
Bottle, 8 oz., French dressing, blown, #5031	195.00
Bowl, finger, #3309	60.00
Bowl, 5½", ftd., mint	32.50
Bowl, 5¾", ftd., mint, CABOCHON	67.50
Bowl, 6", ftd., mint, QUEEN ANN	40.00
Bowl, 6", jelly, 2 hdld., ftd., QUEEN ANN	42.50
Bowl, 6", oval, lemon, w/cover, WAVERLY	250.00
Bowl, 6½", 2 pt., oval, dressing, WAVERLY	57.50
Bowl, 6½", ftd., honey/cheese, WAVERLY	55.00
Bowl, 6½", ftd., jelly, WAVERLY	45.00
Bowl, 6½", lemon, w/cover, WAVERLY	157.50
Bowl, 7", ftd., honey, WAVERLY	40.00
Bowl, 7", ftd., jelly, WAVERLY	40.00
Bowl, 7", lily, QUEEN ANN	45.00
Bowl, 7", relish, 3 pt., round, WAVERLY	67.50
Bowl, 7", salad, WAVERLY	52.50
Bowl, 7", salad dressings, QUEEN ANN	50.00
Bowl, 9", ftd., fruit or salad, WAVERLY	120.00
Bowl, 9", salad, WAVERLY	85.00
Bowl, 9", 4 pt., rnd., relish, WAVERLY	90.00
Bowl, 9½", crimped, floral, WAVERLY	65.00
Bowl, 10", gardenia, WAVERLY	65.00
Bowl, 10", crimped, floral, WAVERLY	82.50
Bowl, 11", 3 pt., relish, WAVERLY	77.50
Bowl, 11", 3 ftd., floral, WAVERLY	125.00
Bowl, 11", floral, WAVERLY	67.50
Bowl, 11", oval, 4 ftd., WAVERLY	125.00
Bowl, 12", crimped, floral, WAVERLY	75.00
Bowl, 13", crimped, floral, WAVERLY	80.00
Bowl, 13", floral, WAVERLY	80.00
Bowl, 13", gardenia, WAVERLY	75.00
Butter, w/cover, 6", WAVERLY	165.00
Butter, w/cover, ¼ lb., CABOCHON	250.00
Candlestick, 1-lite, #112	40.00
Candlestick, 2-lite, FLAME	65.00
Candlestick, 3-lite, #142, CASCADE	77.50
Candlestick, 3-lite, WAVERLY	85.00
Candlestick, 5", 2-lite, #134, TRIDENT	65.00
Candlestick, 6", epergnette, deep, WAVERLY	325.00
Candy, w/cover, 5", ftd., WAVERLY	160.00
Candy, w/cover, 6", low, bowknot cover	165.00
Candy, w/cover, 6¼", #1951, CABOCHON	125.00
Celery tray, 12", WAVERLY	50.00
Celery tray, 13", WAVERLY	60.00
Cheese compote, 4½", & cracker (11" plate) WAVERLY	125.00
Cheese compote, 5½", & cracker (12" plate) QUEEN ANNE	125.00
Chocolate, w/cover, 5", WAVERLY	125.00
Cigarette holder, #4035	85.00

	Crystal
Cocktail icer, w/liner, #3304, UNIVERSAL	100.00
Cocktail shaker, #4225, COBEL	125.00
Comport, 6½", low ft., WAVERLY	60.00
Comport, 7", oval, ftd., WAVERLY	125.00
Creamer, ftd., WAVERLY	27.50
Creamer, indiv., WAVERLY	25.00
Cup, WAVERLY	50.00
Decanter, 1 pt., #4036½, #101 stopper	195.00
Hurricane lamp, w/12" globe, #5080	300.00
Hurricane lamp, w/12" globe, PLANTATION	300.00
Ice bucket, dolp. ft., QUEEN ANN	250.00
Ice tub, 2 hdld., WAVERLY	250.00
Mayonnaise, 5½", 2 hdld., WAVERLY	55.00
Mayonnaise, 5½", div., 1 hdld., WAVERLY	55.00
Mayonnaise, 5½", ftd., WAVERLY	60.00
Oil, 3 oz., ftd., WAVERLY	165.00
Pitcher, 73 oz., #4164	500.00
Plate, 7", salad, WAVERLY	20.00
Plate, 7", mayonnaise, WAVERLY	20.00
Plate, 8", salad, WAVERLY	30.00
Plate, 10½", dinner	135.00
Plate, 10½", service, WAVERLY	75.00
Plate, 11", sandwich, WAVERLY	75.00
Plate, 11", demi-torte, WAVERLY	65.00
Plate, 12", ftd., salver, WAVERLY	200.00
Plate, 15", ftd., cake, WAVERLY	275.00
Plate, 14", torte, WAVERLY	90.00
Plate, 14", sandwich, WAVERLY	90.00
Plate, 14", ctr. hdld., sandwich, WAVERLY	185.00
Salt & pepper, ftd., pr., WAVERLY	65.00
Saucer, WAVERLY	10.00
Stem, #5072, 1 oz., cordial	130.00
Stem, #5072, 3 oz., wine	100.00
Stem, #5072, 3½ oz., oyster cocktail, ftd.	27.50
Stem, #5072, 4 oz., claret	90.00
Stem, #5072, 4 oz., cocktail	40.00
Stem, #5072, 6 oz., sherbet	27.50
Stem, #5072, 6 oz., saucer champagne	30.00
Stem, #5072, 9 oz., water	42.50
Sugar, indiv., WAVERLY	25.00
Sugar, ftd., WAVERLY	25.00
Tumbler, #5072, 5 oz., ftd., juice	45.00
Tumbler, #5072, 12 oz., ftd., tea	45.00
Tray, indiv. creamer/sugar, QUEEN ANN	50.00
Vase, 3½", ftd., violet, WAVERLY	85.00
Vase, 4", ftd., violet, WAVERLY	95.00
Vase, 7", ftd., fan, WAVERLY	95.00
Vase, 8", #4198	100.00
Vase, 8", sq., ftd., urn	100.00
Vase, 10", #4198	175.00
Vase, 10", sq., ftd, urn	100.00
Vase, 12", sq., ftd., urn	175.00

Colors: crystal; some crystal with gold

There is over a week of sixteen hour days in the next eight pages, not including photography time. There are several individual shots to point out including stacking ashtrays, pressed Rose Point stems with etched Rose Point tops, and the punch bowl set. Throughout the photographs are many unusual and rare pieces, but in order to **show** them, I have no space to mention them except to say enjoy! For beginners #3500 line has what my wife calls a pie crust edge (creamer, sugar and plate on top 137).

	Crystal		Crystal
Ashtray, stack set on metal pole, #1715	195.00	Bowl, 10", 2 hdld. (#3500/28)	75.00
Ashtray, 2½", sq. #721	32.50	Bowl, 10", 4 tab ftd., flared (#3900/54)	57.50
Ashtray, 3¼" (#3500/124)	32.50	Bowl, 10½", crimp edge, #1351	70.00
Ashtray, 3¼", sq. (#3500/129)	55.00	Bowl, 10½", flared (#3400/168)	62.50
Ashtray, 3½" (#3500/125)	35.00	Bowl, 10½", 3 part, #222	160.00
Ashtray, 4" (#3500/126)	40.00	Bowl, 10½", 3 part (#1401/122)	200.00
Ashtray, 4", oval (#3500/130)	75.00	Bowl, 11", ftd. (#3500/16)	85.00
Ashtray, 4¼" (#3500/127)	45.00	Bowl, 11", ftd., fancy edge (#3500/19)	110.00
Ashtray, 4½" (#3500/128)	50.00	Bowl, 11", 4 ftd., oval (#3500/109)	250.00
Ashtray, 4½", oval (#3500/131)	60.00	Bowl, 11", 4 ftd., shallow, fancy edge (#3400/48)	65.00
Basket, 3", favor (#3500/79)	225.00	Bowl, 11", fruit (#3400/1188)	75.00
Basket, 5", 1 hdld. (#3500/51)	175.00	Bowl, 11", low foot (#3400/3)	110.00
Basket, 6", 1 hdld. (#3500/52)	195.00	Bowl, 11", tab hdld. (#3900/34)	65.00
Basket, 6", 2 hdld. (#3400/1182)	35.00	Bowl, 11½", ftd., w/tab hdl. (#3900/28)	67.50
Basket, 6", sq., ftd., 2 hdld (#3500/55)	35.00	Bowl, 12", 4 ftd., oval (#3400/1240)	75.00
Basket, 7", 1 hdld., #119	365.00	Bowl, 12", 4 ftd., oval, w/"ears" hdl. (#3900/65)	75.00
Basket, 7", wide (#3500/56)	45.00	Bowl, 12", 4 ftd., fancy rim oblong (#3400/160)	75.00
Basket, sugar, w/handle and tongs (#3500/13)	225.00	Bowl, 12", 4 ftd., flared (#3400/4)	65.00
Bell, dinner, #3121	125.00	Bowl, 12", 4 tab ftd., flared (#3900/62)	65.00
Bowl, 3", 4 ftd., nut (#3400/71)	65.00	Bowl, 12", ftd., (#3500/17)	90.00
Bowl, 3½", bonbon, cupped, deep (#3400/204)	70.00	Bowl, 12", ftd., oblong (#3500/118)	135.00
Bowl, 3½", cranberry (#3400/70)	75.00	Bowl, 12", ftd., oval w/hdl. (#3500/21)	135.00
Bowl, 5", hdld. (#3500/49)	35.00	Bowl, 12½", flared, rolled edge (#3400/2)	125.00
Bowl, 5" fruit (#3500/10)	40.00	Bowl, 12½", 4 ftd., #993	75.00
Bowl, 5" fruit, blown #1534	65.00	Bowl, 13", #1398	90.00
Bowl, 5¼" fruit (#3400/56)	40.00	Bowl, 13", 4 ftd., narrow, crimped (#3400/47)	110.00
Bowl, 5¼", 2 hdld., bonbon (#3400/1180)	30.00	Bowl, 13", flared (#3400/1)	65.00
Bowl, 5½", nappy (#3400/56)	42.50	Bowl, 14", 4 ftd., crimp edge, oblong, #1247	110.00
Bowl, 5½", 2 hdld., bonbon (#3400/1179)	30.00	Bowl, cream soup, w/liner (#3400)	135.00
Bowl, 6", bonbon, crimped (#3400/203)	80.00	Bowl, cream soup, w/liner (#3500/2)	125.00
Bowl, 6", bonbon, cupped, shallow (#3400/205)	75.00	Bowl, finger, w/liner, #3106	75.00
Bowl, 6", cereal (#3400/53)	55.00	Bowl, finger, w/liner, #3121	75.00
Bowl, 6", cereal (#3400/10)	55.00	Butter, w/cover, round, #506	175.00
Bowl, 6", cereal (#3500/11)	52.50	Butter, w/cover, 5" (#3400/52)	165.00
Bowl, 6", hdld. (#3500/50)	40.00	Butter dish, ¼ lb. (#3900/52)	275.00
Bowl, 6", 2 hdld. (#1402/89)	35.00	Candelabrum, 2-lite w/bobeches & prisms, #1268	110.00
Bowl, 6", 2 hdld., ftd., bonbon (#3500/54)	35.00	Candelabrum, 2-lite (#3500/94)	75.00
Bowl, 6", 4 ftd., fancy rim (#3400/136)	125.00	Candelabrum, 3-lite, #1338	55.00
Bowl, 6½" bonbon, crimped (#3400/202)	80.00	Candelabrum, 5½", 3-lite w/#19 bobeche & #1 prisms, #1545	85.00
Bowl, 7", bonbon, crimped, shallow (#3400/201)	75.00	Candelabrum, 6½", 2-lite, w/bobeches & prisms, (Martha #496)	150.00
Bowl, 7", tab hdld., ftd., bonbon (#3900/130)	35.00	Candle, torchere, cup ft. (#3500/90)	165.00
Bowl, 8", ram's head, squared (#3500/27)	250.00	Candle, torchere, flat ft. (#3500/88)	150.00
Bowl, 8½", rimmed soup, #361	225.00	Candlestick, sq. base & lites (#1700/501)	150.00
Bowl, 8½", 3 part, #221	135.00	Candlestick, 2½" (#3500/108)	30.00
Bowl, 9", 4 ftd., (#3400/135)	165.00	Candlestick, 3½", #628	35.00
Bowl, 9", ram's head (#3500/25)	300.00	Candlestick, 4", #627	45.00
Bowl, 9½", pickle (like corn), #477	45.00		
Bowl, 9½", ftd., w/hdl. (#3500/115)	110.00		
Bowl, 9½", 2 hdld. (#3400/34)	65.00		
Bowl, 2 hdld. (#3400/1185)	70.00		

	Crystal		Crystal
Candlestick, 4", ram's head (#3500/74)	85.00	Comport, 7", keyhole (#3400/20)	125.00
Candlestick, 5" (#3900/68)	40.00	Comport, 7", keyhole, low (#3400/28)	75.00
Candlestick, 5", 1-lite keyhole (#3400/646)	30.00	Creamer (#3400/68)	20.00
Candlestick, 5", inverts to comport (#3900/67)	50.00	Creamer (#3500/14)	20.00
Candlestick, 5½", 2-lite (Martha #495)	45.00	Creamer, flat #137	100.00
Candlestick, 6" (#3500/31)	75.00	Creamer, flat, #944	110.00
Candlestick, 6", 2-lite keyhole (#3400/649)	35.00	Creamer, ftd., (#3400/16)	60.00
Candlestick, 6", 2-lite (#3900/72)	40.00	Creamer, ftd., (#3900/41)	20.00
Candlestick, 6", 3-lite (#3900/74)	40.00	Creamer, indiv. (#3500/15) pie crust edge	25.00
Candlestick, 6", 3-lite keyhole (#3400/638)	42.50	Creamer, indiv. (#3900/40) scalloped edge	20.00
Candlestick, 6", 3-tiered lite, #1338	55.00	Cup, 3 styles (#3400/54, #3500/1, #3900/17)	30.00
Candlestick, 6½", Calla Lily, #499	175.00	Cup, 5 oz., punch, #488	35.00
Candlestick, 7", #3121	60.00	Cup, after dinner (#3400/69)	210.00
Candlestick, 7½", w/prism (Martha #497)	125.00	Decanter, 12 oz., ball, w/stopper (#3400/119)	195.00
Candy box,w/cover, 5", apple shape, #316	750.00	Decanter, 14 oz., ftd. #1320	325.00
Candy box,w/cover, 5⅜", #1066 stem	130.00	Decanter, 26 oz., sq., #1380	
Candy box,w/cover, 5⅜" (#3121/3)	135.00	Decatner, 28 oz., tall, #1372	
Candy box,w/cover, 5⅜" (#3121/4)	125.00	Decanter, 28 oz., w/stopper, #1321	250.00
Candy box,w/cover, blown, 5⅜" (#3500/103)	135.00	Decanter, 32 oz., ball, w/stopper (#3400/92)	325.00
Candy box,w/cover, 6", ram's head (3500/78)	200.00	Dressing bottle, flat, #1263	250.00
Candy box,w/rose finial, 6", 3 ftd., #300	235.00	Dressing bottle, ftd., #1261	275.00
Candy box,w/cover, 7" (#3400/9)	125.00	Epergne (candle w/vases) (#3900/75)	150.00
Candy box,w/cover, 7", round #103	135.00	Grapefruit, w/liner, #187	110.00
Candy box,w/cover, 8", 3 pt. (#3500/57)	70.00	Hat, 5", #1704	300.00
Candy box,w/cover, rnd. (#3900/165)	95.00	Hat, 6", #1703	350.00
Celery, 12" (#3400/652)	45.00	Hat, 8", #1702	400.00
Celery, 12" (#3500/652)	45.00	Hat, 9", #1701	450.00
Celery, 12", 5 pt. (#3400/67)	55.00	Honey dish, w/cover (#3500/139)	235.00
Celery, 14", 4 pt., 2 hdld. (#3500/97)	135.00	Hot plate or trivet (shown: bottom 139)	65.00
Celery & relish, 9", 3 pt. (#3900/125)	45.00	Hurricane lamp, w/prisms, #1613	250.00
Celery & relish, 12", 3 pt. (#3900/126)	57.50	Hurricane lamp, candlestick base, #1617	175.00
Celery & relish, 12", 5 pt. (#3900/120)	65.00	Hurricane lamp, keyhole base, w/prisms,	
Cheese (5" comport) & cracker (13" plate)		#1603	195.00
(#3900/135)	100.00	Hurricane lamp, 8", etched chimney, #1601	195.00
Cheese (5½" comport) & cracker (11½" plate)		Hurricane lamp, 10", etched chimney & base,	
(#3400/6)	100.00	#1604	225.00
Cheese (6" comport) & cracker (12" plate)		Ice bucket (#1402/52)	185.00
(#3500/162)	110.00	Ice bucket, w/chrome hand. (#3900/671)	125.00
Cheese dish, w/cover, 5", #980	375.00	Ice pail, #1705	175.00
Cigarette box,w/cover, #615	110.00	Ice pail (#3400/851)	100.00
Cigarette box,w/cover, #747	125.00	Ice tub, #671	135.00
Cigarette holder, oval, w/ashtray ft., #1066	135.00	Icer, cocktail, #968	75.00
Cigarette holder, round, w/ashtray ft., #1337	125.00	Marmalade, 8 oz., #147	125.00
Coaster #1628	42.50	Marmalade, w/cover, 7 ox., ftd., #157	150.00
Cocktail icer, 2 pc. (#3600)	70.00	Mayonnaise (sherbet type w/ladle) #19	50.00
Cocktail shaker, metal top (#3400/157)	125.00	Mayonnaise, div., w/liner & 2 ladles	
Cocktail shaker, metal top (#3400/175)	110.00	(#3900/111)	75.00
Cocktail shaker, 12 oz., metal top, #97	275.00	Mayonnaise, 3 pc. (#3400/11)	65.00
Cocktail shaker, 32 oz., w/glass stopper, #101	135.00	Mayonnaise, 3 pc. (#3900/129)	65.00
Cocktail shaker, 46 oz., metal top, #98	125.00	Mayonnaise, w/liner & ladle (#3500/59)	70.00
Cocktail shaker, 48 oz., glass stopper, #102	130.00	Mustard, 3 oz., #151	125.00
Comport, 5" (#3900/135)	35.00	Oil, 2 oz., ball, w/stopper (#3400/96)	57.50
Comport, 5", 4 ftd., (#3400/74)	60.00	Oil, 6 oz., ball, w/stopper (#3400/99)	95.00
Comport, 5½", scalloped edge (#3900/136)	50.00	Oil, 6 oz., hdld (#3400/193)	75.00
Comport, 5⅜", blown (#3500/101)	60.00	Oil, 6 oz., hdld., #293	150.00
Comport, 5⅜", blown, #3121	55.00	Oil, 6 oz., loop hdld., w/stopper (#3900/100)	110.00
Comport, 5⅜", blown, #3121 stem	60.00	Oil, 6 oz., w/stopper, ftd., hdld. (#3400/161)	175.00
Comport, 5⅜", blown, #1066 stem	65.00	Pickle, 9" (#3400/59)	50.00
Comport, 6" (#3500/36)	100.00	Pickle or relish, 7", (#3900/123)	35.00
Comport, 6" (#3500/111)	100.00	Pitcher, 20 oz., (#3900/117)	210.00
Comport, 6", 4 ftd., (#3400/13)	35.00	Pitcher, 20 oz. w/ice lip, #70	210.00
Comport, 7", 2 hdld. (#3500/37)	95.00	Pitcher, 32 oz. (#3900/118)	250.00

	Crystal
Pitcher, 32 oz. martini (slender) w/metal insert, (#3900/114)	400.00
Pitcher, 60 oz., martini, #1408	1,650.00
Pitcher, 76 oz. (#3900/115)	165.00
Pitcher, 76 oz., ice lip (#3400/100)	165.00
Pitcher, 76 oz., ice lip (#3400/152)	250.00
Pitcher, 80 oz., ball (#3400/38)	175.00
Pitcher, 80 ox., ball (#3900/116)	165.00
Pitcher, 80 oz., Doulton (#3400/141)	255.00
Pitcher, nite set, 2 pc., w/tumbler insert top, #103	500.00
Plate, 6", bread/butter (#3400/60)	12.50
Plate, 6", bread/butter (#3500/3)	12.50
Plate, 6", 2 hdld. (#3400/1181)	17.50
Plate, 6⅛" canape	215.00
Plate, 6½", bread/butter (#3900/20)	12.50
Plate, 7½" (#3500/4)	15.00
Plate, 7½", salad (#3400/176)	15.00
Plate, 8", salad (#3900/22)	17.50
Plate, 8", 2 hdld., ftd., (#3500/161)	60.00
Plate, 8", tab hdld., ftd., bonbon (#3900/131)	35.00
Plate, 8½", breakfast (#3400/62)	18.00
Plate, 8½", salad (#3500/5)	18.00
Plate, 9½" crescent salad	195.00
Plate, 9½", luncheon (#3400/63)	35.00
Plate, 10½", dinner (#3400/64)	115.00
Plate, 10½", dinner (#3900/24)	115.00
Plate, 10½" dinner (#3900/24)	115.00
Plate, 11", 2 hdld. (#3400/35)	50.00
Plate, 12", 4 ftd., (#3900/26)	65.00
Plate, 12", 4 ftd., service (#3900/26)	65.00
Plate, 12", ftd. (#3500/39)	85.00
Plate, 12½", 2 hdld. (#3400/1186)	65.00
Plate, 13", rolled edge, ftd. (#3900/33)	70.00
Plate, 13", 4 ftd., torte (#3500/110)	110.00
Plate, 13", ftd., cake (Martha #170)	225.00
Plate, 13", torte (#3500/38)	150.00
Plate, 13½", #242	135.00
Plate, 13½", rolled edge, #1397	70.00
Plate, 13½", tab hdld., cake (#3900/35)	70.00
Plate, 14", rolled edge (#3900/166)	55.00
Plate, 14", service (#3900/167)	70.00
Plate, 14", torte (#3400/65)	110.00
Plate, 18", punch bowl liner (Martha #129)	350.00
Punch bowl, 15", Martha #478	3,000.00
Punch set, 15-pc. (Martha)	3,750.00
Relish, 5½", 2 pt. (#3500/68)	22.50
Relish, 5½", 2 pt., hdld. (#3500/60)	27.50
Relish, 6", 2 pt. (#3400/90)	32.50
Relish, 6", 2 pt., 1 hdl. (#3400/1093)	75.00
Relish, 6½", 3 pt. (#3500/69)	32.50
Relish, 6½", 3 pt., hdld. (#3500/61)	35.00
Relish, 7", 2 pt. (#3900/124)	37.50
Relish, 7½", 3 pt., center hdld. (#3500/71)	110.00
Relish, 7½", 4 pt. (#3500/70)	35.00
Relish, 7½", 4 pt., 2 hdld. (#3500/62)	50.00
Relish, 8", 3 pt., 3 hdld. (#3400/91)	37.50
Relish, 10", 2 hdld. (#3500/85)	65.00
Relish, 10", 3 pt., 2 hdld. (#3500/86)	50.00
Relish, 10", 3 pt., 4 ftd., 2 hdld. (#3500/64)	50.00

	Crystal
Relish, 10", 4 pt. (#3500/65)	60.00
Relish, 10", 4 pt., 2 hdld. (#3500/87)	55.00
Relish, 11", 2 pt., 2 hdld. (#3400/89)	75.00
Relish, 11", 3 pt. (#3400/200)	55.00
Relish, 12", 5 pt. (#3400/67)	60.00
Relish, 12", 6 pc. (#3500/67)	185.00
Relish, 14", w/cover, 4 pt., 2 hdld. (#3500/142)	350.00
Relish, 15", 4 pt., hdld. (#3500/113)	165.00
Salt & pepper, egg shape, pr., #1468	80.00
Salt & pepper, individual, rnd., glass base, pr., #1470	80.00
Salt & pepper, individual, w/chrome tops, pr., #360	55.00
Salt & pepper, lg., rnd., glass base, pr., #1471	80.00
Salt & pepper, w/chrome tops, pr., #395	150.00
Salt & pepper, w/chrome tops, pr. (#3400/37)	135.00
Salt & pepper, w/chrome tops, pr., ftd. (#3400/77)	50.00
Salt & pepper w/chrome tops, pr., flat (#3900/1177)	40.00
Sandwich tray, 11", center handled (#3400/10)	125.00
Saucer, after dinner (#3400/69)	40.00
Saucer, 3 styles (#3400, #3500, #3900)	5.00
Stem, #3104, 3½ oz., cocktail	250.00
Stem, #3106, ¾ oz., brandy	85.00
Stem, #3106, 1 oz., cordial	85.00
Stem, #3106, 1 oz., pousse cafe	85.00
Stem, #3106, 2 oz., sherry	40.00
Stem, #3106, 2½ oz., wine	40.00
Stem, #3106, 3 oz., cocktail	30.00
Stem, #3106, 4½ oz., claret	45.00
Stem, #3106, 5 oz., oyster cocktail	30.00
Stem, #3106, 7 oz., high sherbet	30.00
Stem, #3106, 7 oz., low sherbet	25.00
Stem, #3106, 10 oz., water goblet	35.00
Stem, #3121, 1 oz., brandy	85.00
Stem, #3121, 1 oz., cordial	67.50
Stem, #3121, 3 oz., cocktail	32.50
Stem, #3121, 3½ oz., wine	55.00
Stem, #3121, 4½ oz., claret	75.00
Stem, #3121, 4½ oz., low oyster cocktail	37.50
Stem, #3121, 5 oz., low ft. parfait	75.00
Stem, #3121, 6 oz., low sherbet	18.00
Stem, #3121, 6 oz., tall sherbet	21.00
Stem, #3121, 10 oz., water	27.50
Stem, #3500, 1 oz., cordial	65.00
Stem, #3500, 2½ oz., wine	55.00
Stem, #3500, 3 oz., cocktail	35.00
Stem, #3500, 4½ oz., claret	75.00
Stem, #3500, 4½ oz., low oyster cocktail	37.50
Stem, #3500, 5 oz., low ft. parfait	75.00
Stem, #3500, 7 oz., low ft. sherbet	16.00
Stem, #3500, 7 oz., tall sherbet	21.00
Stem, #3500, 10 oz. water	27.50
Stem, #37801, 4 oz., cocktail	45.00
Stem, #7801, 4 oz. cocktail, plain stem	40.00
Stem, #7966, 1 oz., cordial, plain ft.	110.00
Stem, #7966, 2 oz., sherry, plain ft.	80.00
Sugar (#3400/68)	20.00
Sugar (#3500/14)	20.00

ROSE POINT, Cambridge Glass Company, 1936 – 1953 (continued)

	Crystal		Crystal
Sugar, flat, #137	100.00	Tumbler, #3500, 12 oz., low ft., ice tea	30.00
Sugar, flat, #944	110.00	Tumbler, #7801, 5 oz., ftd.	35.00
Sugar, ftd. (#3400/16)	60.00	Tumbler, #7801, 12 oz., ftd., ice tea	50.00
Sugar, ftd. (#3900/41)	20.00	Tumbler, #3900/117, 5 oz.	40.00
Sugar, indiv. (#3500/15) pie crust edge	22.50	Tumbler, #3400/115, 13 oz.	45.00
Sugar, indiv. (#3900/40) scalloped edge	21.50	Urn, 10", w/cover (#3500/41)	425.00
Syrup, w/drip stop top, #1670	325.00	Urn, 12", w/cover (#3500/42)	550.00
Tray, 6", 2 hdld., sq. (#3500/91)	150.00	Vase, 5", #1309	60.00
Tray, 12", 2 hdld., oval, service (#3500/99)	175.00	Vase, 5", globe (#3400/102)	65.00
Tray, 12", rnd. (#3500/67)	135.00	Vase, 5", ftd., #6004	45.00
Tray, 13", 2 hdld., rnd. (#3500/72)	135.00	Vase, 6", high ftd., flower, #6004	50.00
Tray, sugar/creamer, (#3900/37)	25.00	Vase, 6½", globe (#3400/103)	75.00
Tumbler, #498, 2 oz., straight side	95.00	Vase, 7", ivy, ftd., ball, #1066	175.00
Tumbler, #498, 5 oz., straight side	45.00	Vase, 8", #1430	125.00
Tumbler, #498, 8 oz., straight side	45.00	Vase, 8", flat, flared, #797	110.00
Tumbler, #498, 10 oz., straight side	45.00	Vase, 8", ftd. (#3500/44)	35.00
Tumbler, #498, 12 oz., straight side	50.00	Vase, 8", high ftd., flower, #6004	55.00
Tumbler, #3000, 5 oz., cone, ftd.	100.00	Vase, 9", ftd., keyhole, #1237	75.00
Tumbler, #3106, 3 oz., ftd.	25.00	Vase, 9½" ftd., keyholde, #1233	65.00
Tumbler, #3106, 5 oz., ftd.	25.00	Vase, 10", bud, #1528	75.00
Tumbler, #3106, 9 oz., ftd.	25.00	Vase, 10", cornucopia (#3900/575)	150.00
Tumbler, #3106, 12 oz., ftd.	30.00	Vase, 10", flat, #1242	110.00
Tumbler, #3106, 2½ oz., ftd.	60.00	Vase, 10", ftd., #1301	75.00
Tumbler, #3121, 5 oz., low ft., juice	30.00	Vase, 10", ftd., #6004	65.00
Tumbler, #3121, 10 oz., low ft., water	25.00	Vase, 10", ftd. (#3500/45)	135.00
Tumbler, #3121, 12 oz., low ft., ice tea	30.00	Vase, 10", slender, #274	50.00
Tumbler, #3400/1341, 1 oz., cordial	85.00	Vase, 11", ftd., flower, #278	95.00
Tumbler, #3400/92, 2½ oz.	95.00	Vase, 11", ped. ftd., flower, #1299	115.00
Tumbler, #3400/38, 5 oz.	45.00	Vase, 12", ftd., #6004	75.00
Tumbler, #3400/38, 12 oz.	50.00	Vase, 12", ftd., keyhole, #1234	75.00
Tumbler, #3900/115, 13 oz.	40.00	Vase, 12", ftd., keyhole, #1238	125.00
Tumbler, #3500, 2½ oz., ftd.	50.00	Vase, 13", ftd., flower, #279	175.00
Tumbler, #3500, 5 oz., low ft., juice	30.00	Vase, sweet pea, #629	225.00
Tumbler, #3500, 10 oz., low ft., water	25.00		

ROYAL, Plate Etching #273, Fostoria Glass Company

Colors: amber, black, blue, green

Royal is a Fostoria pattern that is often confused with Vesper since both designs are similar and both are found in the same colors on the #2350 blank. There are more collectors for Vesper at the present time because that pattern has been more publicized than Royal. That may be changing as new collectors are finding that the less expensive Royal is very comparable to Vesper in many other ways. Cost is a great determining factor; so we shall see what the future holds.

I will miss George's critique's of my work. In three years he is the only one that noticed the Seville cordial that was in the Royal picture by mistake.

Several pieces to watch for include the covered cheese, cologne bottles and the pitchers. Both the amber and green can be collected in sets; but only a few pieces can be found in blue and black. Fostoria's blue color found with Royal etching was called "Blue" as opposed to the "Azure" blue which is the lighter color found with June etching.

	*Amber, Green		*Amber, Green
Ashtray, #2350, 3½"	22.50	Ice bucket, #2378	45.00
Bowl, #2350, bouillon, flat	11.00	Mayonnaise, #2315	25.00
Bowl, #2350½, bouillon, ftd.	12.50	Pickle, 8", #2350	20.00
Bowl, #2350, cream soup, flat	13.00	Pitcher, #1236	350.00
Bowl, #2350½, cream soup, ftd.	15.00	Pitcher, #5000, 48 oz.	250.00
Bowl, #869, 4½", finger	16.00	Plate, 8½", deep soup/underplate	35.00
Bowl, #2350, 5½", fruit	11.00	Plate, #2350, 6", bread/butter	3.00
Bowl, #2350, 6½", cereal	14.00	Plate, #2350, 7½", salad	4.00
Bowl, #2267, 7", ftd.	30.00	Plate, #2350, 8½", luncheon	8.00
Bowl, #2350, 7¾", soup	18.00	Plate, #2321, 8¾, Maj Jongg (canape)	30.00
Bowl, #2350, 8", nappy	30.00	Plate, #2350, 9½", small dinner	13.00
Bowl, #2350, 9", nappy	32.00	Plate, #2350, 10½", dinner	27.50
Bowl, #2350, 9", oval, baker	35.00	Plate, #2350, 13", chop	27.50
Bowl, #2324, 10", ftd.	40.00	Plate, #2350, 15", chop	38.00
Bowl, #2350, 10", salad	35.00	Platter, #2350, 10½"	30.00
Bowl, #2350, 10½", oval, baker	45.00	Platter, #2350, 12"	40.00
Bowl, #2315, 10½", ftd.	45.00	Platter, #2350, 15½"	75.00
Bowl, #2329, 11", console	22.00	Salt and pepper, #5100, pr.	55.00
Bowl, #2297, 12", deep	22.00	Sauce boat, w/liner	95.00
Bowl, #2329, 13", console	30.00	Saucer, #2350/#2350½	3.00
Bowl, #2324, 13", ftd.	45.00	Saucer, #2350, demi	5.00
Bowl, #2371, 13", oval, w/flower frog	75.00	Server, #2287, 11", center hdld.	25.00
Butter, w/cover #2350	195.00	Stem, #869, ¾ oz., cordial	60.00
Candlestick, #2324, 4"	14.00	Stem, #869, 2¾ oz., wine	27.50
Candlestick, #2324, 9"	40.00	Stem, #869, 3 oz., cocktail	22.50
Candy, w/cover, #2331, 3 part	60.00	Stem, #869, 5½ oz., oyster cocktail	15.00
Candy, w/cover, ftd., ½ lb.	125.00	Stem, #869, 5½ oz., parfait	27.50
Celery, #2350, 11"	25.00	Stem, #869, 6 oz., low sherbet	12.50
Cheese, w/cover/plate #2276 (plate 11")	85.00	Stem, #869, 6 oz., high sherbet	16.00
Cologne, #2322, tall	30.00	Stem, #869, 9 oz., water	20.00
Cologne, #2323, short	25.00	Sugar, flat, w/lid	125.00
Cologne/powder jar combination	150.00	Sugar, #2315, ftd., flat	17.00
Comport, #1861½, 6", jelly	25.00	Sugar, #2350½, ftd.	12.00
Comport, #2327, 7"	28.00	Sugar lid, #2350½	95.00
Comport, #2358, 8" wide	30.00	Tumbler, #869, 5 oz., flat	22.50
Creamer, flat	14.00	Tumbler, #859, 9 oz., flat	25.00
Creamer, #2315½, ftd., fat	18.00	Tumbler, #859, 12 oz., flat	27.50
Creamer, #2350½, ftd.	13.00	Tumbler, #5000, 2½ oz., ftd.	25.00
Cup, #2350, flat	12.00	Tumbler, #5000, 5 oz., ftd.	14.00
Cup, #2350½, ftd.	13.00	Tumbler, #5000, 9 oz., ftd.	16.00
Cup, #2350, demi	22.50	Tumbler, #5000, 12 oz., ftd.	22.00
Egg cup, #2350	22.50	Vase, #2324, urn, ftd.	65.00
Grapefruit, w/insert	65.00	Vase, #2292, flared	85.00

* Add 50% more for blue or black!

144

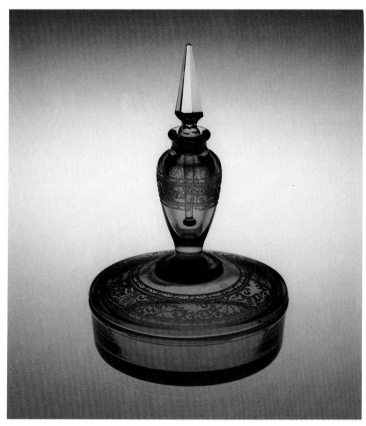

145

SANDWICH, #41, Duncan & Miller Glass Company, 1924 – 1955

Colors: crystal, amber, pink, green, red, cobalt blue

Lancaster Colony is making some of this for their lines today. The bright blue, green and amberina are from Duncan moulds and were sold by Montgomery Ward in the early 1970's. Tiffin also made some Sandwich pieces in milk glass. Stemware abounds and it is the serving pieces that are in demand. Anyone can find stemware to use if you like this pattern.

	Crystal		Crystal
Ashtray, 2½" x 3¾", rect.	10.00	Bowl, 10", lily, vertical edge	50.00
Ashtray, 2⅜", sq.	8.00	Bowl, 11", cupped nut	45.00
Basket, 6½", w/loop hdld.	115.00	Bowl, 11½", crimped flower	50.00
Basket, 10", crimped, w/loop hdl.	145.00	Bowl, 11½", gardenia	45.00
Basket, 10", oval, w/loop hdl.	145.00	Bowl, 11½", ftd., crimped fruit	50.00
Basket, 11½", w/loop hdl.	175.00	Bowl, 12", fruit, flared edge	45.00
Bonbon, 5", heart shape, w/ring hdl.	15.00	Bowl, 12", shallow salad	40.00
Bonbon, 5½", heart shape, hdld.	15.00	Bowl, 12", oblong console	40.00
Bonbon, 6", heart shape, w/ring hdl.	20.00	Bowl, 12", epergne, w/ctr. hole	50.00
Bonbon, 7½", ftd., w/cover	35.00	Butter, w/cover, ¼ lb.	37.50
Bowl, 2½", salted almond	8.00	Cake stand, 11½", ftd., rolled edge	85.00
Bowl, 3½", nut	8.50	Cake stand, 12", ftd., rolled edge, plain	
Bowl, 4", finger	12.50	pedestal	75.00
Bowl, 5½", hdld.	15.00	Cake stand, 13", ftd., plain pedestal	75.00
Bowl, 5½", ftd., grapefruit, w/rim liner	15.00	Candelabra, 10", 1-lite, w/bobeche & prisms	65.00
Bowl, 5½", ftd., grapefruit, w/fruit cup liner	15.00	Candelabra, 10", 3-lite, w/bobeche & prisms	135.00
Bowl, 5", 2 pt., nappy	12.00	Candelabra, 16", 3-lite, w/bobeche & prisms	195.00
Bowl, 5", ftd., crimped ivy	22.00	Candlestick, 4", 1-lite	14.00
Bowl, 5", fruit	10.00	Candlestick, 4", 1-lite, w/bobeche & stub.	
Bowl, 5", nappy, w/ring hdl.	12.00	prisms	30.00
Bowl, 6", 2 pt., nappy	14.00	Candlestick, 5", 3-lite	35.00
Bowl, 6", fruit salad	12.00	Candlestick, 5", 3-lite, w/bobeche & stub.	
Bowl, 6", grapefruit, rimmed edge	15.00	prisms	85.00
Bowl, 6", nappy, w/ring hdl.	17.50	Candlestick, 5", 2-lite, w/bobeche & stub.	
Bowl, 10", salad, deep	60.00	prisms	60.00
Bowl, 10", 3 pt., fruit	67.50	Candlestick, 5", 2-lite	25.00

	Crystal
Candy, 6" square	100.00
Candy box, w/cover, 5", flat	35.00
Candy jar, w/cover, 8½", ftd.	50.00
Cheese, w/cover (cover 4¾", plate 8")	90.00
Cheese/cracker (3" compote, 13" plate)	42.50
Cigarette box, w/cover, 3½"	22.00
Cigarette holder, 3", ftd.	27.50
Coaster, 5"	12.00
Comport, 2¼"	15.00
Comport, 3¼", low ft., crimped candy	20.00
Comport, 3¼", low ft., flared candy	17.50
Comport, 4¼", ftd.	20.00
Comport, 5", low ft.	20.00
Comport, 5½", ftd., low crimped	25.00
Comport, 6", low ft., flared	22.50
Condiment set (2 cruets; 3¾" salt & pepper; 4 pt. tray)	85.00
Creamer, 4", 7 oz., ftd.	9.00
Cup, 6 oz., tea	10.00
Epergne, 9", garden	85.00
Epergne, 12", 3 pt., fruit or flower	175.00
Jelly, 3", indiv.	7.00
Mayonnaise set, 3 pc.: ladle, 5" bowl, 7" plate	32.00
Oil bottle, 5¾"	35.00
Pan, 6¾" x 10½", oblong, camelia	55.00
Pitcher, 13 oz., metal top	50.00
Pitcher, w/ice lip, 8", 64 oz.	110.00
Plate, 3", indiv. jelly	6.00
Plate, 6", bread/butter	6.00
Plate, 6½", finger bowl liner	8.00
Plate, 7", dessert	7.50
Plate, 8", mayonnaise liner, w/ring	5.00
Plate, 8", salad	10.00
Plate, 9½", dinner	30.00
Plate, 11½", hdld., service	35.00
Plate, 12", torte	45.00
Plate, 12", ice cream, rolled edge	50.00
Plate, 12", deviled egg	60.00
Plate, 13", salad dressing, w/ring	32.00
Plate, 13", service	50.00
Plate, 13", service, rolled edge	55.00
Plate, 13", cracker, w/ring	25.00
Plate, 16", lazy susan, w/turntable	85.00
Plate, 16", hostess	75.00
Relish, 5½", 2 pt., rnd., ring hdl.	15.00
Relish, 6", 2 pt., rnd., ring hdl.	17.00
Relish, 7", 2 pt., oval	20.00
Relish, 10", 4 pt., hdld.	25.00

	Crystal
Relish, 10", 3 pt., oblong	27.50
Relish, 10½", 3 pt., oblong	27.50
Relish, 12", 3 pt.	37.50
Salad dressing set: (2 ladles; 5" ftd. mayonnaise; 13" plate w/ring)	80.00
Salad dressing set: (2 ladles; 6" ftd. div. bowl; 8" plate w/ring)	65.00
Salt & pepper, 2½", w/glass tops, pr.	18.00
Salt & pepper, 2½", w/metal tops, pr.	18.00
Salt & pepper, 3¾", w/metal top (on 6" tray), 3 pc.	30.00
Saucer, 6", w/ring	4.00
Stem, 2½", 6 oz., ftd., fruit cup/jello	11.00
Stem, 2¾", 5 oz., ftd., oyster cocktail	15.00
Stem, 3½", 5 oz., sundae (flared rim)	12.00
Stem, 4¼", 3 oz., cocktail	15.00
Stem, 4¼", 5 oz., ice cream	12.50
Stem, 4¼", 3 oz., wine	20.00
Stem, 5¼", 4 oz., ftd., parfait	25.00
Stem, 5¼", 5 oz., champagne	20.00
Stem, 6", 9 oz., goblet	18.50
Sugar, 3¼", ftd., 9 oz.	8.00
Sugar, 5 oz.	7.50
Sugar (cheese) shaker, 13 oz., metal top	60.00
Tray, oval (for sugar/creamer)	10.00
Tray, 6" mint, rolled edge, w/ring hdl.	17.50
Tray, 7", oval, pickle	15.00
Tray, 7", mint, rolled edge, w/ring hdl.	20.00
Tray, 8", oval	18.00
Tray, 8", for oil/vinegar	20.00
Tray, 10", oval, celery	18.00
Tray, 12", fruit epergne	40.00
Tray, 12", ice cream, rolled edge	40.00
Tumbler, 3¾", 5 oz., ftd., juice	12.00
Tumbler, 4¾", 9 oz., ftd., water	14.00
Tumbler, 5¼", 13 oz., flat, iced tea	20.00
Tumbler, 5¼", 12 oz., ftd., iced tea	17.50
Urn, w/cover, 12", ftd.	100.00
Vase, 3", ftd., crimped	17.50
Vase, 3", ftd., flared rim	15.00
Vase, 4", hat shape	20.00
Vase, 4½", flat base, crimped	20.00
Vase, 5", ftd., flared rim	22.50
Vase, 5", ftd., crimped	25.00
Vase, 5", ftd., fan	35.00
Vase, 7½", epergne, threaded base	45.00
Vase, 10", ftd.	50.00

SATURN, Blank #1485, A.H. Heisey & Co.

Colors: crystal, "Zircon" or "Limelight" green, "Dawn"

Shakers in "Zircon" are quite rare as you can see by the price. "Limelight" and "Zircon" are the same color. Originally made in 1937, this color was called "Zircon." In 1955, it was made again by Heisey, but called "Limelight."

	Crystal	Zircon/ Limelight
Ashtray	9.00	
Bitters bottle, w/short tube, blown	32.50	
Bowl, baked apple	5.00	55.00
Bowl, finger	4.00	
Bowl, rose, lg.	32.50	
Bowl, 4½", nappy	4.00	
Bowl, 5", nappy	6.00	
Bowl, 5", whipped cream	10.00	75.00
Bowl, 7", pickle	12.00	
Bowl, 9", 3 part, relish	17.50	
Bowl, 10", celery	13.00	
Bowl, 11", salad	30.00	
Bowl, 12", fruit, flared rim	32.50	
Bowl, 13", floral, rolled edge	35.00	
Bowl, 13", floral	35.00	
Candelabrum, w/"e" ball drops, 2-lite	125.00	500.00
Candle block, 2-lite	75.00	325.00
Candlestick, 3", ftd., 1-lite	25.00	145.00
Comport, 7"	30.00	250.00
Creamer	10.00	95.00
Cup	9.00	125.00
Hostess Set, 8 pc. (low bowl w/ftd. ctr. bowl, 3 toothpick holders & clips)	20.00	225.00
Marmalade, w/cover	30.00	
Mayonnaise	6.00	80.00
Mustard, w/cover and paddle	35.00	295.00
Oil bottle, 2 oz., w/#1 stopper	40.00	350.00
Parfait, 5 oz.	5.00	65.00
Pitcher, 70 oz., w/ice lip, blown	60.00	350.00
Pitcher, juice	35.00	245.00
Plate, 6"	3.00	30.00
Plate, 7", bread	5.00	30.00
Plate, 8", luncheon	7.00	55.00
Plate, 13", torte	15.00	
Plate, 15", torte	10.00	
Salt & pepper, pr.	45.00	550.00
Saucer	3.00	25.00
Stem, 3 oz., cocktail	7.00	55.00
Stem, 4 oz., fruit cocktail or oyster cocktail	6.00	75.00
Stem, 4½ oz., sherbet	2.50	60.00
Stem, 5 oz., sherbet	5.00	55.00
Stem, 6 oz., saucer champagne	4.00	75.00
Stem, 10 oz.	12.00	90.00
Sugar	12.50	90.00
Sugar shaker (pourer)	27.50	
Sugar, w/cover, no handles	20.00	
Tray, tidbit, 2 sides turned as fan	20.00	75.00
Tumbler, 5 oz., juice	5.00	65.00
Tumbler, 7 oz., old fashioned	20.00	
Tumbler, 8 oz., old fashioned	8.00	
Tumbler, 9 oz., luncheon	9.00	
Tumbler, 10 oz.	15.00	40.00
Tumbler, 12 oz., soda	8.00	65.00
Vase, violet	20.00	85.00
Vase, 8½", flared	25.00	175.00
Vase, 8½", straight	25.00	175.00

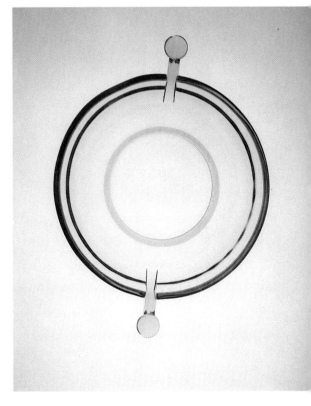

SEVILLE, Fostoria Glass Company, 1926-1931

Colors: amber, green

This new listing would be a good starting pattern for someone who would like an inexpensive Fostoria pattern. It will not that way for long as there is not that much to go around. Green would be easier to collect than amber.

	Amber	Green		Amber	Green
Ashtray, #2350, 4"	17.50	22.50	Grapefruit, #945½, blown	40.00	45.00
Bowl, #2350, fruit, 5½"	10.00	12.00	Grapefruit, #945½, liner, blown	30.00	35.00
Bowl, #2350, cereal, 6½"	16.00	18.00	Grapefruit, #2315, molded	22.50	25.00
Bowl, #2350, soup, 7¾"	17.50	20.00	Ice bucket, #2378	50.00	52.00
Bowl, #2315, low foot, 7"	16.00	18.00	Pickle, #2350, 8"	13.50	15.00
Bowl, #2350, vegetable	20.00	25.00	Pitcher, #5084, ftd.	195.00	225.00
Bowl, #2350, nappy, 9"	30.00	35.00	Plate, #2350, bread and butter, 6"	3.50	4.00
Bowl, #2350, oval, baker, 9"	25.00	30.00	Plate, #2350, salad, 7½"	5.00	5.50
Bowl, #2315, flared, 10½", ftd.	25.00	30.00	Plate, #2350, luncheon, 8½"	6.00	6.50
Bowl, #2350, oval, baker, 10½"	35.00	40.00	Plate, #2321, Maj Jongg (canape),		
Bowl, 10", ftd.	30.00	35.00	8¾"	30.00	35.00
Bowl, #2350, salad, 10"	30.00	35.00	Plate, #2350, sm. dinner, 9½"	12.00	13.50
Bowl, #2329, rolled edge, console,			Plate, #2350, dinner, 10½"	30.00	35.00
11"	27.50	32.50	Plate, #2350, chop, 13¾"	30.00	35.00
Bowl, #2297, deep, flared, 12"	30.00	32.50	Plate, #2350, round, 15"	35.00	40.00
Bowl, #2371, oval, console, 13"	35.00	40.00	Plate, #2350, cream soup liner	5.00	6.00
Bowl, #2329, rolled edge, console,			Platter, #2350, 10½"	22.50	25.00
13"	30.00	32.50	Platter, #2350, 12"	35.00	40.00
Bowl, #2350, bouillon, flat	13.50	15.00	Platter, #2350, 15"	65.00	75.00
Bowl, #2350½, bouillon, ftd.	14.00	16.00	Salt and pepper shaker, #5100, pr.	60.00	65.00
Bowl, #2350, cream soup, flat	14.50	16.00	Sauce boat liner, #2350	20.00	22.50
Bowl, #2350½, cream soup, ftd.	15.50	17.00	Sauce boat, #2350	50.00	60.00
Bowl, #869/2283, finger, w/6" liner	17.50	20.00	Saucer, #2350	3.00	3.00
Butter, w/cover, #2350, round	150.00	200.00	Saucer, after dinner, #2350	5.00	5.00
Candlestick, #2324, 2"	15.00	17.50	Stem, #870, cocktail	15.00	16.00
Candlestick, #2324, 4"	12.50	15.00	Stem, #870, cordial	60.00	65.00
Candlestick, #2324, 9"	25.00	30.00	Stem, #870, high sherbet	15.00	16.00
Candy jar, w/cover, #2250,			Stem, #870, low sherbet	12.50	13.50
½ lb., ftd.	75.00	100.00	Stem, #870, oyster cocktail	16.50	17.50
Candy jar, w/cover, #2331, 3 pt., flat	60.00	75.00	Stem, #870, parfait	27.50	30.00
Celery, #2350, 11"	15.00	17.50	Stem, #870, water	20.00	22.50
Cheese and cracker, #2368,			Stem, #870, wine	22.50	25.00
(11" plate)	35.00	40.00	Sugar cover, #2350½	65.00	75.00
Comport, #2327, 7½",			Sugar, fat, ftd., #2315	13.50	14.50
(twisted stem)	20.00	22.50	Sugar, ftd., #2350½	12.50	13.50
Comport, #2350, 8"	27.50	32.50	Tray, 11", center handled, #2287	27.50	30.00
Creamer, #2315½, flat, ftd.	13.50	15.00	Tumbler, #5084, ftd., 2 oz.	30.00	32.50
Creamer, #2350½, ftd.	12.50	13.50	Tumbler, #5084, ftd., 5 oz.	13.50	15.00
Cup, #2350, after dinner	25.00	30.00	Tumbler, #5084, ftd., 9 oz.	15.00	16.50
Cup, #2350, flat	10.00	12.50	Tumbler, #5084, ftd., 12 oz.	18.00	20.00
Cup, #2350½, ftd.	10.00	12.50	Urn, small, #2324	65.00	75.00
Egg cup, #2350	30.00	35.00	Vase, #2292, 8"	50.00	60.00

"SPIRAL FLUTES," Duncan & Miller Glass Company, Introduced 1924

Colors: amber, green, pink, crystal

Not many collectors flock to this pattern, but those who do have found the going difficult on many pieces. Everyone can locate the 6¾" flanged bowls, 7 oz. footed tumblers and 7½" plates, but after that there is very little found.

	Amber, Green, Pink		Amber, Green, Pink
Bowl, 2", almond	10.00	Ice tub, handled	40.00
Bowl, 3¾", bouillon	15.00	Lamp, 10½", countess	225.00
Bowl, 4⅜", finger	6.00	Mug, 6½", 9 oz., handled	27.50
Bowl, 4¾", ftd., cream soup	15.00	Mug, 7", 9 oz., handled	35.00
Bowl, 4" w., mayonnaise	17.50	Oil, w/stopper, 6 oz.	135.00
Bowl, 5", nappy	6.00	Pickle, 8⅝"	12.00
Bowl, 6½", cereal, sm. flange	25.00	Pitcher, ½ gal.	125.00
Bowl, 6¾", grapefruit	7.50	Plate, 6", pie	3.00
Bowl, 6", handled nappy	22.00	Plate, 7½", salad	4.00
Bowl, 6", handled nappy, w/cover	60.00	Plate, 8⅜", luncheon	4.00
Bowl, 7", nappy	15.00	Plate, 10⅜", dinner	22.50
Bowl, 7½", flanged (baked apple)	22.50	Plate, 13⅝", torte	27.50
Bowl, 8", nappy	15.00	Plate, w/star, 6", (fingerbowl item)	6.00
Bowl, 8½", flanged (oyster plate)	22.50	Platter, 11"	32.50
Bowl, 9", nappy	27.50	Platter, 13"	42.50
Bowl, 10", oval, veg., two styles.	40.00	Relish, 10" x 7⅜", oval, 3 pc. (2 inserts)	65.00
Bowl, 10½", lily pond	40.00	Saucer	3.00
Bowl, 11¾" w. x 3¾" t., console, flared	30.00	Saucer, demi	5.00
Bowl, 11", nappy	30.00	Seafood sauce cup, 3" w. x 2½" h.	22.00
Bowl, 12", cupped console	30.00	Stem, 3¾", 3½ oz., wine	17.50
Candle, 3½"	15.00	Stem, 3¾", 5 oz., low sherbet	8.00
Candle, 7½"	55.00	Stem, 4¾", 6 oz., tall sherbet	12.00
Candle, 9½"	60.00	Stem, 5⅝", 4½ oz., parfait	17.50
Candle, 11½"	95.00	Stem, 6¼", 7 oz., water	17.50
Celery, 10¾" x 4¾"	17.50	Sugar, oval	8.00
* Chocolate jar, w/cover	200.00	Sweetmeat, w/cover, 7½"	85.00
Cigarette holder, 4"	30.00	Tumbler, 3⅜", ftd., 2½ oz., cocktail (no stem)	7.00
Comport, 4⅜"	15.00	Tumbler, 4¼", 8 oz., flat	27.50
Comport, 6⅝"	17.50	Tumbler, 4⅜", ftd., 5½ oz., juice (no stem)	14.00
Comport, 9", low ft., flared	50.00	Tumbler, 4¾", 7 oz., flat, soda	27.50
Console stand, 1½" h. x 4⅝" w.	12.00	Tumbler, 5⅛", ftd., 7 oz., water (1 knob)	8.00
Creamer, oval	8.00	Tumbler, 5⅛", ftd., 9 oz., water (no stem)	20.00
Cup	9.00	Tumbler, 5½", 11 oz., gingerale	50.00
Cup, demi	22.50	Vase, 6½"	12.00
* Fernery, 10" x 5½", 4 ftd., flower box	300.00	Vase, 8½"	17.50
Grapefruit, ftd.	20.00		

*Crystal, $135.00

154

TEAR DROP, #301, Duncan & Miller Glass Company, 1936 – 1955

Colors: crystal

I still have trouble selling stemware in Tear Drop just as I have trouble finding dinner plates and serving pieces. Even cordials are easily found when compared to finding cordials in other patterns. This is another good starting pattern for beginners. You can buy a lot of it without mortgaging the farm.

	Crystal		Crystal
Ashtray, 3" indiv.	6.00	Coaster/ashtray, 3", rolled edge	7.00
Ashtray, 5"	8.00	Comport, 4¾", ftd.	12.00
Bonbon, 6", 4 hdld.	12.00	Comport, 6", low foot., hdld.	15.00
Bottle, w/stopper, 12", bar	95.00	Condiment set: 5 pc. (salt/pepper, 2	
Bowl, 4¼", finger	7.00	3 oz. cruets, 9", 2 hdld. tray)	85.00
Bowl, 5", fruit nappy	6.00	Creamer, 3 oz.	5.00
Bowl, 5", 2 hdld., nappy	8.00	Creamer, 6 oz.	6.00
Bowl, 6", dessert, nappy	6.00	Creamer, 8 oz.	8.00
Bowl, 6", fruit, nappy	6.00	Cup, 2½ oz., demi	10.00
Bowl, 7", fruit, nappy	7.00	Cup, 6 oz., tea	6.00
Bowl, 7", 2 hdld., nappy	10.00	Flower basket, 12", loop hdl.	95.00
Bowl, 8" x 12", oval, flower	32.00	Ice bucket, 5½"	55.00
Bowl, 9", salad	25.00	Marmalade, w/cover, 4"	35.00
Bowl, 9", 2 hdld., nappy	20.00	Mayonnaise, 4½" (2 hdld. bowl, ladle,	
Bowl, 10", crimped console, 2 hdld.	27.50	6" plate)	27.50
Bowl, 10", flared, fruit	25.00	Mayonnaise set, 3 pc. (4½" bowl, ladle,	
Bowl, 11½", crimped, flower	30.00	8" hdld. plate)	32.50
Bowl, 11½", flared, flower	30.00	Mustard jar, w/cover, 4¼"	35.00
Bowl, 12", salad	35.00	Nut dish, 6", 2 pt.	10.00
Bowl, 12", crimped, low foot	37.00	Oil bottle, 3 oz.	20.00
Bowl, 12", ftd., flower	40.00	Olive dish, 4¼", 2 hdld., oval	15.00
Bowl, 12", sq., 4 hdld.	42.50	Olive dish, 6", 2 pt.	15.00
Bowl, 13", gardenia	35.00	Pickle dish, 6"	15.00
Bowl, 15½", 2½ gal. punch	85.00	Pitcher, 5", 16 oz., milk	50.00
Butter, w/cover, ¼ lb., 2 hdld.	22.00	Pitcher, 8½", 64 oz., w/ice lip	90.00
Cake salver, 13", ftd.	40.00	Plate, 6", bread/butter	4.00
Canape set: (6" plate w/ring, 4 oz., ftd.,		Plate, 6", canape	10.00
cocktail)	25.00	Plate, 7", 2 hdld., lemon	12.50
Candlestick, 4"	9.00	Plate, 7½", salad	5.00
Candlestick, 7", 2-lite, ball loop ctr.	18.00	Plate, 8½", luncheon	7.00
Candlestick, 7", lg. ball ctr. w/bobeches,		Plate, 10½", dinner	27.50
prisms	35.00	Plate, 11", 2 hdld.	27.50
Candy basket, 5½" x 7½", 2 hdld., oval	55.00	Plate, 13", 4 hdld.	25.00
Candy box, w/cover, 7", 2 pt., 2 hdld.	40.00	Plate, 13", salad liner, rolled edge	27.50
Candy box, w/cover, 8", 3 pt., 3 hdld.	45.00	Plate, 13", torte, rolled edge	30.00
Candy dish, 7½", heart shape	22.00	Plate, 14", torte	35.00
Celery, 11", 2 hdld.	15.00	Plate, 14", torte, rolled edge	35.00
Celery, 11", 2 pt., 2 hdld.	18.00	Plate, 16", torte, rolled edge	37.50
Celery, 12", 3 pt.	20.00	Plate, 18", lazy susan	50.00
Cheese & cracker (3½" comport, 11"		Plate, 18", punch liner, rolled edge	50.00
2 hdld. plate)	42.50		

	Crystal
Relish, 7", 2 pt., 2 hdld.	15.00
Relish, 7½", 2 pt., heart shape	18.00
Relish, 9", 3 pt., 3 hdld.	25.00
Relish, 11", 3 pt., 2 hdld.	25.00
Relish, 12", 3 pt.	25.00
Relish, 12", 5 pt., rnd.	25.00
Relish, 12", 6 pt., rnd.	25.00
Relish, 12", sq., 4 pt., 4 hdld.	25.00
Salad set, 6" (compote, 11" hdld. plate)	37.50
Salad set, 9", (2 pt. bowl, 13" rolled edge plate)	70.00
Salt & pepper, 5"	25.00
Saucer, 4½", demi	3.00
Saucer, 6"	1.50
Stem, 2½", 5 oz., ftd., sherbet	5.00
Stem, 2¾", 3½ oz., ftd., oyster cocktail	7.50
Stem, 3½", 5 oz., sherbet	6.00
Stem, 4", 1 oz., cordial	30.00
Stem, 4½", 1¾ oz., sherry	27.50
Stem, 4½", 3½ oz., cocktail	20.00
Stem, 4¾", 3 oz., wine	22.00
Stem, 5", 5 oz., champagne	10.00
Stem, 5½", 4 oz., claret	15.00
Stem, 5¾", 9 oz.	11.00
Stem, 6¼", 8 oz., ale	15.00
Stem, 7", 9 oz.	15.00
Sugar, 3 oz.	5.00
Sugar, 6 oz.	6.00

	Crystal
Sugar, 8 oz.	8.00
Sweetmeat, 5½", star shape, 2 hdld.	27.50
Sweetmeat, 6½", ctr. hdld.	27.50
Sweetmeat, 7", star shape, 2 hdld.	30.00
Tray, 5½", ctr. hdld. (for mustard jar)	11.00
Tray, 6", 2 hdld. (for salt/pepper)	10.00
Tray, 7¾", ctr. hdld. (for cruets)	12.50
Tray, 8", 2 hdld. (for oil/vinegar)	12.50
Tray, 8", 2 hdld. (for sugar/creamer)	7.50
Tray, 10", 2 hdld (for sugar/creamer)	8.00
Tumbler, 2¼", 2 oz., flat, whiskey	17.50
Tumbler, 2¼", 2 oz., ftd., whiskey	15.00
Tumbler, 3", 3 oz., ftd., whiskey	15.00
Tumbler, 3¼", 3½ oz., flat, juice	8.00
Tumbler, 3¼", 7 oz., flat, old fashioned	10.00
Tumbler, 3½", 5 oz., flat, juice	8.00
Tumbler, 4", 4½ oz., ftd., juice	9.00
Tumbler, 4¼", 9 oz., flat	9.00
Tumbler, 4½", 8 oz., flat, split	9.00
Tumbler, 4½", 9 oz., ftd.	9.00
Tumbler, 4¾", 10 oz., flat, hi-ball	12.00
Tumbler, 5", 8 oz., ftd., party	10.00
Tumbler, 5¼", 12 oz., flat, iced tea	15.00
Tumbler, 5¾", 14 oz., flat, hi-ball	17.50
Tumbler, 6", 14 oz., iced tea	17.50
Urn, w/cover, 9", ftd.	100.00
Vase, 9", ftd., fan	25.00
Vase, 9", ftd., round	35.00

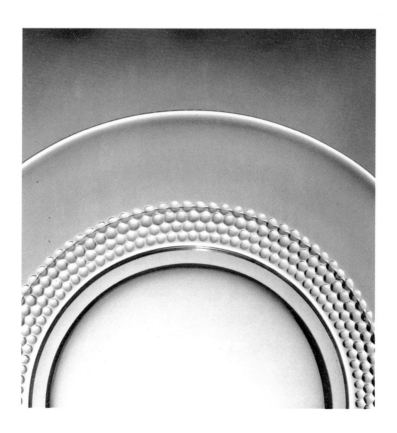

TROJAN, Fostoria Glass Company, 1929 – 1944

Colors: "Rose" pink, "Topaz" yellow; some green seen

Trojan is collected more in yellow than in pink because pink serving pieces are difficult to find. Very few Trojan decanters have been found, but you can see one here.

Having bought several Fostoria collections in the last few years, I can say that clarets are almost nonexistent in any pattern. If you need them, you had better buy them whenever you find them.

	Rose	Topaz		Rose	Topaz
Ashtray, #2350, lg.	50.00	40.00	Ice dish liner (tomato, crab, fruit)		
Ashtray, #2350, sm.	30.00	25.00	#2451	20.00	10.00
Bottle, salad dressing, #2983	400.00	250.00	Mayonnaise ladle	30.00	30.00
Bowl, baker, #2375, 9"		50.00	Mayonnaise, w/liner, #2375	60.00	50.00
Bowl, bonbon, #2375		13.00	Oil, ftd., #2375	295.00	235.00
Bowl, bouillon, #2375, ftd.		18.00	Oyster, cocktail, #5099, ftd.	30.00	27.50
Bowl, cream soup, #2375, ftd.	27.50	22.00	Parfait, #5099	65.00	45.00
Bowl, finger, #869/2283,			Pitcher, #5000	350.00	275.00
w/6¼" liner	40.00	35.00	Plate, #2375, canape	25.00	20.00
Bowl, lemon, #2375	18.00	16.00	Plate, #2375, bread/butter, 6"	6.00	5.00
Bowl, #2394, 3 ftd., 4½", mint.	25.00	22.00	Plate, #2375, salad, 7½"	9.00	8.00
Bowl, #2375, fruit, 5"	20.00	18.00	Plate, 2375, cream soup or		
Bowl, #2354, 3 ftd., 6"	30.00	35.00	mayo liner, 7½",	9.00	8.00
Bowl, cereal, #2375, 6½"	35.00	25.00	Plate, #2375, luncheon, 8¾"	17.50	15.00
Bowl, soup, #2375, 7"	50.00	40.00	Plate, #2375, sm., dinner, 9½"	20.00	17.50
Bowl, lg. dessert, #2375, 2-handled	55.00	50.00	Plate, #2375, cake, handled, 10"	35.00	32.50
Bowl, #2395, 10"	85.00	65.00	Plate, #2375, grill, rare, 10¼"	75.00	65.00
Bowl, #2395, scroll, 10"	65.00	55.00	Plate, #2375, dinner, 10¼"	65.00	45.00
Bowl, combination #2415,			Plate, #2375, chop, 13"	50.00	45.00
w/candleholder handles,	135.00	120.00	Plate, #2375, round, 14"	50.00	40.00
Bowl, #2375, centerpiece, flared			Platter, #2375, 12"	65.00	55.00
optic, 12"	45.00	40.00	Platter, #2375, 15"	125.00	100.00
Bowl, #2394, centerpiece, ftd., 12"	45.00	40.00	Relish, #2375, 8½"		15.00
Bowl, #2375, centerpiece,			Relish, #2350, 3 pt., rnd., 8¾"	45.00	40.00
mushroom, 12"	45.00	40.00	Sauce boat, #2375	100.00	90.00
Candlestick, #2394, 2"	18.00	16.00	Sauce plate, #2375	40.00	35.00
Candlestick, #2375, flared, 3"	20.00	18.00	Saucer, #2375, after dinner	10.00	10.00
Candlestick, #2395½, scroll, 5"	60.00	55.00	Saucer, #2375	6.00	5.00
Candy, w/cover, #2394, ¼ lb.	225.00	200.00	Shaker, #2375, pr., ftd.	90.00	75.00
Candy, w/cover, #2394, ½ lb.	150.00	125.00	Sherbet, #5099, high, 6"	25.00	20.00
Celery, #2375, 11½"	35.00	27.50	Sherbet, #5099, low, 4¼"	20.00	16.00
Cheese & cracker, set, #2375, #2368	65.00	60.00	Sugar, #2375½, ftd.	22.50	20.00
Comport, #5299 or #2400, 6"	35.00	30.00	Sugar cover, #2375½	100.00	85.00
Comport, #2375, 7"	45.00	40.00	Sugar pail, #2378	125.00	110.00
Creamer, #2375, ftd.	22.50	20.00	Sugar, tea, #2375½	50.00	45.00
Creamer, tea, #2375½	50.00	45.00	Sweetmeat, #2375	15.00	15.00
Cup, after dinner, #2375	45.00	35.00	Tray, 11", ctr. hdld., #2375	35.00	32.50
Cup, #2375½, ftd.	20.00	18.00	Tray, #2429, service & lemon insert		200.00
Decanter, #2439, 9"		750.00	Tumbler, #5099, ftd., 2½ oz.	50.00	40.00
Goblet, claret, #5099, 4 oz., 6"	85.00	75.00	Tumbler, #5099, ftd., 5 oz., 4½"	30.00	25.00
Goblet, cocktail, #5099, 3 oz., 5¼"	30.00	27.50	Tumbler, #5099, ftd., 9 oz., 5¼"	22.50	17.50
Goblet, cordial, #5099, ¾ oz., 4"	85.00	70.00	Tumbler, #5099, ftd., 12 oz., 6"	30.00	27.50
Goblet, water, #5299, 10 oz., 8¼"	37.50	27.50	Vase, #2417, 8"	135.00	120.00
Goblet, wine, #5099, 3 oz., 5½"	55.00	45.00	Vase, #4105, 8"	195.00	160.00
Grapefruit, #5282½	50.00	45.00	Vase, #2369, 9"		195.00
Grapefruit liner, #945½	45.00	40.00	Whipped cream bowl, #2375	15.00	12.00
Ice bucket, #2375	75.00	65.00	Whipped cream pail, #2378	125.00	110.00
Ice dish, #2451, #2455	40.00	35.00			

Note: See page 83 for stem identification.

TWIST, Blank #1252, A.H. Heisey & Co.

Colors: crystal, "Flamingo" pink, "Moongleam" green, "Marigold" amber/yellow; some "Alexandrite" (rare)

	Crystal	Pink	Green	Marigold Sahara
Baker, 9", oval	10.00	20.00	25.00	60.00
Bonbon	5.00	12.00	17.00	30.00
Bonbon, 6", 2 hdld.	5.00	12.00	17.00	30.00
Bottle, French dressing	35.00	75.00	95.00	125.00
Bowl, cream soup/bouillon	15.00	25.00	32.00	50.00
Bowl, ftd., almond/indiv. sugar	15.00	30.00	37.50	60.00
Bowl, indiv. nut	5.00	20.00	27.50	45.00
Bowl, 4", nappy	5.00	12.00	16.00	17.00
Bowl, 6", 2 hdld.	7.00	15.00	18.00	20.00
Bowl, 6", 2 hdld., jelly	7.00	15.00	18.00	20.00
Bowl, 6", 2 hdld., mint	7.00	15.00	18.00	20.00
Bowl, 8", low ftd.	25.00	35.00	40.00	65.00
Bowl, 8", nappy, grnd. bottom	12.00	25.00	30.00	40.00
Bowl, 8", nasturtium, rnd.	25.00	30.00	40.00	60.00
Bowl, 8", nasturtium, oval	25.00	30.00	40.00	60.00
Bowl, 9", floral	25.00	35.00	40.00	65.00
Bowl, 9", floral, rolled edge	30.00	35.00	40.00	65.00
Bowl, 12", floral, oval, 4 ft.	30.00	40.00	50.00	65.00
Bowl, 12", floral, rnd., 4 ft.	30.00	40.00	50.00	65.00
Candlestick, 2", 1-lite	7.50	10.00	15.00	20.00
Cheese dish, 6", 2 hdld.	5.00	10.00	17.50	20.00
Cocktail shaker, metal top			400.00	
Comport, 7", tall	25.00	60.00	85.00	150.00
Creamer, hotel, oval	15.00	35.00	45.00	50.00
Creamer, individual (unusual)	18.00	35.00	35.00	65.00
Creamer, zigzag handles, ftd.	20.00	30.00	37.50	60.00
Cup, zigzag handles	10.00	25.00	32.00	35.00
Grapefruit, ftd.	10.00	15.00	22.50	30.00
Ice tub	25.00	65.00	85.00	125.00
Pitcher, 3 pint	35.00	110.00	160.00	
Mayonnaise	15.00	20.00	30.00	40.00
Mayonnaise, #1252½	15.00	22.50	32.00	50.00
Mustard, w/cover, spoon	25.00	50.00	70.00	90.00
Oil bottle, 2½ oz., w/#78 stopper	30.00	65.00	85.00	125.00
Oil bottle, 4 oz., w/#78 stopper	35.00	70.00	90.00	135.00
Plate, cream soup liner	5.00	7.00	10.00	15.00
Plate, 8", Kraft cheese	15.00	30.00	40.00	60.00
Plate, 8", grnd. bottom	7.00	12.00	15.00	20.00
Plate, 10" utility, 3 ft.	25.00	30.00	42.00	
Plate, 12", 2 hdld., sandwich	25.00	40.00	50.00	55.00
Plate, 12", muffin, 2 hdld., turned sides	30.00	40.00	55.00	65.00
Plate, 13", 3 part, relish	10.00	17.00	22.00	35.00
Platter, 12"	15.00	40.00	60.00	75.00
Salt & pepper, 2 styles	35.00	65.00	135.00	125.00
Saucer	3.00	5.00	7.00	10.00
Stem, 2½ oz., wine	15.00	30.00	35.00	40.00
Stem, 3 oz., oyster cocktail	5.00	15.00	22.00	25.00
Stem, 3 oz., cocktail	5.00	15.00	22.00	25.00
Stem, 5 oz., saucer champagne	7.00	16.00	22.00	25.00
Stem, 5 oz., sherbet	7.50	12.00	18.00	22.50
Stem, 9 oz., luncheon (1 block in stem)	15.00	25.00	35.00	45.00
Sugar, ftd.	20.00	30.00	37.50	60.00
Sugar, hotel, oval	15.00	35.00	40.00	50.00
Sugar, individual (unusual)	18.00	35.00	38.00	65.00
Sugar, w/cover, zigzag handles	15.00	27.00	40.00	70.00
Tray, 7", pickle, grnd. bottom	7.00	15.00	22.00	25.00
Tray, 10", celery	10.00	20.00	27.00	30.00
Tray, 13", celery	12.00	25.00	37.00	50.00
Tumbler, 5 oz., fruit	4.00	12.00	20.00	25.00
Tumbler, 6 oz., ftd. soda	5.00	13.00	20.00	25.00
Tumbler, 8 oz., flat, grnd. bottom	7.00	15.00	21.00	30.00
Tumbler, 8 oz., soda, straight & flared	7.00	15.00	21.00	30.00
Tumbler, 9 oz., ftd. soda	8.00	16.00	24.00	31.00
Tumbler, 12 oz., iced tea	12.00	25.00	35.00	45.00
Tumbler, 12 oz., ftd. iced tea	15.00	30.00	40.00	50.00

VALENCIA, Cambridge Glass Company

Colors: crystal, pink

A pink Valencia console set has been found. These are the only known colored pieces in this pattern. Another Cambridge pattern often confused with Valencia is Minerva. Note the pattern shot of Valencia with the lines meeting perpendicular. On Minerva, the lines are on the diagonal.

This little-known Cambridge pattern has many unusual and interesting pieces in its repertoire. Note the covered honey dish, six-piece relish on #3500 12" plate, and the 15" long, three-part, two-handled relish. All of these pieces are highly coveted in Rose Point, but are just beginning to be noticed in Valencia. Pieces in a highly-promoted pattern such as Rose Point were made in larger quantities than those of Valencia. Since there are thousands of collectors searching for Rose Point, and only a small number looking for Valencia, there is a large discrepancy in price on the same pieces in the two patterns. Of course, the Rose Point is the higher priced.

The little metal-handled piece on the right is called a sugar basket by Cambridge. This is similar to Fostoria's sugar pail. Terminology used by the different companies causes collectors problems in figuring out which piece is called what.

	Crystal		Crystal
Ashtray, #3500/124, 3¼", round.	10.00	Relish, #3500/64, 10", 3 comp.	27.50
Ashtray, #3500/126, 4", round	14.00	Relish, #3500/65, 10", 4 comp.	30.00
Ashtray, #3500/128, 4½", round	18.00	Relish, #3500/67, 12", 6 pc.	85.00
Basket, #3500/55, 6", 2 hdld., ftd.	22.00	Relish, #3500/112, 15", 3 pt./2 hdld.	75.00
Bowl, #3500/49, 5", hdld.	18.00	Relish, #3500/13, 15", 4 pt./2 hdld.	85.00
Bowl, #3500/37, 6", cereal	20.00	Salt and pepper, #3400/18	50.00
Bowl, #1402/89, 6", 2 hdld.	18.00	Saucer, #3500/1	3.00
Bowl, #1402/88, 6", 2 hdld., div.	20.00	Stem, #1402, cordial	60.00
Bowl, #3500/115, 9½", 2 hdld., ftd.	35.00	Stem, #1402, wine	30.00
Bowl, #1402/82, 10"	32.50	Stem, #1402, cocktail	20.00
Bowl, #1402/88, 11"	35.00	Stem, #1402, claret	35.00
Bowl, #1402/95, salad dressing, div.	40.00	Stem, #1402, oyster cocktail	16.00
Bowl, #1402/100, finger, w/liner	25.00	Stem, #1402, low sherbet	12.50
Bowl, #3500, ftd., finger	27.50	Stem, #1402, tall sherbet	15.00
Candy dish, w/cover, #3500/103	80.00	Stem, #1402, goblet	20.00
Celery, #1402/94, 12"	30.00	Stem, #3500, cordial	60.00
Cigarette holder, #1066, ftd.	35.00	Stem, #3500, wine, 2½ oz.	27.50
Comport, #3500/36, 6"	27.50	Stem, #3500, cocktail, 3 oz	18.00
Comport, #3500/37, 7"	40.00	Stem, #3500, claret, 4½ oz.	35.00
Creamer, #3500/14	15.00	Stem, #3500, oyster cocktail, 4½ oz.	15.00
Creamer, #3500/15, individual	17.50	Stem, #3500, low sherbet, 7 oz.	12.50
Cup, #3500/1	17.50	Stem, #3500, tall sherbet, 7 oz.	15.00
Decanter, #3400/92, 32 oz., ball	95.00	Stem, #3500, goblet, long bowl	20.00
Decanter, #3400/119, 12 oz., ball	75.00	Stem, #3500, goblet, short bowl	18.00
Honey dish, w/cover, #3500/139	85.00	Sugar, #3500/14	15.00
Ice pail, #1402/52	50.00	Sugar, #3500/15, individual	17.50
Mayonnaise, #3500/59, 3 pc.	40.00	Sugar basket, #3500/13	75.00
Nut, #3400/71, 3", 4 ftd.	45.00	Tumbler, #3400/92, 2½ oz.	11.50
Perfume, #3400/97, 2 oz., perfume	65.00	Tumbler, #3400/100, 13 oz.	20.00
Plate, #3500/167, 7½", salad	10.00	Tumbler, #3400/115, 14 oz.	22.00
Plate, #3500/5, 8½", breakfast	12.00	Tumbler, #3500, 2½ oz., ftd.	16.00
Plate, #1402, 11½", sandwich, hdld.	22.50	Tumbler, #3500, 3 oz., ftd.	14.00
Plate, #3500/39, 12", ftd.	27.50	Tumbler, #3500, 5 oz., ftd.	12.50
Plate, #3500/67, 12"	22.50	Tumbler, #3500, 10 oz., ftd.	14.00
Plate, #3500/38, 13", torte	25.00	Tumbler, #3500, 12 oz., ftd.	18.00
Relish, #3500/68, 5½", 2 comp.	17.50	Tumbler, #3500, 13 oz., ftd.	17.50
Relish, #3500/69, 6½", 3 comp.	20.00	Tumbler, #3500, 16 oz., ftd.	20.00
Relish, #1402/91, 8", 3 comp.	25.00		

VERSAILLES, Fostoria Glass Company, 1928–1944

Colors: blue, yellow, pink, green

I have tried to list all of Fostoria line numbers for each piece of Versailles. These numbers can also be used for items listed in June.

Several things I need to point out this time include the following: liners for cream soups and mayonnaise liners are the same piece; two handled cake plate comes with and without an indent in the center and the indented serves as plate for one of two styles of cheese and cracker (both styles are shown in yellow); bonbon, lemon dish, sweetmeat and whipped cream bowl all come with a loop handle or a bow handle; sugars come with a straight top and a ruffled top but it is the ruffled top that requires a lid.

Be sure to see page 83 for the Fostoria stems that many people confuse because heights are so similar. Shapes are more important. Clarets are the difficult stem to find with cordials the next most difficult.

	Pink, Green	Blue	Yellow
Ash tray, #2350	24.00	30.00	25.00
Bottle, #2083, salad dressing, crystal glass top	275.00		325.00
Bottle, #2375, salad dressing, w/ sterling top or colored top	300.00		350.00
Bowl, #2375, baker, 9"	50.00	95.00	55.00
Bowl, #2375, bonbon	15.00	22.50	17.50
Bowl, #2375, bouillon, ftd.	20.00	32.00	20.00
Bowl, #2375, cream soup, ftd.	22.00	27.50	20.00
Bowl, #869/2283, finger, w/6" liner	25.00	40.00	30.00
Bowl, lemon	15.00	22.00	17.50
Bowl, 4½", mint, 3 ftd.	25.00	35.00	25.00
Bowl, #2375, fruit, 5"	17.50	25.00	20.00
Bowl, #2394, 3 ftd., 6"			30.00
Bowl, #2375, cereal, 6½"	22.50	35.00	25.00
Bowl, #2375, soup, 7"	35.00	50.00	35.00
Bowl, #2375, lg., dessert, 2 hdld.	45.00	70.00	40.00
Bowl, #2375, baker, 10"	45.00	75.00	40.00
Bowl, #2395, centerpiece, scroll, 10"	45.00	65.00	45.00
Bowl, #2375, centerpiece, flared top, 12"	35.00	50.00	40.00
Bowl, #2394, ftd., 12"	35.00	50.00	45.00
Bowl, #2375½, oval, centerpiece 13"	50.00	65.00	
Candlestick, #2394, 2"	20.00	22.50	17.50
Candlestick, #2395, 3"	17.50	27.50	20.00
Candlestick, #2395½, scroll, 5"	25.00	35.00	25.00
Candy, w/cover, #2331, 3 pt.	125.00	165.00	
Candy, w/cover, #2394, ¼ lb.			150.00
Candy, w/cover, #2394, ½ lb.			125.00
Celery, #2375, 11½"	35.00	45.00	40.00
Cheese & cracker, #2375 or #2368, set	65.00	85.00	65.00
Comport, #5098, 3"	25.00	35.00	25.00
Comport, #5099/2400, 6"	30.00	40.00	30.00
Comport, #2375, 7"	32.50	50.00	
Comport, #2400, 8"	65.00	85.00	
Creamer, #2375½, ftd.	17.50	22.50	15.00
Creamer, #2375½, tea	42.50	50.00	42.50
Cup, #2375, after dinner	35.00	45.00	35.00
Cup, #2375½, ftd.	17.50	21.00	19.00
Decanter, #2439, 9"	250.00	1,500.00	575.00
Goblet, cordial, #5098 or #5099, ¾ oz., 4"	80.00	85.00	65.00
Goblet, #5098 or #5099, claret, 4 oz., 6"	65.00	85.00	65.00
Goblet, cocktail, #5098 or #5099, 3 oz., 5¼"	25.00	35.00	28.00
Goblet, water, #5098 or #5099, 10 oz., 8¼"	27.50	35.00	30.00
Goblet, wine, #5098 or #5099, 3 oz., 5½"	40.00	60.00	45.00
Grapefruit, #5082½	40.00	65.00	40.00

	Pink, Green	Blue	Yellow
Grapefruit liner, #945½	35.00	45.00	35.00
Ice bucket, #2375	62.50	80.00	75.00
Ice dish, #2451	30.00	40.00	30.00
Ice dish liner (tomato, crab, fruit), #2451	20.00	20.00	10.00
Mayonnaise, w/liner, #2375	35.00	50.00	40.00
Mayonnaise ladle	30.00	40.00	30.00
Oil, #2375, ftd.	300.00	450.00	250.00
Oyster cocktail, #5098 or #5099	22.50	32.50	25.00
Parfait, #5098 or #5099	35.00	45.00	35.00
Pitcher, #5000	265.00	395.00	295.00
Plate, #2375, bread/butter, 6"	4.00	5.00	4.00
Plate, #2375, canape, 6"	20.00	35.00	30.00
Plate, #2375, salad, 7½"	6.00	10.00	7.00
Plate, #2375, cream soup or mayo liner, 7½"	6.00	10.00	7.00
Plate, #2375, luncheon, 8¾"	8.00	12.50	9.00
Plate, #2375, sm., dinner, 9½"	15.00	30.00	17.50
Plate, #2375, cake, 2 hdld., 10"	26.00	37.50	30.00
Plate, #2375, dinner, 10¼"	60.00	75.00	55.00
Plate, #2375, chop, 13"	45.00	60.00	40.00
Platter, #2375, 12"	60.00	75.00	60.00
Platter, #2375, 15"	90.00	125.00	90.00
Relish, #2375, 8½"	30.00	40.00	35.00
Sauce boat, #2375	65.00	100.00	65.00
Sauce boat plate, #2375	20.00	30.00	20.00
Saucer, #2375, after dinner	4.00	6.00	5.00
Saucer, #2375	4.00	6.00	5.00
Shaker, #2375, pr., ftd.	90.00	125.00	85.00
Sherbet, #5098/5099, high, 6"	20.00	27.50	22.50
Sherbet, #5098/5099, low, 4¼"	20.00	25.00	22.00
Sugar, #2375½, ftd.	15.00	20.00	15.00
Sugar cover, #2375½	120.00	150.00	110.00
Sugar pail, #2378	135.00	195.00	125.00
Sugar, #2375½, tea	42.50	50.00	42.50
Sweetmeat, #2375	14.00	18.00	15.00
Tray, #2375, ctr. hdld., 11"	30.00	45.00	35.00
Tray, service & lemon	275.00		200.00
Tumbler, flat, old fashioned (pink only)	85.00		
Tumbler, flat, tea (pink only)	90.00		
Tumbler, #5098 or #5099 2½ oz., ftd.,	32.50	45.00	37.50
Tumbler, #5098 or #5099, 5 oz., ftd., 4½",	20.00	27.50	22.00
Tumbler, #5098 or #5099, 9 oz., ftd., 5¼"	20.00	30.00	21.50
Tumbler, #5098 or #5099 12 oz., ftd., 6",	30.00	45.00	27.50
Vase, #2417, 8"			135.00
Vase, #4100, 8"	125.00	195.00	
Vase, #2385, fan, ftd., 8½"	110.00	175.00	
Whipped cream bowl, #2375	15.00	18.00	13.00
Whipped cream pail, 2378	100.00	145.00	100.00

Note: See page 83 for stem identification.

VESPER, Fostoria Glass Company, 1926 – 1934

Colors: amber, green; some blue

If you like amber Fostoria, this is the pattern to collect. There are a multitude of pieces, many of which are easily found. Others will take some patience and searching. Amber Fostoria etched patterns may be the "sleepers" in the Elegant glass collecting field because many people have an aversion to the color. That could be a big mistake. Besides, I've seen gorgeous table settings made with amber glass. Don't sell it short!

The 8¾" canape plate which is large by most standards, was called a Maj Jongg set by Fostoria. They are quite rare. The butter dish in amber is the only one known at this time, so you might want to keep your eyes open for another.

This pattern cost me more time to get photographed than any other in the book. I packed it last June and took it to Paducah to be photographed. After the photography session, I took it to be displayed at a glass show in Springfield, Missouri. When I finally saw the prints in December, the glassware was not fully shown on one side. The glass had to be found, repacked and taken back to Paducah to be done again. I was less than amused at this procedure!

	Green	Amber	Blue
Ashtray, #2350, 4"	25.00	30.00	
Bowl, #2350, bouillon, ftd.	12.00	15.00	20.00
Bowl, #2350, cream soup, flat	25.00	30.00	
Bowl, #2350, cream soup, ftd.	20.00	20.00	25.00
Bowl, #2350, fruit, 5½"	10.00	12.50	20.00
Bowl, #2350, cereal, sq. or rnd., 6½"	18.00	20.00	25.00
Bowl, #2267, low, ftd., 7"	20.00	25.00	
Bowl, #2350, soup, shallow, 7¾"	18.00	22.00	35.00
Bowl, soup, deep, 8¼"		25.00	
Bowl, 8"	25.00	30.00	
Bowl, #2350, baker, oval, 9"	40.00	60.00	50.00
Bowl, #2350, baker, oval, 10½"	60.00	70.00	90.00
Bowl, #2375, flared bowl, 10½"	30.00	32.00	
Bowl, #2329, console, rolled edge, 11"	30.00	32.50	
Bowl, #2375, 3 ftd., 12½"	35.00	38.00	
Bowl, #2371, oval, 13"	35.00	37.50	
Bowl, #2329, rolled edge, 13"	35.00	37.50	
Bowl, #2329, rolled edge, 15"	40.00	45.00	
Butter dish, #2350		750.00	
Candlestick, #2324, 2"	17.50	22.50	
Candlestick, #2394, 3"	15.00	15.00	30.00
Candlestick, #2324, 4"	15.00	17.50	
Candlestick, #2394, 9"	50.00	65.00	50.00
Candy jar, w/cover, #2331, 3 pt.	85.00	85.00	150.00
Candy jar, w/cover, #2250, ftd., ½ lb.	200.00	145.00	
Celery, #2350	17.00	22.00	30.00
Cheese, #2368, ftd.	18.00	20.00	
Comport, 6"	22.50	25.00	35.00
Comport, #2327, (twisted stem), 7½"	27.50	30.00	45.00
Comport, 8"	40.00	45.00	50.00
Creamer, #2350½, ftd.	14.00	16.00	
Creamer, #2315½, fat, ftd.	18.00	20.00	25.00
Creamer, #2350½, flat		20.00	
Cup, #2350	14.00	15.00	25.00
Cup, #2350, after dinner	25.00	25.00	50.00
Cup, #2350½, ftd.	14.00	15.00	
Egg cup, #2350		35.00	
Finger bowl and liner, #869/2283, 6"	22.00	25.00	35.00
Grapefruit, #5082½, blown	40.00	40.00	65.00

	Green	Amber	Blue
Grapefruit liner, #945½, blown	35.00	35.00	40.00
Grapefruit, #2315, molded	40.00	45.00	
Ice bucket, #2378	60.00	62.50	
Oyster cocktail, #5100	16.00	18.00	30.00
Pickle, #2350	20.00	22.00	30.00
Pitcher, #5100, ftd.	275.00	295.00	450.00
Plate, #2350, bread/butter, 6"	4.50	5.00	10.00
Plate, #2350, salad, 7½"	6.00	6.50	12.00
Plate, #2350, luncheon, 8½"	7.50	8.50	15.00
Plate, #2321, Maj Jongg (canape), 8¾"		40.00	
Plate, #2350, sm., dinner, 9½"	15.00	16.00	20.00
Plate, dinner, 10½"	23.00	29.00	
Plate, #2287, ctr. hand., 11"	22.50	25.00	45.00
Plate, chop, 13¼"	32.00	37.50	60.00
Plate, #2350, server, 15"	45.00	55.00	75.00
Plate, w/indent for cheese, 11"	18.00	20.00	
Platter, #2350, 10½"	30.00	35.00	
Platter, #2350, 12"	40.00	50.00	75.00
Platter, #2350, 15",	75.00	85.00	95.00
Salt & pepper, #5100, pr.	65.00	75.00	
Sauce boat, w/liner, #2350	95.00	110.00	
Saucer, #2350, after dinner	7.50	9.00	15.00
Saucer, #2350	4.00	4.50	5.00
Stem, #5093, high sherbet	16.00	17.50	25.00
Stem, #5093, water goblet	25.00	27.50	35.00
Stem, #5093, low sherbet	15.00	17.00	22.00
Stem, #5093, parfait	30.00	35.00	40.00
Stem, #5093, cordial, ¾ oz.	70.00	75.00	100.00
Stem, #5093, wine, 2¾ oz.	32.00	35.00	45.00
Stem, #5093, cocktail, 3 oz.	25.00	27.50	30.00
Sugar, #2350½, flat		20.00	
Sugar, #2315, fat ftd.	18.00	20.00	25.00
Sugar, #2350½, ftd.		14.00	16.00
Sugar, lid		135.00	150.00
Tumbler, #5100, ftd., 2 oz.	30.00	35.00	45.00
Tumbler, #5100, ftd., 5 oz.	15.00	18.00	25.00
Tumbler, #5100, ftd., 9 oz.	16.00	18.00	30.00
Tumbler, #5100, ftd., 12 oz.	22.00	25.00	40.00
Urn, #2324, small		60.00	65.00
Urn, large		70.00	75.00
Vase, #2292, 8"	70.00	75.00	110.00
Vanity set, combination cologne/ powder & stopper	150.00	175.00	225.00

Note: See stemware identification on page 83.

WAVERLY, Blank #1519, A.H. Heisey & Co.

Colors: crystal; rare in amber

	Crystal
Bowl, 6", oval, lemon, w/cover	30.00
Bowl, 6½", 2 hdld., ice	50.00
Bowl, 7", 3 part, relish, oblong	25.00
Bowl, 7", salad	20.00
Bowl, 9", 4 part, relish, round	25.00
Bowl, 9", fruit	35.00
Bowl, 9", vegetable	35.00
Bowl, 10", crimped edge	17.50
Bowl, 10", gardenia	15.00
Bowl, 11", seahorse foot, floral	65.00
Bowl, 12", crimped edge	37.50
Bowl, 13", gardenia	20.00
Box, 5", chocolate, w/cover	45.00
Box, 5" tall, ftd., w/cover, seahorse hand.	65.00
Box, 6", candy, w/bow tie knob	45.00
Box, trinket, lion cover (rare)	750.00
Butter dish, w/cover, 6", square	65.00
Candleholder, 1-lite, block (rare)	135.00
Candleholder, 2-lite	20.00
Candleholder, 2-lite, "flame" center	50.00
Candleholder, 3-lite	60.00
Candle epergnette, 5"	10.00
Candle epergnette, 6", deep	13.00
Candle epergnette, 6½"	10.00
Cheese dish, 5½", ftd.	10.00
Cigarette holder	30.00
Comport, 6", low ftd.	8.00
Comport, 6½", jelly	10.00
Comport, 7", low ftd., oval	30.00
Creamer, ftd.	15.00
Creamer & sugar, individual, w/tray	35.00
Cruet, 3 oz., w/#122 stopper	40.00
Cup	11.00
Honey dish, 6½", ftd.	10.00
Mayonnaise, w/liner & ladle, 5½"	25.00
Plate, 7", salad	4.00
Plate, 8", luncheon	6.00
Plate, 10½", server	20.00
Plate, 11", sandwich	12.00
Plate, 13½", ftd., cake salver	60.00
Plate, 14", center handle, sandwich	55.00
Plate, 14", sandwich	20.00
Salt & pepper, pr.	25.00
Saucer	3.00
Stem, 1 oz., cordial	95.00
Stem, 3 oz., wine, blown	55.00
Stem, 3½ oz., cocktail	32.50
Stem, 5½ oz., sherbet/champagne	15.00
Stem, 10 oz., blown	20.00
Sugar, ftd.	15.00
Tray, 12", celery	13.00
Tumbler, 5 oz., ftd., juice, blown	15.00
Tumbler, 13 oz., ftd., tea, blown	20.00
Vase, 3½", violet	30.00
Vase, 7", ftd.	25.00
Vase, 7", ftd., fan shape	30.00

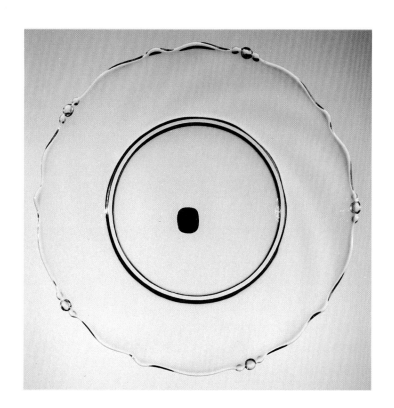

WILDFLOWER, Cambridge Glass Company, 1940's – 1950's

Colors: crystal, mainly; some few pieces in color

You will find additional pieces of Wildflower on different Cambridge blanks. I have tried to show the major portion, but (as with other Cambridge patterns) there seems to be a never ending list. I have given you the "ball park" to start. Price yellow about 10% to 20% higher.

	Crystal		Crystal
Basket, #3400/1182, 2 hdld., ftd., 6"	25.00	Plate, #3900/20, bread/butter, 6½"	7.50
Bowl, #3400/1180, bonbon, 2 hdld., 5¼"	18.00	Plate, #3900/130, bonbon, 2 hdld., 7"	17.50
Bowl, bonbon, 2 hdld., ftd., 6"	17.50	Plate, #3400/176, 7½"	9.00
Bowl, #3400/90, 2 pt., relish, 6"	17.50	Plate, #3900/161, 2 hdld., ftd., 8"	20.50
Bowl, 3 pt., relish, 6½"	17.50	Plate, #3900/22, salad, 8"	11.00
Bowl, #3900/123, relish, 7"	18.00	Plate, #3400/62, 8½"	13.00
Bowl, #3900/130, bonbon, 2 hdld., 7"	20.00	Plate, #3900/24, dinner, 10½"	65.00
Bowl, #3900/124, 2 pt., relish, 7"	22.00	Plate, #3900/26, service, 4 ftd., 12"	30.00
Bowl, #3400/91, 3 pt., relish, 3 hdld., 8"	25.00	Plate, #3900/35, cake, 2 hdld., 13½"	32,50
Bowl, #3900/125, 3 pt., celery & relish, 9"	25.00	Plate, #3900/167, torte, 14"	35.00
Bowl, #477, pickle (corn), ftd., 9½"	25.00	Plate, #3900/65, torte, 14"	32.50
Bowl, #3900/54, 4 ft., flared, 10"	35.00	Salt & pepper, #3400/77, pr.	35.00
Bowl, #3900/34, 2 hdld., 11"	40.00	Salt & pepper, #3900/1177	32.50
Bowl, #3900/28, w/tab hand., ftd., 11½"	40.00	Saucer, #3900/17 or #3400/54	3.50
Bowl, #3900/126, 3 pt., celery & relish, 12"	35.00	Set: 2 pc. Mayonnaise, #3900/19 (ftd. sherbet w/ladle)	25.00
Bowl, #3400/4, 4 ft., flared, 12"	29.50	Set: 3 pc. Mayonnaise, #3900/129 (bowl, liner, ladle)	28.00
Bowl, #3400/1240, 4 ft., oval, "ears" hand., 12"	42.00	Set: 4 pc. Mayonnaise #3900/111 (div. bowl, liner, 2 ladles)	32.00
Bowl, 5 pt., celery & relish, 12"	35.00	Stem, #3121, cordial, 1 oz.	50.00
Butter dish, #3900/52, ¼ lb.	150.00	Stem, #3121, cocktail, 3 oz.	22.50
Butter dish, #3400/52, 5"	110.00	Stem, #3121, wine, 3½ oz.	30.00
Candlestick, #3400/638, 3-lite, ea.	32.00	Stem, #3121, claret, 4½ oz.	35.00
Candlestick, #3400/646, 5"	25.00	Stem, #3121, 4½ oz., low oyster cocktail	18.00
Candlestick, #3400/647, 2-lite, "fleur de lis," 6"	30.00	Stem, #3121, 5 oz., low parfait	27.00
Candy box, w/cover, #3900/165	55.00	Stem, #3121, 6 oz., low sherbet	15.00
Candy box, w/cover, #3900/165, rnd.	50.00	Stem, #3121, 6 oz., tall sherbet	17.50
Cocktail icer, #968, 2 pc.	65.00	Stem, #3121, 10 oz., water	20.00
Cocktail shaker, #3400/175	75.00	Sugar, 3900/41	12.50
Comport, #3900/136, 5½"	30.00	Sugar, indiv., 3900/40	17.00
Comport, #3121, blown, 5⅜"	40.00	Tray, creamer & sugar, 3900/37	15.00
Creamer, #3900/41	12.50	Tumbler, #3121, 5 oz., juice	15.00
Creamer, #3900/40, individual	17.00	Tumbler, #3121, 10 oz., water	17.00
Cup, #3900/17 or #3400/54	16.50	Tumbler, #3121, 12 oz., tea	20.00
Hat, #1704, 5"	125.00	Tumbler, #3900/115, 13 oz.	25.00
Hat, #1703, 6"	150.00	Vase, #3400/102, globe, 5"	30.00
Hurricane lamp, #1617, candlestick base,	125.00	Vase, #6004, flower, ftd., 6"	30.00
Hurricane lamp, #1603, keyhole base & prisms	150.00	Vase, #6004, flower, ftd., 8"	35.00
Ice bucket, w/chrome hand., #3900/671	65.00	Vase, #1237, keyhole ft., 9"	40.00
Oil, w/stopper, #3900/100, 6 oz.	60.00	Vase, #1528, bud, 10"	30.00
Pitcher, ball, #3400/38, 80 oz.	110.00	Vase, #278, flower, ftd., 11"	42.00
Pitcher, #3900/115, 76 oz.	100.00	Vase, #1299, ped. ft., 11"	45.00
Pitcher, Doulton, #3400/141	225.00	Vase, #1238, keyhole ft., 12"	60.00
		Vase, #279, ftd., flower, 13"	75.00

Note: See Pages 182-183 for stem identification.

YEOMAN, Blank #1184, A.H. Heisey & Co.

Colors: crystal, "Flamingo" pink, "Sahara" yellow, "Moongleam" green, "Hawthorne" orchid/pink, "Marigold" deep, amber/yellow; some cobalt

Etched patterns on Yeoman blanks will bring 15% to 25% more than the prices listed below. Empress etch is the most commonly found pattern on Yeoman blanks.

	Crystal	Pink	Sahara	Green	Hawth.	Marigold
Ashtray, 4", hdld. (bow tie)	10.00	20.00	22.00	25.00	30.00	35.00
Bowl, 2 hdld., cream soup	10.00	16.00	22.00	24.00	28.00	32.00
Bowl, finger	5.00	11.00	17.00	20.00	27.50	30.00
Bowl, ftd., banana split	7.00	23.00	30.00	35.00	40.00	45.00
Bowl, ftd., 2 hdld., bouillon	10.00	20.00	25.00	30.00	35.00	40.00
Bowl, 4½", nappy	4.00	7.50	10.00	12.50	15.00	17.00
Bowl, 5", low, ftd., jelly	12.00	20.00	25.00	27.00	30.00	40.00
Bowl, 5", oval, lemon	7.00	10.00	15.00	18.00	19.00	25.00
Bowl, 5", rnd., lemon	6.00	10.00	15.00	18.00	19.00	25.00
Bowl, 5", rnd., lemon, w/cover	15.00	20.00	25.00	30.00	40.00	50.0
Bowl, 6", oval, preserve	7.00	12.00	17.00	22.00	27.00	30.00
Bowl, 6", vegetable	5.00	10.00	14.00	16.00	20.00	24.00
Bowl, 6½", hdld., bonbon	5.00	10.00	14.00	16.00	20.00	24.00
Bowl, 8", rect., pickle/olive	12.00	15.00	20.00	25.00	30.00	35.00
Bowl, 8½", berry, 2 hdld.	14.00	22.00	25.00	30.00	35.00	50.00
Bowl, 9", 2 hdld., veg., w/cover	30.00	45.00	55.00	65.00	90.00	150.00
Bowl, 9", oval, fruit	20.00	25.00	35.00	45.00	55.00	55.00
Bowl, 9", baker	20.00	25.00	35.00	45.00	55.00	55.00
Bowl, 12", low, floral	15.00	25.00	35.00	45.00	55.00	55.00
Cigarette box, (ashtray)	25.00	60.00	65.00	70.00	80.00	100.00
Cologne bottle, w/stopper	40.00	90.00	95.00	100.00	110.00	135.00
Comport, 5", high ftd., shallow	15.00	25.00	37.00	45.00	55.00	70.00
Comport, 6", low ftd., deep	20.00	30.00	34.00	40.00	42.00	48.00
Creamer	10.00	15.00	17.00	19.00	22.00	28.00
Cruet, 2 oz., oil	20.00	40.00	45.00	50.00	55.00	65.00
Cruet, 4 oz., oil	25.00	45.00	50.00	55.00	60.00	75.00
Cup	5.00	15.00	20.00	25.00	30.00	40.00
Cup, after dinner	7.00	28.00	30.00	35.00	40.00	50.00
Egg cup	15.00	24.00	32.00	39.00	42.00	52.00
Grapefruit, ftd.	10.00	17.00	24.00	31.00	38.00	45.00
Gravy (or dressing) boat, w/underliner	13.00	25.00	30.00	35.00	40.00	45.00
Marmalade jar, w/cover	25.00	35.00	40.00	45.00	55.00	65.00
Parfait, 5 oz.	10.00	15.00	20.00	25.00	30.00	35.00
Pitcher, quart	35.00	55.00	65.00	75.00	125.00	160.00
Plate, 2 hdld., cheese	5.00	10.00	13.00	15.00	17.00	25.00
Plate, cream soup underliner	5.00	7.00	9.00	12.00	14.00	16.00
Plate, finger bowl underliner	3.00	5.00	7.00	9.00	11.00	13.00
Plate, 4½", coaster	3.00	5.00	10.00	12.00		
Plate, 6"	3.00	6.00	8.00	10.00	13.00	15.00
Plate, 6", bouillon underliner	3.00	6.00	8.00	10.00	13.00	15.00

	Crystal	Pink	Sahara	Green	Hawth.	Marigold
Plate, 6½", grapefruit bowl	7.00	12.00	15.00	19.00	27.00	32.00
Plate, 7"	5.00	8.00	10.00	14.00	17.00	22.00
Plate, 8", oyster cocktail	9.00					
Plate, 8", soup	9.00					
Plate, 9", oyster cocktail	10.00					
Plate, 10½"	12.00				30.00	
Plate, 10½", ctr. hand., oval, div.	15.00	26.00		32.00		
Plate, 11", 4 pt., relish	20.00	27.00		32.00		
Plate, 14"	20.00					
Platter, 12", oval	10.00	17.00	19.00	26.00	33.00	
Salt, ind. tub (cobalt: $30.00)	5.00	8.00		15.00		
Salver, 10", low ftd.	15.00	30.00		42.00		
Salver, 12", low ftd.	10.00	25.00		32.00		
Saucer	3.00	5.00	7.00	7.00	10.00	10.00
Saucer, after dinner	3.00	5.00	7.00	8.00	10.00	10.00
Stem, 2¾ oz., ftd., oyster cocktail	4.00	8.00	10.00	12.00	14.00	
Stem, 3 oz., cocktail	7.00	12.00	17.00	20.00		
Stem, 3½ oz., sherbet	5.00	8.00	11.00	12.00		
Stem, 4 oz., fruit cocktail	3.00	5.00	7.00	9.00		
Stem, 4½ oz., sherbet	3.00	5.00	7.00	9.00		
Stem, 5 oz., soda	5.00	8.00	10.00	12.00		
Stem, 5 oz., sherbet	3.00	5.00	7.00	9.00		
Stem, 6 oz., champagne	6.00	11.00	16.00	18.00		
Stem, 8 oz.	5.00	12.00	18.00	20.00		
Stem, 10 oz., goblet	7.00	15.00	20.00	25.00		
Sugar, w/cover	13.00	25.00	27.00	30.00	35.00	40.00
Sugar shaker, ftd.	50.00	95.00		110.00		
Syrup, 7 oz., saucer ftd.	30.00	75.00				
Tray, 7" x 10", rect.	26.00	30.00	40.00	35.00		
Tray, 9", celery	10.00	14.00	16.00	15.00		
Tray, 11", ctr. hand., 3 pt.	15.00	20.00	24.00			
Tray, 12", oblong	16.00	19.00	24.00			
Tray, 13", 3 pt., relish	20.00	27.00	32.00			
Tray, 13", celery	20.00	27.00	32.00			
Tray, 13", hors d'oeuvre, w/cov. ctr.	32.00	42.00	52.00	75.00		
Tray insert, 3½" x 4½"	4.00	6.00	7.00	8.00		
Tumbler, 2½ oz., whiskey	3.00	8.00	10.00	12.00		
Tumbler, 4½ oz., soda	4.00	6.00	10.00	15.00		
Tumbler, 8 oz.	4.00	12.00	17.00	20.00		
Tumbler, 10 oz., cupped rim	4.00	15.00	20.00	22.50		
Tumbler, 10 oz., straight side	5.00	15.00	20.00	22.50		
Tumbler, 12 oz., tea	5.00	20.00	25.00	30.00		
Tumbler cover (unusual)	35.00					

CAMBRIDGE STEMS

1066
11 oz. Goblet

1402
Brandy Inhaler (Tall)

3025
10 oz. Goblet

3035
3 oz. Cocktail

3077
6 oz. Tall Sherbet

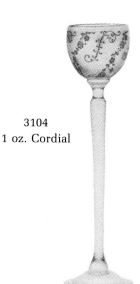

3104
1 oz. Cordial

3106
9 oz. Goblet Tall Bowl

3115
3½ oz. Cocktail

182

3120
6 oz. Tall Sherbet

3121
10 oz. Goblet

CAMBRIDGE STEMS

3122
9 oz. Goblet

3124
3 oz. Wine

3126
7 oz. Tall Sherbet

3130
6 oz. Tall Sherbet

3135
6 oz. Tall Sherbet

3400
9 oz. Lunch Goblet

3500
10 oz. Goblet

3600
2½ oz. Wine

3775
4½ oz. Claret

183

3625
4½ oz. Claret

3779
1 oz. Cordial

HEISEY'S "ALEXANDRITE" COLOR (rare)

Bowl, 12", floral, Twist (1252)	275.00
Candlesticks, pr. (134)	500.00
Cream & sugar, pr., Empress (1401)	425.00
Compote, Albermarle (3368)	125.00
Cup & saucer, Queen Ann (1509)	125.00
Jelly, 6", w/dolphin feet, Queen Ann (1509)	125.00
Mayonnaise, w/dolp. ft. & ladle, Queen Ann (1509)	225.00
Plate, 8", Empress (1401)	60.00
Salt & pepper, pr., Queen Ann (1509)	235.00
Stem, 2½ oz., wine, Creole (3381)	125.00
Stem, 2½ oz., wine, Old Dominion (3380)	140.00
Stem, 6 oz., champagne, Old Dominion (3380)	125.00
Stem, 11 oz., water goblet, Carcassone (3390)	80.00
Stem, 11 oz., water goblet, Creole (3381)	120.00
Vase, 4", ball, Wide Optic (4045)	150.00

HEISEY'S "ALEXANDRITE" COLOR (rare)

Ashtray, Empress (1401)	125.00
Candlesticks, 7", pr. (135)	275.00
Celery tray, 10", Empress (1401)	150.00
Nut, individual, Empress (1401)	95.00
Plate, 6", square, Empress (1401)	25.00
Plate, 7", square, Empress (1401)	40.00
Plate, 8", square, Empress (1401)	60.00
Plate, 10½", square, Empress (1401)	135.00
Tumbler, 1 oz., cordial, Carcassonne (3390)	100.00
Tumbler, 2½ oz., bar, Glenford (3481)	135.00
Tumbler 5 oz., ftd., soda, Creole (3381)	60.00
Tumbler, 8½ oz., ftd., soda, Creole (3381)	65.00
Tumbler, 12 oz., ftd., soda, Creole (3381)	70.00
Vase, 9", ftd., Empress (1401)	625.00

HEISEY'S "COBALT" COLOR (rare)

Bowl, 12", Thumbprint & Panel (1433)	140.00
Candlestick, 2-lite, pr., Thumbprint & Panel (1433)	250.00
Candlestick, 6", pr., Old Sandwich (1404)	325.00
Mug, 12 oz., Old Sandwich, (1404)	190.00
Mug, 16 oz., Old Sandwich (1404)	280.00
Mug, 18 oz., Old Sandwich (1404)	270.00
Pitcher, Old Sandwich (1404)	260.00
Salt and Pepper, pr. (24)	220.00
Sign, Cabochon (crystal)	175.00
Stem, 1 oz., cordial, Spanish (3404)	225.00
Stem, 3½ oz., cocktail, Spanish (3404)	90.00
Stem, 5½ oz., sherbet, Spanish (3404)	60.00
Stem, 5½ oz., saucer champagne, Spanish (3404)	80.00
Stem, 10 oz., water, Spanish (3404)	100.00
Tumbler, 10 oz., ftd., soda, Spanish (3404)	85.00
Vase, ball (4045)	120.00
Vase, favor, Diamond Optic (4229)	250.00
Vase, favor, Diamond Optic (4230)	250.00
Vase, tulip, 9", ftd. (1420)	325.00

HEISEY'S "COBALT" COLOR (rare)

Bowl, 11", floral, Warwick (1428)	280.00
Candlestick, 6", pr. (135)	420.00
Candy, w/cover, 6", Empress (1401)	340.00
Cigarette holder, ftd., Carcassonne (3390)	85.00
Plate, 8", Empress (1401)	65.00
Sign, Cabochon (crystal)	175.00
Stem, 6 oz., saucer champagne, Carcassonne (3390)	45.00
Stem, 11 oz., tall, Carcassonne (3390)	90.00
Tumbler, 2½ oz., wine, ftd., Carcassonne (3390)	85.00
Tumbler, 12 oz., soda, ftd., Carcassonne (3390)	75.00
Vase, 5", Warwick (1428)	140.00
Vase, 9", pr., Warwick (1428)	360.00

HEISEY'S "DAWN" COLOR (rare)

Bowl, 6¾", jelly (1565)	40.00
Bowl, 8½", Town & Country (1637)	100.00
Bowl, 11", salad, Town & Country (1637)	140.00
Butter dish, ¼ pound, Cabochon (1951)	150.00
Cruet, 3 oz., crystal stopper, Saturn (1485)	275.00
Plate, 8⅝", luncheon, Town & Country (1637)	75.00
Plate, 10", dinner, Town & Country (1637)	175.00
Plate, 14", underliner, Town & Country (1637)	100.00
Relish, 3 pt., Cabochon (1951)	75.00
Salt and pepper shaker, pr., Saturn (1485)	250.00
Sherbet, 20th Century (1415)	35.00
Tray, 12", 4 pt., Octagon (500)	300.00
Tumbler, 9 oz., Town & Country (1637)	30.00
Tumbler, 10 oz., water, Coleport (1407)	30.00
Tumbler, 13 oz., iced tea, Coleport (1407)	40.00
Tumbler, 13 oz., iced tea, Town & Country (1637)	40.00

HEISEY'S TANGERINE COLOR (rare)

Plate, 8", Empress blank (1401) 100.00
Stem, champagne, Duquesne blank (3389) 145.00
Stem, cocktail, Gascony (3397) looks red 195.00
Stem, sherbet, Duquesne blank (3389) 125.00
Stem, water, Duquesne blank (3389) 160.00
Tumbler, ice tea, Spanish stem (3404) 375.00
Tumbler, juice, Duquesne blank (3389) 125.00
Tumbler, soda, Gascony (3397) looks red 225.00
Vase, favor (4232) 500.00
Vase, ivy 185.00

HEISEY'S ZIRCON (LIMELIGHT) COLOR (rare)

Ashtray, Kohinoor (1488) 75.00
Ashtray, Ridgeleigh (1469) 45.00
Bowl, 6", hdld., jelly, Fern (1495) 45.00
Bowl, 13", floral, Kohinoor (1488) 400.00
Cigarette box, Ridgeleigh (1469) 140.00
Cigarette holder, Kohinoor (1488) 110.00
Candelabra, pr., Kohinoor (1488) 1000.00
Candle vase, Ridgeleigh (1469) 110.00
Vase, 8", Ridgeleigh (1469½) 160.00

Other Books by Gene Florence

Kitchen Glassware of the Depression Years, 4th Edition $19.95
Pocket Guide to Depression Glass, 7th Edition $9.95
Collector's Encyclopedia of Depression Glass, 9th Edition $19.95
Collector's Encyclopedia of Occupied Japan I $14.95
Collector's Encyclopedia of Occupied Japan II $14.95
Collector's Encyclopedia of Occupied Japan III $14.95
Collector's Encyclopedia of Occupied Japan IV $14.95
Very Rare Glassware of the Depression Years $24.95
Very Rare Glassware of the Depression Years, 2nd Series $24.95
Gene Florence's Standard Baseball Guide Price Guide, 3rd Edition $9.95

A publication I recommend:

DEPRESSION GLASS DAZE

THE ORIGINAL NATIONAL DEPRESSION GLASS NEWSPAPER

Depression Glass Daze, the original national monthly newspaper dedicated to the buying, selling and collecting of colored glassware of the 20's and 30's. We average 60 pages each month, filled with feature articles by top-notch columnists, readers' "finds," club happenings, show news, a china corner, a current listing of new glass issues to beware of and a multitude of ads! You can find it in the **DAZE**! Keep up with what's happening in the dee gee world with a subscription to the **DAZE**. Buy, sell or trade from the convenience of your easy chair.

NAME _____

ADDRESS _____

CITY _____ STATE _____ ZIP _____

☐ 1 YEAR - $15.00   ☐ CHECK ENCLOSED   ☐ PLEASE BILL ME   ☐ MASTERCARD   ☐ VISA

CARD NO. _____ EXP. DATE _____

SIGNATURE _____

SEND ORDER TO: **D.G.D., BOX 57 GF, OTISVILLE, MI 48463-0008** (Please allow 30 days.)

Schroeder's Antiques Price Guide

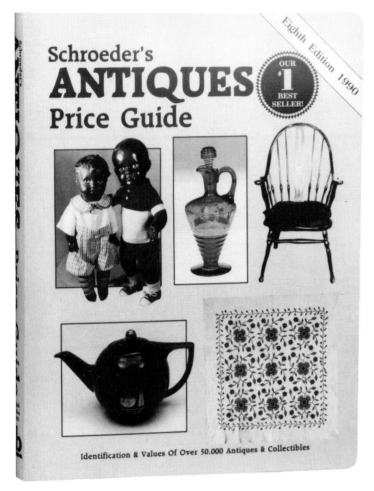

Schroeder's Antiques Price Guide has climbed its way to the top in a field already supplied with several well-established publications! The word is out, *Schroeder's Price Guide* is the best buy at any price. Over 500 categories are covered, with more than 50,000 listings. But it's not volume alone that makes Schroeder's the unique guide it is recognized to be. From ABC Plates to Zsolnay, if it merits the interest of today's collector, you'll find it in Schroeder's. Each subject is represented with histories and background information. In addition, hundreds of sharp original photos are used each year to illustrate not only the rare and the unusual, but the everyday "fun-type" collectibles as well -- not postage stamp pictures, but large close-up shots that show important details clearly.

Each edition is completely re-typeset from all new sources. We have not and will not simply change prices in each new edition. All new copy and all new illustrations make Schroeder's THE price guide on antiques and collectibles.

The writing and researching team behind this giant is proportionately large. It is backed by a staff of more than seventy of Collector Books' finest authors, as well as a board of advisors made up of well-known antique authorities and the country's top dealers, all specialists in their fields. Accuracy is their primary aim. Prices are gathered over the entire year previous to publication, from ads and personal contacts. Then each category is thoroughly checked to spot inconsistencies, listings that may not be entirely reflective of actual market dealings, and lines too vague to be of merit.

Only the best of the lot remains for publication. You'll find *Schroeder's Antiques Price Guide* the one to buy for factual information and quality.

No dealer, collector or investor can afford not to own this book. It is available from your favorite bookseller or antiques dealer at the low price of $12.95. If you are unable to find this price guide in your area, it's available from Collector Books, P. O. Box 3009, Paducah, KY 42001 at $12.95 plus $2.00 for postage and handling.

8½ x 11, 608 Pages $12.95

COLLECTOR BOOKS
A Division of Schroeder Publishing Co., Inc.